ROYAL INDIA

HIS HIGHNESS SIR RANBIR SINGH, SECOND MAHARAJA OF KASHMIR

ROYAL INDIA

*A descriptive and historical study
of India's fifteen principal States
and their Rulers*

BY

MAUD DIVER

Amid the levelling tendencies of the day, the inevitable monotony of Government on scientific lines, the Princes of India keep alive traditions and customs. They sustain the virility and save from extinction the picturesqueness of ancient and noble races. They have that indefinable quality endearing them to the people that arises from being born of the soil. Above all—especially in Rajputana—they constitute a school of manners . . . and show in the persons of their Chiefs that illustrious lineage has not ceased to implant noble and chivalrous ideas, fine standard of public spirit and private courtesy, which have always been instinctive in the aristocracy of India.

With the loss of these—if ever they be allowed to disappear, Indian society would go to pieces like a dismasted vessel in a storm.

LORD CURZON

Essay Index Reprint Series

 BOOKS FOR LIBRARIES PRESS
FREEPORT, NEW YORK

INTERNATIONAL STANDARD BOOK NUMBER:
0-8369-2152-6

LIBRARY OF CONGRESS CATALOG CARD NUMBER:
76-142620

PRINTED IN THE UNITED STATES OF AMERICA

TO

THE PRINCES OF INDIA

IN SINCERE ADMIRATION
FOR ALL THAT HAS BEEN ACCOMPLISHED
BY THEIR ORDER FROM AGE TO AGE
FOR THE WELFARE OF THEIR GREAT COUNTRY

THIS BOOK IS DEDICATED BY

A LOVER OF INDIA

AUTHOR'S NOTE

WITHIN the limits of this book, I have attempted portraits of certain distinguished Maharajas and their immediate predecessors. I would merely add that the varying length of my chapters on each State bears no relation to its size or importance. It merely means that, in some cases, more material has been available than in others ; and I am confined by space to a few of the greater Princes.

I have tried, as far as may be, to keep clear of politics and controversial themes ; but — as I have written elsewhere — ' in India politics have become an epidemic ; though, after all, the problems of India's relation with England out-soar mere politics. It may decide the future of Europe and Asia. There are fine minds at work on both sides, but there are too many tongues.'

In my first and last chapters these things must, of necessity, play a leading part ; and also in my study of a Prince, who has devoted to them all his mental gifts and magnificent energy—the Maharaja of Bikanir.

I gratefully acknowledge the help I have received from the India Office Library, from Sir Stuart Fraser, K.C.S.I., Sir Henry Lawrence, K.C.S.I., Miss E. L. Tottenham, Mr. C. A. Kincaid, C.V.O., and Colonel Graham Seton Hutchison, D.S.O., M.C., for allowing me to quote from his Monarchical Federation plan for all India. My thanks are due also to the *Asiatic Review* for leave to use part of an article on the Indian Princes and the War.

I wish to add that I have no ' axe to grind '. This book has been written at the request of my American publishers, and my sole concern has been to present a living portrayal of Royal India to the best of my ability.

Parkstone : 1942

vi

CONTENTS

PAGE

GUIDE TO PRONOUNCING VOWEL SOUNDS AND CERTAIN NAMES

ā—arn	i—*ee*	ai—as *i* in v*i*ne
a—u in ' but '	ir—*eer*	o—as in note
é—as *ai*	in—*een*	u—*oo*

Gwalior—pronounce as Gwollia
Udaipur—pronounce as Oodypore
Náwanagar—pronounce as Nowanugga
Méwar—pronounce as Maiwa
Begum—pronounce as Baigum

Mrs. Maud Diver writes of India with insight, sympathy and understanding. Through her father she is connected with the Lawrences of the Punjab. Her Life of Honoria Lawrence—wife of Sir Henry Lawrence of Punjab, Rajputana and Lucknow fame—was commended by critics as a ' book of outstanding merit ', a classic of its kind. She has personal knowledge of the country. Her father, Colonel C. H. T. Marshall, served in the Punjab as soldier-civilian and Political Officer for thirty-five years.

The Princes above named will find in this volume a vivid and sympathetic portrayal of their States, their history, their problems, with a full recognition of the part they are clearly destined to play in the coming era, after the War.

LIST OF ILLUSTRATIONS

ix

ADDITIONAL NOTE TO FINAL CHAPTER

THE recent important interlude of the definite offer to India, from His Majesty's Government, seems to call for a brief allusion, since it clearly set forth the readiness of that Government to recognise and accept, immediately after the War, a working constitution framed by Indians themselves : in effect, the creation of an Indian Union that would become a Dominion, to be associated in complete equality, with all other Dominions, in allegiance to the Crown : an offer as generous as it was genuine. To quote *The Times* : ' The significance of the plan lies in the attempt to realise freedom through unity and unity through consent ' : a proffered plan that had at least the merit of making clear to the world at large the patent stumbling-blocks to any practical form of settlement that must rest on that fair-sounding basis.

In sentiment all parties hailed the prospect of Dominion Status ; but discussion of actualities revealed as usual a wide divergence of views among the various Leagues involved. It is too often forgotten that, for India, any form of democracy—in the true sense of the word—automatically involves Hindu domination. The rule of *demos* is majority rule ; and 68 per cent of India's population is Hindu. But the obstinate fact remains that Moslems will not be ruled by Hindus or Sikhs ; Sikhs will not be ruled in Pakistan by Moslems ; Hindus will not be ruled by Moslems ; the Princes will not be overruled by politicians of British India. ' Yet any offer to get Britain out of India must contemplate these things. . . .' No wonder the general public often feels bewildered as to what the ' much speaking ' is all about.

To take the Princes—with whom this book is mainly concerned— their Chamber at once passed a resolution declaring that they would in no way oppose India's attainment of Dominion Status, including a common allegiance to the Crown. Yet they could not be other than concerned at the prospect of reduced representation for themselves and the possibility of a self-governing British India being established without their accession to it : a development that might endanger their whole political future.

Result : after weeks of interminable talk—that may or may not have clarified the issue—the situation remains practically unchanged. True, India's fighting spirit has been intensified ; but nothing has occurred to modify all that has been written and proposed in the last chapter.

The palm still rests with the Princes for sanity of outlook and recognition of realities too often obscured by political phraseology and the need to make out a case for the prevailing point of view.

I cannot do better than refer the reader to the sane words spoken by the Maharaja of Bikanir on p. 273 and in other parts of that chapter ; to the practical conclusions of that notable Moslem Ruler, the Nawab of Bhopāl (p. 277) ; and, not least, to the dictum of India's great and wise reformer Prince, Sir Shahu Chhatrapati of Kolhapur : ' The gift of democratic government may be made or withheld by Parliament ; but no such gift will cause the growth of democracy in India. Educate, educate. . . . Only by means of social progress can political progress become a natural growth from within.'

But education takes time ; and politicians are apt to be in a hurry, often to the detriment of their country and their çause.

April 1942

ROYAL INDIA :
WHAT IT HAS BEEN AND WHAT IT IS

Always, in speaking of India, one must remember the great variety
of human characteristics and natural conditions that it comprises.
Those who know . . . can claim with assurance that there exists
between certain sections of the Indian people and the British a sense
of common service, common ideals and loyalties. . . . Of the Princes
it may be said that they belong to the British ' family ', and feel
personal loyalty to the Sovereign as warm as that of any Briton.—Sir
George Schuster.

In India it is the intangible that grips a man's thoughts and controls
his actions ; and unless we look at India through Eastern as well as
Western eyes, we shall look at her asquint.—Major-General J. F. C.
Fuller, C.B., C.B.E., D.S.O.

I

The chief ruling Princes of India—their names and fame and
devotion to the British Crown—are familiar, more or less, in
almost every country of the world. In England and India the
greatest among them are known individually, if only by repute or
through the Press. Men of high standing and personal experience
frankly regard them as ' one of the most astonishing facts in their
own continent or any other ' : a unique survival from bygone days.
Nowhere else could one find, in this twentieth century, so attractive
a blend of ancient and modern : rulers enjoying all the privilege,
power and prestige of autocrats, yet freed, through their allegiance
to the British Crown, from all risk of serious trouble within or
without their domains.

For over two thousand years India's kingly ideal has proved its
survival value ; proved also that the moderate-sized kingdom is
better suited to Indian tradition and temperament than the larger,
unwieldy Provinces of much-administered British India.

The States themselves, under enlightened Maharajas, are no
mere anachronisms, as they are often styled by the politically-
minded of both races. Changing in form, but not in fundamentals, they have shown, and are showing, a power of adaptation
that qualifies them to survive. The best of their rulers have
reached a high standard of duty and responsibility. Many of
them have adopted Western dress, yet they remain, as a whole,
picturesque personalities ; their outlook still feudal in the finer
sense of the word ; famed for their fabulous jewels, their hospitality
on the grand scale and, not least, for their devotion to the Crown
of England.

Princes we call them, since they owe allegiance to the King-

Emperor, but the fine-sounding title ' Maharaja ' means Great King, as many of them are indeed ; lesser Princes being entitled Raja or Nawab. All told, they number some six hundred principalities ; ranging in size from Hyderabad — almost as large as France—to feudal areas little bigger than a private estate ; ranging also in mentality and outlook from the mediaeval baron to the modern Prince, who sees himself as the father of his people. Of such are the best known Rulers : Hyderabad, Kashmir, Mysore, Baroda, Gwalior and the Rajput soldier-statesman, Bikanir. England does not forget how the forebears of these Princes stood by their Queen-Empress in the critical days of the Mutiny ; even as they flung all their resources into the two later world conflicts between ' the spirit of force and the forces of the spirit '.

In view of all that they are—and of the important part they may play in creating the India of to-morrow—it seems worth trying to present a living picture of these born rulers, through the varied record of their history and lineage and the influences that have moulded their destinies. Though of late years a good many books have been written on the subject of the greater Princes, most of them have been political ; and few, if any, have the personal touch of Sir Walter Lawrence in his delightful book, *The India We Served*, or of Miss Tottenham in her *Highnesses of Hindostan*.

Even the British in India, with notable exceptions, have little more than a surface knowledge of the States. In social and military circles they are mainly connected with tourists and *tamāshas*, big game shooting and unlimited hospitality ; though, in these days, they have become more widely known for what they are—cultivated and travelled men, often keen sportsmen, who fraternise with their guests, like any English host, and even dine at the same table. Increasingly they tend to discard rigid caste rules that hamper social life and progressive ambition.

So varied are they, in type, outlook and personality, that the vice of generalising is more than ever liable to give false impressions of a loyal and gallant body of men.

Outside India, even among educated readers, fantastic and piquant stories are more easily swallowed than unromantic facts. The mere phrase ' Eastern potentate ' suggests a background of Arabian nights, dancing girls, jewels and wealth. The jewels and wealth are true enough of some ; but they do not imply that any Maharaja sits down to breakfast covered with diamonds and rubies, or spends his substance on riotous living.

The Princes themselves, and their whole position in the country, are very imperfectly understood. How many people realise that Indian India is not, and never has been, British territory ; that thousands of bankers, merchants and financiers in Bombay and Calcutta are subjects of Indian States ; that the ubiquitous moneylender is usually a Marwari from Jaipur; that one-third of India and a quarter of her peoples belong to Rulers, who are allies by treaty with the British Crown.

For a clear view of their position, they need to be seen in historical perspective : and India's perspective—history merging into legend—covers close on three thousand years.

Hindu India can look back to a Northern Buddhist Empire more than three hundred years before Christ, to a Golden Age that flourished for a hundred and fifty years ; offset by two centuries of unrecorded darkness. Followed the long-drawn tragedy of invasion on invasion ; the crash of empires ; eight hundred years of anarchy, sharpened by fierce religious feuds and fanaticisms, not wholly resolved even to-day.

The tidal wave of Aryans from the uplands of Central Asia proved all to the good for India's future development. A fair race, fine and warlike as their Rajput descendants, they conquered more than half of northern India, thrusting the Dravidians back and back into the south. Left in peace for a little matter of a thousand years, they evolved a religion, or rather a priestly social system, based on caste—in effect, Hinduism ; a system by which the whole sub-continent is dominated to the present day.

They gave India the brilliant era of Rajput dominion: a number of small kingdoms ruled by Chiefs of a great military caste, kept singularly pure by the strictest rules as to marriage and status ; their men kept virile and courageous by the exercise of sport in every form, not least the kingly sport of war, as it was waged in a more barbarous yet a more chivalrous age. ' A triumph of human breeding ', Count Keyserling has called them ; and Hindu India did well in evolving these Rajputs—Sons of Kings—who were to prove its mainstay against a more formidable invasion than any yet.

For now, in the eighth century, there came crusading out of Asia the world's great fighting races—Arabs and Turks, Tartars and Afghans ; red-hot fanatics, vowed to slay all infidels who could not be persuaded or coerced into accepting the non-idolatrous creed of God and his Prophet.

In this violent fashion began the thousand-year feud between Hindu and Moslem—a fierce and fundamental antagonism, hardly to be realised by those who are not familiar with the all-pervading religious atmosphere of India.

To give Western minds a partial idea of the age-long clash between the two creeds that dominate India, one may roughly compare Hindu with Roman Catholic forms of worship—elaborate ritual, images of gods, and sanctified priesthood; while the Moslem, like the Protestant, worships God direct and sees all men as equal in His sight, at prayer-time and meal-time—the last being a religious function in the East. But, in truth, the cleavage cuts far deeper; and it must be remembered that, in India, religion permeates the whole of life as it rarely does in the West.

The Moslem creed—conceived by an obscure Arab in the seventh century—is, in essence, a fighting faith; and, as such, was destined to challenge the world. The Mogul dream of wholesale dominion, in part fulfilled, was only frustrated by the combined valour and diplomacy of the Rajputs, who may fairly be said to have saved Hindu India ; their supreme claim to renown.

Even so, initial sweeping victories enabled the Moguls to found an Empire, centred in Delhi, that astonished East and West alike, and survived for two hundred years.

The Rajputs, refusing to admit defeat, set up small proud kingdoms in oases of the great Indian desert, now known as Rajputana. Of these there were three chief principalities : Méwar, with its capital city of Udaipur, Jaipur and the desert State of Jōdhpur. In their courts these Rajput Rulers preserved Aryan traditions and culture, while the Brahmins stiffened the spiritual barrier of caste against the oppressor, convinced that ' the age of despair ' could not last for ever.

It could not. Even while the Mogul power was at its height, adventurers from a small and distant island were scouring the seas. A certain Francis Drake had rounded the Cape of Good Hope and ' navigated the globe '—as then known. England, even now, hardly realises the quality of those simple seamen, who carried on Queen Elizabeth's tradition through the discouraging days of James the First.

' Their ships though heavily gunned, were small. When food and water failed, it was chance work replenishing them. Every port was armed and hostile ; every ship an enemy to be fought or run from. (But the English seldom ran.) To reach India was to sail into a nest of wasps. For they sailed as poachers and pirates outside the law ; and navigation was all sheer guess work.' Yet a tale of the wonders they achieved, against odds—the birth of the East India Company and all that sprang from it—would in itself fill more than one book.

It was in September 1599 that eighty City merchants, pledged to the venture, met in Founders' Hall ; and on the last day of that year their Charter was signed by Queen Elizabeth, as ' merchants of London, travelling to the East Indies '.

At a time when trade was despised by the well-born, they 'went honourably, thinking it no shame to be merchants. They walked and sailed through deaths Ulysses never knew, and did it with cool good humour.' Even so, at Dunkirk, in 1940, the Island race proved that four centuries had not dimmed the tradition of that first Elizabeth.

From such modest beginnings—mere grains of mustard seed—sprang the far-spreading tree of the world's greatest Empire.

For close on a hundred years the East India Company lived and worked as simple traders in silks and gems and spices, on the fringe of an India rent by wars, massacres and invasions ; desiring above all to keep clear of political entanglements. Yet, unknown to themselves or their country, they were men of destiny ; strong in their arrogant belief that ' God Almighty's good Providence hath always graciously superintended the affairs of this Company '.

And the sequel might well seem to justify both arrogance and belief.

Certain it is that affairs in India had a more direct bearing on the Company's future than even a major prophet could then have foreseen.

The Mogul Empire, supreme and splendid under Akbar—Guardian of Mankind—was to decline rapidly under the revived cruelty and persecution of his great-grandson, Aurungzeb, who thereby lost the tacit support of the Rajputs and stirred into hostile activity the militant Marathas—a sturdy race of peasants and yeomen from the inaccessible hill country between Poona and Bombay. Under their brilliant leader, Shivaji, they soon became the terror of all neighbouring lands. Against their chain of strong hill forts, the armies of Aurungzeb exhausted themselves in vain ; and his death in 1707 marked the close of an epoch.

It was in 1739 that the Persian Emperor, Nadir Shah, swept down from the North, struck a final blow at Mogul power and conquered Delhi—the tragic city. Mistress of many victors, despoiled by invading armies, she still remains in essence unconquered ; but beneath the iron heel of Nadir Shah, sacked with every circumstance of brutality, she did seem to be dead indeed.

The Persians, carrying off all seizable booty, bled the country almost white ; and to Hindu princes the word went forth bidding them ' walk in the path of submission, or be blotted out from the face of creation ' : a threat that failed to coerce either Rajputs or Marathas.

Those cool, insatiable robbers merely proceeded to raid India more widely than ever ; till the hapless people themselves—crushed by rapine and pillage, by the march and counter-march of armies—became a masterless multitude, clinging to any power that offered protection.

Over the whole Peninsula, during those decades of anarchy, there existed no centralising influence or authority, nothing even approaching national sentiment. The Mogul despotism had kept foreign traders in their place ; but, when it fell, India lapsed into a chaos of warring merchants and plundering Princes. Everywhere the weakest went to the wall. Any ambitious man could seize a fief or principality, and hold it, till some stronger neighbour snatched it from his grasp.

Yet it was during that century of almost unrelieved darkness, that the little company of English merchants, going quietly from strength to strength, built up a thriving trade. In the course of it they had acquired Bombay, by grant from Charles II ; had founded Calcutta and other small settlements on the river Hooghly ; had safeguarded Madras by building the famous Fort St. George. Harassed by local officials and raiding Marathas, with the whole country in apparent dissolution, it soon became pike-staff plain that the Company must be prepared to defend life and goods against all comers.

It was about this time that another European trade rival appeared on the scene. While the Dutch continued their drive for monopoly, a French East India Company was building factories along the Malabar coast, and everywhere increasing its legitimate activities ; not in trade alone.

It was Dupleix, a Frenchman of genius, who made the significant discovery that a small force of Indians trained by Europeans could out-match any rabble army of Rajas or Nawabs. Here was an obvious temptation to intervene in princely quarrels and obtain political influence that might ultimately oust the English. To that end, Dupleix cleverly exploited the policy of closer relations with various Indian rulers, supporting one against another ; a policy that undesignedly led the British—not the French—along the path to Empire.

Neither Company wanted war ; but, as French influence increased, it became clear that the two could not long work in harmony. The inevitable clash occurred over political rivalry at the important Moslem Court of Hyderabad, and the Nizām's feudatory, the Nawab of Arcot, who governed Madras. Disputes over succession provided a chance for Dupleix to install men of his own choice, which led to open friction with the English Company. The French attacked the stronghold of Madras, fell back before the stubborn English defence, and opened a friendly parley with the Nawab of Arcot.

It was then that there slipped out of Madras, in Moorish disguise, a young man of one and twenty, Robert Clive by name, an underpaid clerk in the East India Company, reputed to be of a martial disposition ; a reputation he affirmed with the astonishing speed of genius spurred by ambition. No more office stool for him, but an Ensign's commission, followed up by a note from the Company to those in authority : ' Be sure to encourage Ensign Clive in his martial pursuits '. The event and his own gift of leadership soon proved encouragement enough.

His ' reckless diversion '—the capture of Arcot (capital of the Carnatic), its gallant defence and ensuing victory—are well-known episodes in the story of British Indian history. As a feat of arms the Arcot victory made Captain Clive immediately famous. None could fail to recognise all that the defenders owed to the super-human valour of one man, ' who seemed to care little or nothing for his own life, and thereby won others to a like vivacity of noble-ness '.

Through the play and the film ' Clive of India ', his personality and dramatic story have been made more or less familiar to the English-speaking world. Reckless, ardent, ambitious, he went from triumph to triumph. His victory at Plassey led to stronger measures against French influence, and to installing in Bengal a Nawab who would favour the English. It was not conquest the Company desired, but a friendly Ruler ; not territory, but trade. ' Of all the interloping European nations,' it is written, ' the English were the last and most reluctant to draw the sword even in defence.' The best among them have always recognised, like Sir Charles Metcalfe, that ' carrying their point by equity and moderation is the proudest triumph for British character '.

The prevailing policy of the time was to manœuvre for influ-ence at native courts by the loan of European officers to train and lead their contending armies. It was the age of the Free Lance, of adventures often beyond belief. Every province fell to fighting some other province or intriguing for power. Everywhere the land was full of burning homesteads and the reek of innocent blood. No safety for any man, but in the strength of his own right arm. Between Moslem and Hindu, Rajput and Pathān raged a deadly enmity, each sect or clan aiming at the extirpation of the other. Thus the last years of the eighteenth century became known as the Great Anarchy ; and at the dawn of the nineteenth century all was dark. The stars were paling. It was not by any means certain what the day was likely to be.

By that time the East India Company had become the strongest among many powers contending for provinces lost to the Mogul.

B

Self-preservation was the only principle on which they could deal with their neighbours ; for the powerful and predatory Marathas respected the security of no State weaker than their own. The English, in Clive's words, ' had succeeded in doing to the French all that the French had planned to do to them ' ; but, although dominant in Bengal, they had not taken over the reins of government ; and inevitably abuses crept in, that were as bad for Indians as for the Company's good name. Clearly they must either leave Bengal, and lose valuable trade, or take the responsibility of government, for which they had no taste at all.

It was then that London sent out Warren Hastings, described as ' the greatest Englishman who ever served in India '. Promptly he grasped the situation, took the reins of government and speedily evolved a more just and workable system than any Indian Province had known before his day.

In a few years, working against incredible difficulties, he used the new British power for the benefit of the people to an extent that partly atoned for the evils of an earlier reluctance to govern.

But there still remained the uncrushable Maratha chiefs, whose raids had kept the country in a turmoil for close on a century. Not only had they survived the great Afghan defeat at Paniput, but had renewed their fighting strength with a resilience all their own. Between 1775 and 1818 they fought no less than four major wars with the British. The last one amounted to a trial of strength for the prize of Empire ; and it needed all the military genius of Wellesley and Lake to smash that strong confederation.

The conflict might have been sooner ended—and British power firmly established by Lord Wellesley—but for his premature recall and the lack of vision among Home authorities : a chronic British defect which has been responsible for uncounted tragedies. In this particular case the backing of Lord Wellesley's vigorous far-sighted policy of alliance would have saved Central India and Rajputana from fifteen years of anarchy and chaos unequalled in history. The hapless Rajputs, torn almost to pieces between their main enemy and predatory banditti, were only saved from extinction by the final, hard-fought Maratha war and British victory ; their independent existence at last assured by an alliance, based on the promise of military protection, that has held good for more than a hundred years.

Seldom can peace have descended more gratefully than on those ravaged regions of Central India ; and ' the liberality of the Government ', wrote Sir John Malcolm, ' gave grace to conquest. Men were for the moment satisfied to be at the feet of generous and humane conquerors . . . and the combined effects of power, humanity and fortune were improved to the utmost by the character of our first measures.' The major Princes became subsidiary allies ; smaller vassal States gladly transferred their allegiance to unchallenged British arms. Only Sindh and the Punjab were still outside the picture.

Thus, without flourish of trumpets, the Pax Britannica was born : a power for good that, in time, evolved order and justice out of the anarchy that for decades had convulsed Central India.

Through feats of British arms and diplomacy a kaleidoscope of shifting fragments had been stilled, if only for a time. Uncertainty and tyranny had given place to a measure of stability. By an extraordinary series of chances and changes, by the genius of a few men, and the curious luck of the race, a great commercial Company had won lordship over all but the two Northern Provinces of India. . Even those who know the full facts cannot easily gauge how immense was the task undertaken and achieved ; nor realise that British ascendancy among those warring elements was an essential stage in their social and racial evolution.

The composite entity, resulting from that achievement, consisted of three great Provinces under direct British rule—Bombay, Bengal, Madras—and a number of Indian States—that had been either conquered, conciliated or saved from conquest—bound to Great Britain by treaty, in subordinate alliance : a relation that has no parallel in history.

The Rulers of these manifold States were given a guarantee of military protection from one another—security of succession and independence within their own borders. They, in return, must acknowledge British supremacy, must give up the right of making war on other States, or dealing with them except through the Governor-General : a policy of isolation essential, at the time, to peace and safety ; though, in the event, it was carried on too long. Not yet were their treaties direct with the Paramount Power. Not yet had been created the joint political achievement of Queen Victoria and Disraeli, now known as the Indian Empire. A great upheaval—the Mutiny of 1857—was to shake the foundations of British rule before Victoria proclaimed herself Queen-Empress of India—the ' brightest jewel ' in her Crown—and inaugurated the Golden Age of Britain in India : a period of fifty years and more.

2

Of the States themselves, their number and variety, I have already given some idea. Only certain of the major principalities can be dealt with in detail : but, from greatest to least, they all represent different degrees of autocracy, from its better features to its worst, according to their stages of development.

In many of the smaller States one may step back hundreds of years, on leaving the railway station, into a mediaeval atmosphere incongruously enlivened by the blare of radio or gramophone, the glare of electric light. Many Chiefs of these backward States are survivals from the past that give some colour to the falsifications emitted by political-minded Indians, whose caricatures of the Princes are inevitably coloured by their own extreme bias against kingship and the British connection. Certainly not many Rulers would be likely to confirm the sweeping statement that ' British protection has destroyed their sense of responsibility, killed popular initiative and sapped the vitality of hereditary institutions ' ; or that personal rule ' breeds economic stagnation and social decay '. Nor would they recognise their own people as ' reduced to cringing servility and abysmal despair ; rotting in a foetid atmosphere of vice and corruption : shamelessly exploited and taxed for the benefit of Palace luxuries, their hearts burning with anger and hatred against fantastic misrule '. Unfortunately such palpable distortions are too often credited by readers who forget that in bitterness of political and religious partisanship, East can give points to West.

Admittedly every form of government has its faults. There are good and bad rulers among Eastern maharajas as among Western kings ; but wholesale denunciation must largely defeat its own ends. Such writers conveniently overlook the fact that the Indian Prince—autocrat though he be—is hedged about with restraints and restrictions of a religious nature ; dedicated to the kingly ideal by sacred Hindu texts in his coronation oath ; a dedication that counts for much in principle, if not always in practice, among six hundred or so of normal human beings, at all stages of development. The tyrannical and irresponsible Ruler, still found in backward States, cannot in justice be cited as typical. The old idea that the people exist for the Ruler has long since given place to recognition that the Ruler exists for his people.

For every case of undue extravagance one could name half a dozen Princes whose Palace expenditure is moderate if not frugal : though many of them still evince the curious Eastern craze for quantity. The father of the present Nizām bought spectacles by the hundred. They would be laid out several inches deep all over his billiard table ; and he would derive an almost childish pleasure from trying on pair after pair, putting aside each one that pleased him, till the chosen ones mounted to a pile and were removed. Probably not one of them was ever put on again. There is a

Prince who owns 270 cars : with a silver-plated one for his Maharani ; and Patiāla's last Maharaja had a passion for pedigree dogs, bought by the score and paid for at kingly prices, better housed and cared for than many human beings. But if a Maharaja may not indulge in a few harmless personal tastes, who may, in this mercifully variegated world ?

Most Englishmen, with personal experience of modern Indian States and personal friendship among their Rulers, would confirm the testimony of one who writes that ' emphatically the private lives of the major Princes or Chiefs of India will bear comparison with those of any corresponding number of men in high places anywhere in the world '. Indeed the more important among them could hold their own with almost any Western statesman in personal attainment and mental calibre. To do them justice they have no desire to be treated as demi-gods. That is simply the instinct of their own people. They themselves are genuinely keen to be good Rulers, as progressive as may be ; keeping in view the welfare and happiness of their subjects.

Their success in both respects has been affirmed by many Englishmen equally familiar with the States and the Provinces. They describe, in passing from one to the other, a sense of escape from the over-regulated, over-legislated British Provinces, from the monotony of the same law courts, the same schools and jail, the same schemes for sanitation, welfare and ' uplift ', not always appreciated by the custom-ridden, custom-loving East. The normal, well-run State, in fact, seems better suited to Indian taste and temperament than the efficient but unwieldy administration of British India.

The average Indian craves variety and excitement, as do most natural men and women of every race. He will take up his bed and tramp endless miles in quest of a wedding, a *méla* [1] or religious festival : anything to break the monotony of his day-to-day existence. Above all, the Raja-ruled States provide more opportunities for individual enterprise, for the swift, dramatic settling of family quarrels, for the greatest of all opportunities, a chance to make good if they have fallen from grace ; so that an outlaw, one day, may even live to become an honoured Government colleague.

But if there are high lights, there are also deep shadows. Court life, in the smaller States, impinges closely on the lives of the people ; and many of these could tales unfold that might have been culled from the Arabian Nights. Queer and exciting things can and do happen outside the law. The police may be more corrupt, justice more rough-and-ready ; but it is prompt and

[1] Fair.

personal ; less costly than interminable law-court trials, with their bribed witnesses, hired corpses and greased palms. The British themselves, in early days, recognised the merits of a swift uncomplicated code in dealing with Asiatics. Sir Henry Lawrence, whose knowledge of Indians was unique, advocated ' the very simplest form of equity, carried out by men who mix freely with the people and will do prompt justice in their shirt sleeves, rather than expound law to the discontent of all honest men '. And Sir William Barton, a high authority, expresses a doubt whether the ' complex hierarchy of Bench and Bar ', now favoured by certain progressive States, will prove a real boon to the people.

Beyond everything, the normal Indian craves personal contact with his Ruler : an instinctive desire that has its roots deep in human nature. Everywhere and always intimate relations with the Ruler have been the mainspring of loyalty, as the British Royal Family has good reason to know. And the States, for all their diversity, are alike in preserving, to some extent, that cherished tradition : the extent varying with the habits and personality of the Prince himself.

Industrialism, with certain exceptions, has not yet widely spread its tentacles into the States. The village still survives as a social unit; and the people themselves are less trammelled by hordes of officials. There is more to relieve the monotony of their days ; more fairs and public holidays with their interminable shows, their excuse for gaily-coloured garments. And the great yearly festivals, Hindu and Moslem, are celebrated with princely pomp and splendour ; prancing horses in silver harness ; outriders in royal livery, shouting ' Make way ! make way ! ', painted elephants in procession, their huge forms hung with cloth of gold ; the greatest among them topped by the swaying gilt howdah—a throne for the Maharaja himself.

There, uplifted, he sits in State attire, richly embroidered coat and jewelled turban, scarlet State umbrella held over him from behind—a curious adjunct of royalty that dates from early Rajput days, when the bearer of the royal umbrella rode into battle with his Maharaj, shielding him as far as might be, yet obviously making him a mark for the foe.

The college-bred student of economics may condemn these pageants and processions, implying that money wrung from starving peasants is wasted on royal vanity. To the peasants themselves and the normal Indian townsman they stand for music and dancing, colour and excitement : all that dwells in the magical word *tamāsha*. In a deeper sense they satisfy the common human need for worship, nowhere more prevalent than in the East. The

Maharaj may levy taxes ; his hand, at times, may be heavy upon them ; but he is one of themselves, bound by their traditions, his kingly rank commanding the loyalty of his people. Man, who lives not by bread alone, will neither worship nor die for economic stability or adult suffrage, least of all in India. It takes an idea to equip a human being with wings. He will die for his faith, for his King, his country or his flag. Were it ever to be otherwise, our world would indeed become ' a cattle-yard of a planet '.

It is precisely India's instinct for worship that gives peculiar significance to the intermittent visits of England's Royal Family : visits that have made the British Crown no mere abstraction but an inspiring personal force, with a peculiar appeal to the heart and imagination of India. When King George V and Queen Mary went out, as Prince and Princess of Wales, the deep impression left by their personalities was incalculable. Sir Walter Lawrence, touring with them, found less significance in the enthusiasm of cheering crowds than ' in the quiet yet compelling influence of Prince George himself ' : an influence felt by all who came in contact with him.

As in the West, so, still more in the East, the survival of monarchy depends on the twin elements of kingly prestige and kingly attributes of character : a consideration that shifts our interest from the States as political units, to the men who rule them ; men who, in several instances, have almost created them as they exist to-day.

Portraits of some fifteen Princes will be attempted in this book. The remaining six hundred can only be considered in bulk : and inevitably there are many lesser Rajas untrue to the best type and tradition. But the arm of the Paramount Power is not shortened ; and if any Prince becomes notorious for gross misrule, the Viceroy has right to replace him by a more promising member of the reigning family.

The vast area covered by Indian-ruled States has been well conveyed by Sir William Barton in a paragraph that can be followed on the map :

' From the huge mountain mass of the Pamirs and Himalayas to Cape Comorin, a distance of nearly 2000 miles, one might travel almost entirely through Indian India without once entering British territory. . . . Similarly one may pass from West to East from the Indus almost to Calcutta, through a stretch of independent States.'

Large or small, backward or progressive, they may be taken as a standing proof that ' the Indian political genius has always shown

preference for the moderate-sized Kingdom, more or less the type
of the Indian State to-day '.

In the early eighteen-forties there was a large measure of
justice in the prevailing belief that the Indian people, as a whole,
were better off under British rule than under autocratic Princes,
more congenially engaged in fighting each other than in looking
after their States.

Even so, men of vision and understanding, like Sir Henry
Lawrence, recognised the independent State as best suited to the
taste and temper of the people themselves.

It has already been shown how most of the important Rulers
owed their power and security to British friendship or British
arms : a fact that went far to prevent the Sepoy revolt of 1857 from
spreading into a veritable Indian Mutiny.

It was the loyal help of Sikh Princes in the Punjab that enabled
the stalwart John Lawrence to reinforce the British and Indian
Army during the critical siege of Delhi.   Column after column
of military stores and ammunition travelled safely down the Grand
Trunk Road, kept open by the good offices of the four ' Protected
States '—Patiāla, Kapurthala, Nabha, Jhind : a signal instance of
Asiatic honour upheld in the face of unparalleled temptation.
Notably also a case in which British fair dealing with the States
concerned brought its own reward.

No less vital to victory was the support of Moslem Hyderabad,
where sympathy with fanatics of their own creed must have run
high, though the people themselves are mainly Hindus.   But the
Nizām did not forget all that English friendship had done for the
State since they rescued his grandfather from bandit Maratha
chiefs.   So he and his wise young Minister—the famous Sir Sālar
Jung—threw all their weight into forming a loyal buffer between
North and South India.   In Rajputana, under Sir George Lawrence, British power and prestige were safe.   Farther south,
Mysore and the Marathas, with one doubtful exception, remained
staunch to former friendship.   Thus the day of trouble—as often
happens—proved the day of reward.

3

It was after the Mutiny that a new era dawned for the Princes of
India, who had either remained neutral or actively supported the
British Raj.

In a happy hour Queen Victoria issued her famous proclamation as Empress of India ; removing the menace of annexation,
re-affirming the former treaties and making the Princes direct allies

of the Crown.   In explicit terms the Queen-Empress stated, ' We shall respect the rights and dignity and honour of the Native Princes as our own ' : and she kept her queenly word, even if those who acted for her did, at times, over-emphasise British supremacy. To her and her successors the Princes tendered their allegiance the more willingly because it was no longer given to a great trading company, but to the Sovereign of a mighty Empire.

Like the rest of India they have suffered from the five-yearly change of Viceroy, which often involves a change of policy as well as personality.   In Lord Dufferin (1885) the Princes found a Viceroy of tact and understanding, the first to honour them with those regular Viceregal visits that bring them into personal touch (always a talisman in India) and improve political relations.

The corps of Imperial Service troops began with Lord Dufferin ; the Imperial Cadet Corps with Lord Curzon—a true if forceful friend of the Princes, and perhaps the most variously estimated of England's many notable Viceroys.   He took a genuine interest in the education of minority Princes.   He did not favour public school and university for a coming Ruler ; and in the Cadet Corps he provided younger sons with a useful and honourable profession.   The education problem assumed a supreme importance in the case of long minorities : and it is worth noting that several of the most distinguished Maharajas were enthroned as minors and educated by English tutors on lines that prepared them for their high calling.   Many virtual creators of modern States— Baroda and Mysore, Hyderabad and Bikanir—would gratefully admit the debt they owed to British tutors who became their lasting friends.

No account of India's Princes, however brief, could be complete without mention of their services to the Crown and Empire, whenever there was a fighting toward, in India or elsewhere. Most notably they rose to their supreme opportunity in 1914, when the King's stirring Call to Arms awoke instant response from all India's fighting races ; while the Princes vied with each other in offers of soldierly help and personal service.   Spontaneously they flung themselves, their troops, their money into the war against Germany.   No effort, no cost seemed too great.   Contingents of Imperial State troops, serving with the British Indian Army, helped to hold the Suez Canal, to keep watch on Sinai, and proved their mettle in General Allenby's victorious campaign.

The full tale of their contribution to the Second World War remains to be told : but from the first they have given money and service without stint.   To name a few among many : the Maharaja

of Bikanir, from his desert kingdom, sent his famous Camel Corps
and contributed £1000 for war sufferers in the dastardly air attacks
on London.   The Maharaja of Patiāla also sent money and troops ;
despatching the last, in Eastern fashion, with a votive offering of
flowers.   In a stirring speech to his people, he urged the whole
Sikh brotherhood to sink their differences and rally to the fight for
civilisation.

' This war ', he told them, ' is our war no less than Great
Britain's.   In this time of crisis it is our solemn duty to make the
cause of civilisation our own—the cause for which Great Britain
is staking her all.   Her success or failure will be our success or
failure.'

To the Viceroy he conveyed the inflexible resolve of the Sikhs
to fight to the end, ' in defence of their moral and spiritual heritage '.

These manly words are not the vapourings of an effete autocrat,
bolstered up by England for her own ends.   They are the words of
a born Ruler who wields increasing influence over the whole Sikh
brotherhood.

The Nizām of Hyderabad, very early in the day, presented the
Royal Air Force with a squadron of Hurricanes that bore the name
of his State and did fine work in the south-west of England :   a
prelude to further princely gifts that will be recorded in a chapter
devoted entirely to the generous part played by India's Princes in
the war.

Reverting to their normal way of life and the formalities of
regal recognition, there are certain points on which every Prince
of standing is extremely jealous :   (1) the public indication of his
precedence and prestige by the exact position of his seat at Imperial
Durbars ;   (2) the number of guns that make up his royal salute.
Out of six hundred chiefs, only seventy-three are entitled to that
coveted mark of royalty :   only five of them being accorded the
maximum of twenty-one guns.   These are known as the twenty-
one-gun Princes—Hyderabad, Mysore, Kashmir, Gwalior, Baroda.
The guns of the rest are graded by twos, from twenty-one to
eleven :   and that traditional form of salute is dearer to them all
than the Western mind can realise.   It is more than a mere
recognition of status.   It is a matter of *izzat*—roughly rendered as
prestige.   But the implications of *izzat* go deeper.   It includes
personal honour, and is jealously guarded from any smirch or
slight.

In all matters affecting salutes and seats in Durbar, Political
Officers must walk delicately and season tact with understanding,

even in situations that, to Western minds, may seem to border on the ludicrous.

A case of the kind happened many years ago, when my father was Resident to a blue-blooded young Rajput Prince, whose guns were only eleven, because his State was small. To him came, on a formal visit, a thirteen-gun Raja whose lineage could not compare with that of his host. But he could boast a wealthier State and a higher salute.

On arrival, with imposing suite, he was duly installed in the Guest House, where he awaited a welcoming visit of ceremony. But the Sun-descended Rajput set his pride of birth above the other's wealth and guns. Flatly each refused to stir ; nor could my father, for all his Irish gift of diplomatic persuasion, induce either of them to make the first ceremonial advance.

Baffled but amused, he recognised that this question of the first move was a serious one, and sympathetic understanding produced a happy idea. A man was told off to measure the exact distance between Palace and Guest House, and to draw a line on the open plain midway between the two. To that line each Prince could advance and meet his fellow, without either sacrificing a shred of personal prestige. Both young Princes were sufficiently enlightened to see the humour of the device : but it worked. At the half-way line they exchanged friendly greetings. The royal guest could then proceed to the Palace ; and honour was satisfied.

One may smile at the childish device ; but we have not the key to racial sensibilities : and Western man also has his own little weaknesses, along other lines, that must often seem childish to Eastern wisdom.

First and last there can be no sincerer tribute to the major Princes than the high esteem in which they are held by those Englishmen who have had the widest experience of them as Rulers and as individuals. Whatever their natural human failings, the best of them are great gentlemen, courteous and dignified ; sure of themselves and their lineage ; taking pride in their armies and the well-being of their people : increasingly ready to work with one another, for the good of their own Order and of India as a whole. The record of their long allegiance to the British Crown is an honourable record of pacts faithfully observed, of mutual friendship and esteem strengthened by the passage of time. The finest among them are men of brains and character who will go far to steady the Federal plan for India, if and when it ever assumes a workable form.

Men of diverse personality, they are one in their will and capacity to uphold their country's finest traditions; one in their devotion to the Empire and in their resolve to fulfil the Empire poet's prophecy :

> *So long as the Blood endures,*
> *I shall know that your good is mine : ye shall feel that my strength is*
> *yours ;*
> *In the day of Armageddon, at the last great fight of all,*
> *That Our House stand together and the pillars do not fall.*

THE PRINCES OF INDIA AND THE WAR

England, India, one together,
Thames and Ganges, East and West,
With the same foul storm and weather,
Worst, that still demands the best.
G. ROSTREVOR HAMILTON.

A PLAIN, if partial, statement of India's response to the Imperial call of 1939 and onward is worth setting down, though the tale cannot yet be told in full.

Even so, it is worth recording here how Prince after Prince, from the greater States like Hyderabad and Kashmir, down to some of the least in size and wealth, placed at the King-Emperor's disposal his personal service and the whole resources of his State. All were lavish in gifts of money and supplies. Those that have troops at once despatched them ; and a number of States offered their own forces to stations in British India, thus releasing regular troops, British and Indian, for service elsewhere. Several of the Princes raised war battalions and trained recruits for the expanding of the Indian Army, besides arranging to care for the wounded in convalescent homes.

Gifts and offers of all kinds were received, literally by hundreds ; and although the scope of these varied with the wealth of the donors, the same spirit was manifest in all : a spirit of unbounded generosity, enhanced by the fact that the States are not British territory nor are their people British subjects. Yet the material support given by them has reached remarkable proportions ; and all are agreed that every hampering domestic and political difference should be set aside during the war ; a resolve well expressed by the present Jām Sahib of Náwanagar, in the Chamber of Princes, that India must not ' fritter away her energies in other channels, when the law of the jungle threatens the basic foundations of civilisation and the ordered progress of humanity, including India and the Commonwealth '.

In their spontaneous rally to the support of the British Throne they offered help in every form, without delay and without stint. During the first ten months of the war, their gifts reached a total of £300,000, apart from recurring gifts of some £280,000 to the Viceroy's War Fund, or individual gifts that have, in some cases, amounted to £22,000 and £15,000. Twenty-eight Princes have given sums of one lakh [1] apiece : expressing in this practical

[1] One lakh = £7500.

19

fashion their active resolve to help in achieving absolute victory.

Where such imposing sums of money have flowed in from greatest and least, it is obviously impossible to give a complete list of all. Only a few can be recorded in detail.

To begin with the greatest and wealthiest, Hyderabad—whose Rulers have been our allies since the year 1785—the Nizām not only sent units of State troops to serve with the Army of Empire in Africa, but, immediately on the outbreak of war, his Government made a gift of £100,000 for the formation of a fighting air squadron.

It was known as the ' Hyderabad Hurricane Squadron ', was constantly in action, and soon created a very fine record for itself. Its first success was gained in February 1940, when it shot down a Heinkel off the north-east coast ; and during the ten days August 13th–23rd it brought down no less than twenty-four Junkers and Messerschmitts. The total enemy loss up to August 24th was thirty-four planes. His Exalted Highness may well feel proud of his fighting squadron and be assured that the cost of its creation and maintenance was well justified. The value of this gift was further enhanced by a further gift of £50,000 for maintenance and for a squadron of bombers. Another £150,000 provided a corvette for use in combating submarines.

From His Exalted Highness himself came a personal donation of £50,000 towards the cost of a fighting squadron or a corps of mechanised tanks ; followed up by a further sum of £37,500 to the Viceroy's War Purposes Fund. He also arranged to give a monthly contribution of Rs.150,000 (£11,250) during the war.

That princely lead spurred his people to a like generosity. Thousands, rich and poor, sent sums ranging from a few pence to donations of £10,000. £22,500 was collected towards the cost of one Hurricane. Nobles and landowners have announced their intention of giving three more aircraft.

Such was the prevailing spirit of emulation that during the first fifteen months of hostilities the Nizām and his Government subscribed no less than £750,000, besides meeting the cost of many other activities for war purposes : a noble record for the premier State of India. And Bhopāl, India's second Moslem State, contributed £54,000 worth of American securities.

Among all the great Hindu Princes, the call to arms evoked the same eagerness to serve and to give. Mysore proved invaluable in the industrial field, followed up by large donations for aircraft and to the British Exchequer : a total amounting to six lakhs of rupees. The Maharaja of Baroda added to his earlier gift of £45,000 another £5000, for a flight of fighter aircraft.

That staunch friend and doughty Rajput, the Maharaja of

Bikanir, offered to raise and maintain six battalions of infantry, plus the services of his famous Camel Corps, under the command of his only surviving son. And his Maharani herself gave £1000 when war broke out. ' The loyalty of the Indian States ', declared the Maharaja, ' has no price, nor was it a matter of bargain and barter. Such an unchivalrous attitude has never been part of the policy or creed of the Princes at the hour of the Empire's need.' Characteristically he added : ' No Rajput is ever too old to fight ! '—a statement to which he has given practical proof. Though well into the sixties, he is now on active service in the Middle East, with his eldest grandson, a boy of seventeen ; the first time, in the recent history of the State, that grandfather and grandson have together gone to war for their King-Emperor.

The soldierly spirit of Bikanir was reflected in a hundred other instances. From Gwalior, Indore, Alwar, Jaipur, Udaipur, Cooch Behar, Travancore (in the far South) and many more, came unending offers of service and special gifts for the purchase of fighting aircraft.

The chief Sikh States of the Punjab—Patiāla, Kapurthala, Jhind—were fired with the same generous rivalry in giving. Two Kapurthala Princes, sons of the well-known Maharaja, volunteered to serve personally, the elder having served in the last war. The Maharaja of Patiāla has already been mentioned as having urged the Khālsa (Sikh Brotherhood) to sink their differences and unite in rallying to the British cause. He has also raised thousands of Sikh soldiers for the Indian Army.

Several States raised war battalions ; and, to take another field of service, those who had industrial facilities helped considerably to increase the output of supplies, placing technical plant and industrial machinery at the disposal of the Government for the making of munitions.

Again, many States have given valuable help in dealing with war emergencies, notably in the matter of taking over Italian prisoners after the collapse of Italy in Africa. The Maharaja of Mysore alone undertook to accommodate 20,000 of them at short notice, his favoured State not being hampered by the many difficulties of India's climate.

Everywhere, in fact, new links were forged by the spirit of united war effort : that one aim eclipsing every other, while the war endured.

In brief, India's war record, from start to finish, has proved creditable alike to her hereditary Princes and her people. It has justified the first principles of British rule, that evolved a stable system of government and alliances from the chaos of earlier years ; that transformed enemies into loyal friends, who stood firmly beside the British Empire in its hour of need.

Though political unrealities continued to function in their limited sphere, India's fighting races, from States and Provinces, ' covered themselves with glory ' at Sidi Barrani, Keren and many decisive African engagements ; also in the Irāk, Irān and Syrian victories. The first D.S.O. presented to an Indian officer was won for great gallantry by a nephew of Sir Ranjitsinhji of Náwanagar : an exploit fully recorded in my portrayal of that famous Prince, more widely known as ' Ranji '.

The Rulers themselves, by personal example, set a high standard before their people, appealing to them on moral grounds and urging them to lend every possible help towards victory for the Allies. Their active support of a great World Cause and the noble response of individual Princes drew from their King-Emperor on March 14th, 1941, a glowing tribute that must have fired their pride and lifted their hearts.

His telegram to Lord Linlithgow, his Viceroy, must be quoted in full :

In a message to India after the outbreak of war I expressed my confidence that in the coming struggle I could count on sympathy and support from every quarter of the Indian Continent in face of the common danger. This confidence has been fully justified, for throughout eighteen hard and anxious months the help of the Princes and people of India has been generous and unfailing.

The loyalty of the Indian Princes to their King-Emperor, on which I know that I can rely even more surely in the hour of trial, has never been more openly displayed. From the Provinces of India and the Indian States has flowed a constant and invaluable stream of men, money and material to swell the rising flood of the Empire's war resources. Moreover, while her fighting forces have been upholding, in many widely scattered theatres of war, the military traditions for which India is so justly famed, her people have been giving freely to the relief of suffering and distress.

I thank the Princes and people of India from my heart for their noble response and for their kindly sympathy. I know that the ideals for which we are fighting are as deeply cherished in India as throughout the British Commonwealth, and I am confident that the magnificent support which India has so readily and unsparingly given to the common cause will be maintained until victory crowns our arms.

GEORGE R.I.

In conclusion I would add the more recent tribute paid by

General Sir Archibald Wavell in his New Year broadcast to the people of India—January 1942.

' India ', he said, ' is playing a great, most honourable and increasing part in the struggle.   She can look back with pride on the magnificent achievement of her troops in Libya, East Africa, Syria, Irāk, Irān, Malaya and Hong-Kong.   Never has their reputation stood higher, or their exploits been more admired. Their losses, up to the present, have been comparatively light, in proportion to the results they have achieved.'

And the end is not yet.

FIVE STATES OF RAJPUTANA:
LAND OF KINGS

*Only that which represents an ideal to a man is permanently vitalised.
. . . There are no more noble types than these Rajputs, the greatest
triumph of human breeding that I know of. They are knightly through
and through.*—COUNT KEYSERLING.

UDAIPUR:
CITY OF ISLAND PALACES

I

CERTAIN tracts of earth possess a magic intrinsically their own.
Not least among them may be reckoned Rajputana, land of stirring
tradition and stirring names—Udaipur, Chitor, Jōdhpur, Bikanir ;
each with its own proud or tragic story of ' far-off things and
battles long ago '.

In the north it is a strong, unlovely desert region of sand and
rock, chivalry, cruelty and daring. On its few oases Rajputs have
founded kingdoms ; and the long low range of the Aravāli hills
divides it into unequal parts : their waters converting the southern
half of the land into a region of mountains and lakes, of jungle
and rocky woodland : fit setting for its capital city—immortal
Udaipur.

' The beauty of Méwar is as the beauty of no other State ',
writes one who had seen Indian India with an eye fresh to the
East. ' On occasions of welcome, its men and women, gathered
on every roof, in every doorway, put all other gala decorations to
shame. Udaipur does not proclaim its emotion, except with that
infinitely graceful salutation of the East ; hands to forehead and
swaying figures, like a gust of wind sweeping a field of flowers
—purple and green, scarlet and gold. Far over the plain, towards
Chitor, Rajput horsemen sit erect, sword in hand, shield slung to
the shoulder, streamers of scarlet, green and orange swathing
their horses' heads.'

Udaipur itself—shrine of past glories, in its setting of mountain
and lake—is steeped in a haunting sense of feudal times, of the
age-old strife between Moslem and Hindu that colours all Rajput
history, reaching its climax of tragedy and heroism in the thrice-

repeated sack of Chitor. That sacred city—once the proud capital
of Méwar—crowns a high fortified rock that rises abruptly from
a tangle of scrub and boulder and broken ruins fallen from above.
A dirty little modern town crouches at its base ; and its vast bulk,
against the brightness of morning, justifies the hackneyed simile
of a great battleship breasting rough seas. Kipling began it ; and
as it can hardly be improved upon, others have followed suit.

' The swell of the sides ', he wrote, ' follows the form of a ship
—from bow to stern more than three miles long and from three
to five hundred feet high.'

Derelict for centuries, that proud and lonely vessel has forged
through seas as rough as any in the troubled waters of Rajput
history. She has survived alike the chivalry and splendour of
her warrior kings, the ruthless onslaught of all-conquering Moguls,
the heroism of self-immolated women and self-dedicated men,
who charged through her main gates in the saffron robe of mourning ; pledged to take such terrible toll of the hated Moslem that
triumph might be darkened by the price paid for it.

Three times in her history Chitor endured the horrors of siege
and sacrifice, culminating in the barbarous process of sacking a
conquered city : first in 1303 ; again in 1535, when thirty thousand
Rajputs, in the final charge, reaped so mighty a harvest that victory
did indeed become a terror of desolation.

Finally, in 1567, Akbar himself, a youth of five and twenty,
sought alliance with his kingly neighbours : a wise move that
would have saved Chitor. Unhappily his offer was flouted by the
least kingly of Rajputs, Udai Singh. So he, that might have
come as an ally, came to conquer where he could not conciliate ;
and the despicable Udai Singh, absent from his capital, did not
return when the flower of Méwar arrived post-haste to defend
Chitor.

But Rajputs have never lacked a leader ; and his place was
taken by sixteen-year-old Putta Singh, who fought and died in his
saffron robe, his widowed mother and girl-wife beside him, lances
in their hands, fighting like men.

Many girls, barely old enough to marry, fought to the death
that day beside warriors who might otherwise have been their
bridegrooms. But courage, heroism and sacrifice were unavailing
against Akbar's hordes. Once again the command was given for
the last tragic rite of *johur*. Then did nine Queens, carrying their
cherished infant sons, followed by some thirteen thousand Princesses and women, descend into the caverns below the Palace, where
funeral pyres had been set alight for those who proudly faced the
devouring flame rather than live to sate the lust of the conqueror.

Above them, in the doomed city, eight thousand men, in saffron robes, charged once more through the gates to give and receive death, in the last indomitable onslaught that made Chitor a shrine of valour and a place of desolation for ever.

' By the sin of the sack of Chitor ' passed into the language as the most solemn oath that any Rajput can utter. And Akbar rightly, in later years, recorded his admiration of that last heroic defence by placing, at the gate of his Delhi Palace, two statues of the young Rajput leaders Putta and Jaimul of Bednor—names that will live while Rajasthān endures.

Chitor itself—the ' widowed city '—still remains a living centre of Hindu faith, as it once was the cradle of Hindu chivalry. There the sun is still worshipped daily in a temple more than a thousand years old ; while Udaipur is, even to-day, the stronghold of a tradition so remote and undisturbed as to startle our mush-room vanities.

The Rajputs themselves—though forced in the end to make terms with Delhi—have remained in essence unconquered. According to Captain James Tod—their devout biographer—they present ' the sole example of a people withstanding every outrage that barbarity can inflict, from a foe whose religion commands annihilation ; bent to earth, yet rising buoyant from the pressure, making of calamity a whetstone for courage '.

When Tod wrote those words, he had no foreknowledge that his tribute to Rajputs might, centuries hence, prove apt to the undefeatable spirit of Poles and Czechs, rising buoyant from the pressure of cruelties unmatched even by the worst that Moslem fanaticism could inflict on a prostrate yet unbeaten foe.

As for the despicable Udai Singh, who shirked the defence of his capital, it was he who, by a strange fatality, built Udaipur, immortalising thus his own dishonoured name. There he made a vow that, while Chitor remained ' a widow ', Rajputs would never twist up their beards ; never eat off anything but leaves, nor sleep on anything but straw. And centuries after, the Rānas of Udaipur, in their own fashion, still honour his vow : sleeping in sumptuous beds—laid on straw ; eating off gold and silver plates—laid upon green leaves : and never twisting their beards. That typical Eastern evasion was recorded by their sincere admirer, Sir George Birdwood, in 1915. Whether the vow is still so curiously kept, only the present Maharāna and his court could reveal : and no doubt they would rightly consider it their own private affair.

The Rajputs of Mēwar—neither tribe nor clan, but a military caste—claim descent from the Sun, through Rāma the god-hero of India's sacred epic the *Rāmayāna*. To quote Sir William Barton :

UDAIPUR : THE PALACE FROM PICHOLA LAKE

UDAIPUR : ELEPHANTS WRESTLING WITHIN THE ROYAL PALACE

(From *India of the Princes*, by Rosita Forbes)

' From the Himalayas to the border of Madras, Rajputs have governed kingdoms and principalities for two thousand years. No other race has such an unbroken continuity of rule. Even to-day, these proudest of India's princes rule one-tenth of the land.'

Warriors all—of the Kshattriya caste, that is second only to the Brahmin—they have had their fill of battle and murder and sudden death. From earliest recorded times, Rajasthān has been the Flanders of India : torn and ravaged not only by the greater wars, against Mogul and Maratha, but by perpetual feuds and jealousies among their thirty-six royal houses. These fought one another, as royal houses know how to do, brother against brother, son against father : a tangled tale of force, fraud and cunning, desperate love and more desperate revenge ; crimes worthy of demons and virtues fit for gods.

Yet, for all their human mingling of good and ill, the indubitable fact remains that these astonishing Rajputs—India's oldest aristocracy—did create a new form of Indian chivalry ; that their Rulers did preserve, through all vicissitudes, the religion, the culture and traditions of the Aryan age.

In a practical fashion, by rigid rules of life and marriage, they preserved their own integrity as a sacrosanct military caste ; the only Hindu caste with any quickening and controlling traditions of political power and responsibility.

To-day, having survived the storms of centuries, they form the main bulk of Indian States. They affirm the vitality of the kingly system and the peculiar fitness of one-man rule for a people who will always follow an individual rather than a cause. ' In blood, brawn and bone,' wrote Sir George Birdwood, ' in their ineradicable virility they are one and the same Aryan people as ourselves'; their failings offset by courage and a keen sense of honour, by pride of race and passion for freedom.

Let it not be forgotten—as by them it never is—that these virile Rajputs did virtually save Hindu India from the flood of Moslem invasion ; that they have given her the most enduring of her political institutions, the feudal Rajput State. In this twofold achievement lies their main title to renown : and that same feudal system, based on the bed-rock of human nature, might even now be adapted to the needs of a progressive age.

Apart from all that, their history is full of colour, vitality and unquenchable courage, whether in victory or defeat. Long before Akbar, their conquering armies had reached the Himalayas and set up an Aryan dominion all over Northern India. Kashmir itself is still Rajput-ruled : and many old Rajput families remain in the Himalayas and in the Punjab. Forced to make terms with Akbar, after the final tragedy of Chitor, they continued to hold their own under the son of that worthless·Udai Singh : a son who livingly embodied Rajput chivalry and courage—Rāna Partāp Singh. No easy Palace life for him : no inglorious peace with the Moguls. Till victory returned to the Sun-descended, he decreed that the war-drums of his army should march behind instead of in front. For twenty years he lived roughly as a soldier in the wilds of Méwar ; he and his followers actually sleeping on straw and eating off leaves. He fought and conquered Raja Mān Singh of Jaipur, refusing to dine with him because one of Jaipur's daughters had been given as a bride to Akbar. He won back most of Méwar ; but he could not revive thrice-murdered Chitor.

While Akbar lived, comparative peace prevailed. Inherently noble, he aimed at dissolving all religious and social barriers between man and man : an achievement beyond even one of the greatest Emperors of all time. Illiterate to the last, he made others read to him ; and he learnt to understand the minds of men by slipping out of his Palace at night in disguise, wandering through street and bazaars, mingling with the crowd, talking, listening and watching their behaviour, especially that of Hindus. Unable to wean these from their age-old creed, he could and did advance them to his highest State appointments, where they served him faithfully, while maintaining their own beliefs and customs.

But Akbar's nobility and tolerance died with him. Under his great-grandson Aurungzeb, fanatical persecution again reared its evil head. An orgy of destruction and desecration of Hindu temples dishonoured a truly imperial line and brought it to an ignominious end.

For, as Mogul power waned, the pirate Princes of Central India came down from strongholds in the Western Ghauts under their brilliant leader, Shivaji. Later still, in the dark days of anarchy and chaos, it was these same bandit chiefs who persistently harassed and often conquered all regions north, east and west of their own. More especially they menaced the Rajputs, fighters of equal prowess, handicapped by inter-State jealousies and intrigues. Recklessly independent, proud and vengeful, they were never able to combine effectively against the common foe. The whole region of Méwar was scoured from end to end ; lovely Udaipur squeezed like an orange : a process from which it had barely recovered more than a hundred years later. The Marathas might, in fact, have seized all Rajputana, but for the rising power of British arms, and the military genius of Lake and Wellesley, to whom, ultimately, the States of Rajasthān owed their very existence.

By an evil fate, when the Maratha peril was at its height—in 1805—Mewar was held by a weak and incompetent Ruler, as in the last fatal days of Chitor : and thereby hangs a tale of tragedy that has thrown a lasting shade of melancholy over the princely House of Udaipur.

The tragedy sprang from a quarrel between the Princes of Jaipur and Jōdhpur, rivals for the hand of a young and lovely Udaipur Princess, daughter of a worthless father, Bhim Singh. At the age of twelve she was betrothed to the Prince of Jōdhpur ; and when he died the bride-to-be was claimed by his successor, on the specious plea that her betrothal was not merely to the Prince but to his throne of Jōdhpur.

Now it so happened that his claim had been successfully forestalled by the debauched and effeminate Prince of Jaipur. Here was matter for fierce rivalry between two warlike States, both swift to seize any excuse for flying at each other's throats.

Incredible as it sounds, all Rajputana was convulsed, for seven long years, by that fierce battle for the hand of Udaipur's child-Princess—famous everywhere for her beauty and charm. Like another Helen, she became the cause of wholesale death to half the youth and valour of the land ; each Chief or Prince taking sides in the conflict.

Sindhia, Maharaja of Gwalior, supported Jōdhpur and laid siege to Udaipur. The poor-spirited Rāna, alarmed by the storm he had raised, appealed at last to Lord Lake, begging the British to intervene : a move that was prevented by a ' cruel and ignorant order from England ', where the tragic facts were probably neither realised nor understood. British refusal hastened the fatal climax. Bhim Singh, hard pressed by rival claimants, yielded at last to the brutal demand that he should either give his daughter to the rightful bridegroom, or have her murdered so that none might possess her. By that time she was nineteen—pure Greek in the grace of her perfected loveliness ; a second Iphigenia ; for her craven father, fearing the vengeance of Jaipur if he gave her to his rival, chose the cruel alternative—death in cold blood for his own daughter.

The order was given ; but no man in the Palace household could be found to use a dagger against defenceless youth and beauty. So the dire deed was entrusted to the women of the harem, who must persuade or compel the Princess to drink a draught of poison.

In the event, there was no need for compulsion. The spirit of that young girl shamed the cowardice of her own father. Obediently she accepted the decree that would bring peace to her loved country. It was she who comforted the wailing women, when her mother, shaken with grief, proffered her the deadly drink.

Dressed as a royal bride, she calmly looked out over the serene Pichola Lake and its island palaces, lifted the bowl and cried out gallantly, ' *This* is the bridegroom destined for me '. Then she fell down in a fatal swoon at the feet of her weeping handmaids : and, in dying, made her name immortal. Even now the heroine of Méwar is a theme for Rajput ballad-makers and poets.

The cruel, senseless tragedy stirred all India ; stirred even distant, uncomprehending England to belated horror and remorse. A weak Home Government had much to answer for in those dark days. Timidity and lack of vision among responsible Home authorities condemned Central India and Rajputana to fifteen years of anarchy and chaos almost unprecedented in history.

It was the Marquis of Hastings—India's seventh Governor-General—who was chosen to carry out a more virile policy of active intervention, to save Rajputana and ensure British supremacy in that part of India. Then were the harassing banditti destroyed, Gwalior isolated, the power of British arms reasserted by victory after victory, under the fine generalship of Sir Arthur Wellesley ; till, in 1818, the Marathas were finally defeated ; and all India, except the Punjab and Sindh, acknowledged British dominion. Gratefully the rescued Rajputs contracted a protective alliance with the power that had saved them from annihilation and secured their independence for ever.

Since that day—a hundred and twenty-two years ago—they have dwelt secure in their many States, great and small ; too secure, perhaps, for a soldier race of men who regard war, religiously, as ' an open door to heaven '.

Undeniably the protectorate, by abolishing risk of war, tended to sap the virility of Rajput manhood and weaken its moral fibre. The great nobles, a fine body of men, grown richer and more prosperous, found themselves left with no practical *raison d'être*. Yet, taking them all round, they have remained true to their tradition of chivalry, courage and sportsmanship.

Certain Indians, who can perceive no merit in British rule, insist that it has emasculated India and her princely families. No doubt there are many regrettable cases in point, since every good is shadowed by its attendant ill ; but to postulate lack of courage in the protected Indian States is to libel the race. The great days of Indian knighthood may be past, but the spirit of it survives—and will survive.

In these days, one need only mention names as familiar as Sir Pratāp Singh, Sir Ganga Singh of Bikanir, the young Princes of Jaipur and Jōdhpur, who probably give the measure of hundreds less widely known. Undeniably, in long periods of peace and prosperity, the men of most races tend to grow effete and comfort-loving. But when the trumpet-call ' To Arms ' challenged British and Indian manhood—as in the years of the First World War—their instant response proved that it was not dead, but sleeping. In 1914 the soldier races of India vied with each other in readiness to defend their one-time defenders ; even as our own over-civilised young men—on land and sea and on the wing—proved over and over all the ingrained qualities that are " for ever England '.

Generations may come and go, standards of faith and courage and leadership may rise and fall, but the spirit of race is immortal, renewed from age to age in those great men who most shiningly embody it—' and their name liveth for ever more '.

2

Thus, through the vicissitudes of a history as brave, tragic and stirring as any on earth, we come to comparatively modern Udaipur. Steeped in tradition, remote and serene among its lakes and hills, it has made less obvious progress, in the accepted sense, than the other great cities of Rajasthān. Partly this has been deliberate ; a refreshing change from the persistent pursuit of progress else-where. No Rāna of Udaipur has been to Europe ; and the city's unusual beauty, its feudal atmosphere, have been safeguarded by one of its most distinguished Maharānas, the late Sir Fateh Singh, himself the embodiment of Rajput royalty with his height, his fine features and his cleft beard. In full Durbar, surrounded by his nobles, he might have stepped straight out of the twelfth century ; and during his rule, the duties and privileges of feudal times were strictly enforced. Even now the peasant ploughs his land with the Rajput shield strapped to his shoulders, and with sword or spear at his side. The whole setting of city and Palace harmonised with the picturesque figure of its revered Ruler.

A life of austerity and restraint so preserved his vigour and energy that he could stick pig and shoot tigers up to late middle age. Stoutly he refused to let the ' fire carriage ' enter his sacred city, that is like no other on earth. The railway ends in a small station three miles off. Only cars and carriages, horses, elephants and camels can fitly enter through the tall Gate of the Sun studded with iron spikes ; a relic of distant days when the elephant's head was used as a battering-ram. In the same spirit he chose to use the waters of Udaipur for adornment rather than for irrigation ; preferring, no doubt, that its people should die of no drains, rather than of too much efficiency.

When apostles of progress asked why he did not develop his State, he would answer with his unemphatic courtesy : ' I am Rajput : soldier and sportsman. Not bunnia.'[1]

Something of the old heroic spirit breathed in his resistance to change ; ' something immense and pathetic ', wrote Miss Fitzroy, ' in the challenge he flung to those new forces that the West cannot control and dare not defy '. Behind his aloof and exquisite manner there lurked a strain of melancholy ; a shadow of the curse that is said to rest on Udaipur ever since that young and lovely Princess was sacrificed to avert the threat of war.

' He had '—wrote Sir Walter Lawrence, who knew him as well as any could know a being so remote—' the most perfect manners in the world ; gracious and inscrutable alike to all. It was interesting to watch the effect of that wonderful manner on diverse persons. Even the great Lord Curzon fell under its charm. Little might be said, but much was conveyed in the atmosphere of that noble presence. It was a privilege merely to sit with him.' Nor could any ever guess what he really thought of the polite strangers from the West, who talked, in well-meaning ignorance, of things they could not know ; things that none could know unless the blood of Rajputs ran in his veins.

But there needs no Rajput heritage to awaken a responsive stir of mind and imagination at the first sight of Udaipur—one of the few experiences, in a land of wonders, that can be counted on to better expectation.

The glory of that unbelievable city may be of the past ; her beauty remains inextinguishable, while two and a half miles of steel-blue water mirrors her infinite variety, and the setting sun baptizes with light and colour the dead-white walls of Palace and city and marble *bund*. Massed trees, against the brightness, glow darkly as if carved in jade ; and as light fades colour deepens. Water turns to wine, reflecting island palaces, more dream than reality, in that flaming end of evening that fades too soon into a ghostly dusk. So much breath-taking beauty everywhere, that details escape the eye, lost in wonder at the whole. There is nothing quite like it anywhere.

Aloof and impenetrable, as Sir Fateh Singh himself, that imposing pile of marble and shorn granite seems to breathe the haughty spirit of Rajput valour and pride of race : grey-white

---

[1] Shopkeeper, moneylender.

houses, domes and towers, fretted balconies and the royal zenana building a precipice of blind white wall, its foundations set deep in water.

From this oldest part, the rest seems to lean back in bastions, terraces and winding stairs, crowning the ridge along all its lifted length : a profusion of exquisite detail that almost defeats design. Has anyone ever tried to count the minarets, the fretted windows, the arches, the balconies ?

Drained of colour in the brief dusk, it looms majestic ; a shrine of the kingly ideal rather than of kings human and fallible. Its true period long past, it continues its magnificent existence unconcerned. Guarding its human secrets, tragic and squalid and heroic, it remains at this late hour a stately symbol of autocracy in a reeling world.

More than a symbol it was to the eighty-year-old Maharāna, who ruled his kingdom as absolutely as any old-time autocrat, however benevolent : no authority other than his own ; no system of finance ; no supervision of local officers. Here was fertile soil for intrigue and political agitation directed from Ajmir. These gave rise to so much trouble among the indigenous tribes that the Government, regrettably, felt obliged to curtail the powers of India's most revered Ruler ; as loyal at heart as he was splendid in aspect. That drastic measure caused no small alarm among his fellow Princes ; and embittered, not without reason, the last years of his own life.

During those years the State was practically ruled by his son Sir Bhupāl Singh, who needed a large measure of tact and forbearance to pull him through the difficult position in which he was placed by the Paramount Power.

By one of Nature's ironical twists, the son of that magnificent figure of a man is slight and frail and partially paralysed ; true Rajput, in that he has refused to let that cruel disability hinder him from moving about his State on business and shooting expeditions. Though he can never be a rider, he is a first-rate shot ; and occasionally he entertains distinguished strangers from England. But, like his father, he has never crossed the sea and very seldom travels beyond his own borders. Perhaps because of his bodily limitation, he possesses a curiously subtle brain ; and there are not many who can penetrate the shell of his reserve. He seldom visits Delhi ; cares very little for politics and less than nothing for the Chamber of Princes, an assembly favoured by few of the greater ones, who pride themselves on their personal relation to the British Crown.

With the passing of youth—he is over fifty-five—his life has

been more or less restricted to the ample confines of his vast and
varied Palace, almost a town in itself ; with its own store-houses,
farmyards and wells ; as large if not larger than the city that climbs
to it up the hillside from the Gate of the Sun. There gaily-
painted houses lean towards each other across narrow winding
streets thronged with the mixed, leisurely traffic of the East ;
scarlet horsemen with small turbans and large curved swords ;
golden-skinned women of the desert crowned with brass lotahs ;
children everywhere and chickens and stray dogs ; milk-white
bulls, privileged and sacred ; panniered camels with drooping
underlip and scornful eye. Now and again, shouldering through
the crowd, comes the vast bulk of an elephant flapping impossible
ears. And everywhere a kaleidoscope of colour—amber, ver-
milion, orange, purple and palest green.

There we have the very aspect and atmosphere of feudal India,
rooted in the past, centuries removed from hybrid Bombay : and
at dusk silver bells ring the fairy city to rest.

Sun-drenched streets and shrines and temples climb up and up
to the Palace, epitome of power in possession ; and not far from it,
symbol of spiritual power, rises the mighty cone of Jagadésh
temple, carved from base to summit with a confused mingling of
gods and goddesses, monsters and men.

Outside that curiously self-contained world, politicians may
wrangle and non-violence violently rage, Hindus and Moslems
may annihilate each other, so long as the sons of Kings hold their
own land and a descendant of Rāma rules in Udaipur.

Up and up, till at last one reaches the outer Palace ; the great
gateway leading into a courtyard crowded, like the streets, with the
varied animal population of India : monkeys, camels, donkeys,
and again the sacred bull *en famille* ; the jewelled gleam of peacocks
—royal birds of Rajasthān—self-consciously sunning their
splendour on coping or battlement. Here also the royal elephants
are picketed, monsters of flesh and sinew nervous of their own
bulk, meekly obedient to slips of brown men whom they could kill
at a stroke. High above the spacious open roof over the wide
gateway looms the main bulk of the Palace, blinding white against
the blue. Below it—far below—gleams the silver shield of Pichola
Lake, with its island palaces and fringe of wooded hills ; one bold
outline cleaving the sky.

The Palace itself, behind imposing walls and towers, seems
quite another world. Curiously haphazard and lacking in design,
it has the fascination of some fairy-tale castle ; a maze of low
doorways and twisting stairs ; little secret rooms and blind court-
yards ; glimpses of sunlit lake and sky through carven arches ; a

UDAIPUR : ENTRANCE TO THE WATER PALACE

(High Commissioner for India)

UDAIPUR : RUINED CITY OF CHITOR

(From *Great Men of India*)

small open terrace, shaded with orange trees, and a splash of scarlet uniforms—peons lounging on guard.

Up a ladder-like staircase cut in the wall, you may climb to one of the many-arcaded towers, where His Highness, Sir Bhupāl Singh, sits cross-legged, Indian fashion, in English garb and expensive English boots that never touch the ground. Here he receives his few European guests talking to them in fluent English, untravelled though he is. From his eyrie, he looks down upon a wide fair view of lake-side and city and low hills, merging into a troubled sea of mountains that range northward to Mount Abu and Ajmir.

There remains one aspect of Udaipur that should, if possible, not be missed—the yearly celebration of the Dewáli Festival, Feast of Lights, when Lakshmi, Goddess of Fortune, is worshipped in the living gold of fire and the dead gold of minted coin ; when women worship their jewels and each man worships the tools of his trade, tossing coins or dice to discover his luck.

And at sunset, when a breeze ripples the lake, young girls go in groups down to the water, each carrying her *chirāgh*, the lamp of life, a cotton wick alight in a clay saucer of oil. These they set afloat on lake or tank, praying that Mai Lakshmi may guide them safely to the farther shore. If the prayer is heard, omens are good. If the little *chirāgh* be wrecked or broken, omens are evil. So—apart from the beauty and wonder of its elaborate illuminations—it is a feast of intensely human significance in a land saturated with superstition. And it culminates, after sundown, in a fairy-like illumination hardly credible in this machine age.

For weeks beforehand every potter's wheel is turning out little *chirāghs* by the thousand, each with its lip in which the cotton wick may rest. These are placed, edge to edge, everywhere along roofs and walls and balconies ; along places possible and impossible, to await the moment of nightfall on that day of days.

As the flaming sunset dies into the brief dusk of India, city and palaces and island pavilions appear to stand like ghosts under a darkening sky. Then the first thin points of fire flicker and waver, ' dancing alive from nothing, lovely and mad '. Deepening from amber to gold, the little blown flames run along walls and window-frames, over roof and arches, as if they caught fire from each other ; so skilful and swift are the unseen hands at work. More lights, and more, spring to life everywhere ; thousands, tens of thousands, till the transformation scene is complete. Palaces, temples, islands, even boats by the shore—the whole of Udaipur blossoms on darkness, in flickering delicate lines of fire. Flame palaces float on the waters of an enchanted lake, where stars are put out by a restless shimmer of gold that seems hardly to be of earth.

Slowly, as night deepens, the quavering lights burn low and lower, till the magic scene dies out, leaving Palace and city and lake just visible in the ghostly gleam of starshine and a waning moon. The fairy scene, that dazzled the eye with its wonder, is eclipsed by the immortal beauty of the heavens that lifts the mind to worship and speaks direct to the soul.

The goddess of Fortune should surely favour her votaries who worship her with this yearly unforgettable vision of all Udaipur, printed in fire on the night sky of Rajasthān.

JŌDHPUR:
THE WARRIOR STATE

I

AFTER immortal Udaipur, loveliest of Rajput cities, we go northward to the Indian desert and Jōdhpur, the largest and perhaps the most soldierly Rajput State, known chiefly through the fame of one man—best-loved of his kind and generation outside India—Lt.-General His Highness Sir Pratāp Singh, K.C.S.I.

As third son of the Maharaja, his father, he never actually ruled over Jōdhpur ; but three times he acted as Regent during minorities : a total of twelve years in all ; and, in addition, he was made Prime Minister, when his elder brother succeeded his father. For twenty years, in fact, he was the life and soul of Jōdhpur public affairs ; coercing wild tribes and handling truculent barons in his effective, summary fashion. It was he who raised the Jōdhpur Lancers and created a polo team that, for a time, held the Indian championship, besides winning laurels at Hurlingham and Ranelagh.

The State itself geographically has nothing in common with the lake and hill setting of Udaipur. Mile on mile of sand, burned to the colour of amber, blossoms here and there into an oasis, where the parched earth is watered by the Luni river. Marwar, Land of Death, the whole region was aptly named before modern irrigation works helped to fertilise some sixty thousand barren acres ; and reservoirs, with pump stations, banished drought from the city. Good motor roads have revolutionised transport. The close-cropped green polo ground, in its desert setting, looks as if it had been lifted on a magic carpet straight from England ; and, in this natural abode of camels, ships of the desert are now rivalled by dragons of the air.

Jōdhpur was founded in 1459 by the Rathore Chief Rāo Jōdha, who christened it Jōdhpur, City of Jōdh. He built part of the town and the fortress on its pinnacle of rock, four hundred feet above the clustered white houses, the temples and palaces crouching at its base.

' Hardly, in all Europe,' it has been said, ' could one find any stronghold so menacing, so cold as that elephantine fort, yellowish on its yellow hill, dominating the yellow desert under the golden Indian sun ; a stronghold that might have been built by demi-gods.' Walls monumentally thick seem a veritable emanation from the rock itself. Only in a land of elephants could such masses of stone have been lifted and shifted into position. For the fort is set upon a pinnacle rather than a plateau ; and its immense walls, guarded by towers, are pierced by seven fortified gates. No enemy could enter except by forcing those huge main gates that open wide to admit distinguished visitors—but not their cars.

These must be deserted for carrying chairs, slung on poles, that will bear them up the steep narrow ascent between high blank walls on one side, and on the other eight storeys of the Royal Palace, with its thousand-columned hall, its carved balconies and windows hanging against a narrow strip of sky : the kind of thing that only India's architectural genius could achieve—in how many years of building ? But none reckoned time, in ancient India—a timeless land, where perfection of design and craftsmanship was the workers' sole concern.

The Fort—a world in itself—contains more palaces, barracks, armouries, the royal zenana and treasury, guarding State jewels to the value of some three million pounds. Here are shields and scabbards and writing sets crusted with precious stones : shoes of some vanished Queen so thickly cased in diamonds that no material can be seen ; pearls and more pearls, literally in handfuls : the garnered wealth of centuries.

Indian India is a mine of such hoarded treasure : millions' worth of hidden beauty ; ' frozen riches ' amounting to an iron ration, against the possibility of lean years or evil days. For the wealth of an Indian Prince is more than a personal affair. It must be on a par with the cost of his whole State ; since he is father and deity, as well as ruler of his people. Troops, police, army, schools, cripples and beggars—the whole upkeep of his country—must all be paid for out of his revenue and exchequer. To whom much is given, from him much is required ; and even the wealthiest principality has its ebb tides of fortune. But modern Jōdhpur prospers ; and the glory of its past survives for those who have eyes to see.

In almost every Indian State there is some special feature—building, personality, legend—that seizes one's interest and imagination. In Udaipur, it is the Palace and the tragic ruin of Chitor. In Jaipur, it is the deserted city of Amber. In Jōdhpur, it is that work of demi-gods, the Fort ; fit birthplace of the incomparable Sir Pratāp Singh, whose name aptly signifies ' Lion of Glory '. Dead nearly twenty years, his influence still lives. Still they can say of him, ' He has no equal—he must have lived many times. Perhaps he will never need to live on earth again.' His record is unique among the Princes of India ; and before his death he added lustre to a brilliant beginning.

Far-famed and widely loved, intimate friend of three British sovereigns, he has been aptly named ' the first gentleman in the British Empire ', using the demoded word in its higher meaning. A Rajput of bluest blood, he reckoned himself beyond all rules and codes except those dictated by his own sense of fitness, which was of the most exacting ; a trait finely shown in the familiar story of an English subaltern who died at Jōdhpur, and whose coffin could not be moved because one of the officers detailed to carry it was down with fever. No Hindu of caste could touch a coffin without defilement. An outcast scavenger seemed the only solution ; but the officers reckoned without Sir Pratāp. The young man had been his friend ; and he promptly offered himself as pall-bearer with the characteristic remark, 'A soldier knows no caste with a brother soldier'. Perhaps only a Hindu could appreciate the spiritual significance of that simple courteous action.

Rightly he belonged to the warrior desert tribe of Rajputs, the Rahtores. ' Famous in battle ', and Sun-descended like the Seesodias of Udaipur, they trace back their pedigree for over fourteen hundred years. According to legend, the first Rahtore sprang from the spine of Indra, God of storms and thunderbolts ; a legend in keeping with their history, that is mainly a red page written in their own blood. Always in the thick of danger or trouble, they welcomed any sacrifice that might save their land from the fanatic fury of Islam ; and their unshakable courage has been embodied in the proverb, ' A wall may give way : a Rajput stands fast '. Of such was Sir Pratāp, devotee of England and Englishmen, and of all that they stand for, East and West : a devotion partly inherited from his father, Takat Singh, who ruled Jōdhpur during the Mutiny.

At that time the boy Pratāp was twelve years old, living with his parents and family in the Fort Palace. There were, then, neither railways nor telegraph wires in Rajputana. Even in British India these were still recent marvels introduced by Lord Dalhousie. So news of the upheaval did not travel post-haste into the desert. But one day there came a runner, with letters that told of a sepoy revolt in Bengal, of the men murdering their officers, British and Indian. Followed wild rumours that the last remaining Mogul had been enthroned at Delhi, that all Rajas were tendering allegiance to him, and British power was at an end. The rebels were killing white women and children without mercy ; and Takat

Singh was urged to send his own representative at once to the court of Delhi.

The Rajput Prince—British friend and ally—scorned alike their rumours and their advice. In his fury, he·caught at the throat of his twelve-year-old son.

' Even if my children were killed *that* way,' he thundered, ' I would never desert the Sahibs. We have sworn friendship. And no Rajput will ever betray a friend.'

In that creed the boy was reared ; and his own personal affection for the Sahibs was deepened, no doubt, by early association with Englishmen of the best type, notably Sir Edward Bradford, A.G.G.[1] of Rajputana, and Colonel Powlett, Resident of Jōdhpur in the days of Pratāp's early manhood. To both personalities he attributed a large share in the moulding of his character ; and both would have readily admitted that they had fine material to work upon, in his generous nature, his courage and uprightness, and the iron will that curbed his proud and hasty temper.

So lasting was his devotion to Colonel Powlett that, on his retirement, Pratāp would never fail to seek him out, when he visited England ; would bend down and touch his knees as a mark of affection and respect.

It is hardly possible to over-estimate the influence, for good or ill, of the Englishman in India ; and, one might add, of the Englishwoman also. It would be well for both races if the last were more actively alive to the fact.

It was about this time that Pratāp—always eager for fresh experience—decided to take service with his sister's husband, the Maharaja of Jaipur, a wise and statesman-like young Ruler, who very soon recognised the latent ability of his untiring brother-in-law. Their friendship led him to offer Pratāp an important post in Jaipur ; a tempting offer for a young man not yet thirty, as ambitious as he was adventurous. But Pratāp's heart was in Jōdhpur. He would accept no post that might prevent him from returning there, if he happened to be needed by his brother Jaswant Singh, who had succeeded their father. And in a few years' time he had his reward.

An urgent message from Jaswant Singh begged him to return at once and help to reorganise Jōdhpur. The Prime Minister had proved a failure : money spent like water, with nothing to show for it ; things in general going from bad to worse. With Pratāp as Prime Minister, they might, between them, give the whole disorganised State a lift. Nor was he disappointed of his

[1] Agent to Governor-General.

hope, in spite of the fact that Pratāp had to hold his own against persistent, hostile intrigues, engineered by the discredited official whom he had supplanted. He found the office of Prime Minister very much to his taste. His activities were unbounded : tackling unruly tribes, checking wholesale bribery, restoring law and order, and effectively reforming the whole State machinery. For the first time he had a chance to prove, in practice, how well he had profited by the statesman-like teaching of Rām Singh and the shining example of his revered Colonel Powlett. In his new capacity, also, he found full scope for more than soldierly qualities : his resolute will, his faith in iron discipline, for himself and others ; his power to win affection in spite of a tendency to summary methods. In effect, it may be said that he found himself and spent himself, without stint, to the lasting benefit of Jōdhpur.

It was in 1887, the year of Queen Victoria's Golden Jubilee, that he was chosen to carry congratulations from the Rathore State to Her Majesty in person. He had only been once to England, and his limited English, his ignorance of the country, led him to ask for the services of an English officer. The choice fell on Captain Bruce Hamilton with two young Rajputs of his own standing. His friend Sir Edward Bradford was also a fellow passenger ; and the two Englishmen coached him assiduously in their difficult language. His twists and turns and odd phrases caused so much mirth, that although he did, in time, learn to speak English fluently, he clung more or less to his own version of certain phrases and his taste for the present participle. To his pride and delight many of his odd phrases were treasured by four generations of the English Royal Family—all his devoted admirers and friends. Whether or no he could have improved his shrewd and effective broken English, none who knew him would have wished his racy talk to be other than it was.

By that time he had become Sir Pratāp, having received his K.C.S.I. from Lord Dufferin in 1885. At Suez he disembarked and travelled overland to see something of Europe. Enchanted with the beauties of Vienna, his pleasure was dashed by the news that his ship, the *Tasmania*, had been ' drowned ' with all his belongings and £22,000 worth of jewellery to be worn in honour of the Queen—he that wore none at any other time. For their rescue he offered £1000 ; and the divers were surprisingly successful in recovering the jewels ; but none of his wardrobe could be salved. How London was to produce Indian brocades and embroideries for so great an occasion remained to be seen.

Meantime he travelled on to Paris, where rooms had been booked for a week. But within three days, in his decisive fashion, he turned down the supreme city of Europe.

' I did not like it at all,' was the emphatic verdict of that desert-bred, spare-living Prince of Rathores. ' The moral atmosphere seemed to me quite noxious. Only pleasure-seekers resort there. And on this account I got disgusted with the city.'

Though he had paid for a week in advance he could not be persuaded to stay it out.

' I care nothing for the money,' was his characteristic answer. ' It is improper for men of high birth and good breeding to stay in such a city.'

London, where he found ' every sort of comfort ', did not so prickle his fastidious moral sense ; and from Indian material, given him by Lady Rosebery, he acquired a fit garment for his interview with the Queen Empress : one of the ' most sacred memories ' in his eventful life.

His own simple record of that meeting can hardly be improved upon.

' The august Queen Empress was pleased to send for me ; and in obedience I presented myself. Reaching near her, I made my salute, Indian fashion, placing my sword on the ground : then, coming closer, I kissed her gracious hand, extended in English style ; and immediately I raised it to my eyes. All English officers present were astounded at the eccentricity of this salutation : and after the reception was over they asked me about it. I explained that, according to Indian ideas, it was thought ill to salute one's master bearing arms. So I laid down my sword. Further, after kissing Her Majesty's hand, I raised it to my eyes, because there is nothing dearer to a man than his eyes. This explanation seemed to satisfy everyone.'

No doubt it also satisfied Queen Victoria, that gesture so purely Eastern, with its depth of double meaning : and a further episode increased the good feeling that was to remain constant between them. Distinctions had been showered on him ; and, as Honorary Colonel of the British Army, he was soon placed on the Royal Staff ; proudly in attendance on the Queen, when his fellow Princes came to make their bow and present their nazars—the Indian gesture of a formal offering to royalty. These nazars are often costly ; and they are only accepted in the form of ' touch and remit, after the manner of Kings '.

Sir Pratāp, being on the Staff, had not thought to prepare one : and when his name was called for presentation, he found himself in a dilemma. But his alert mind was never at a loss. Promptly he plucked from his turban the gold and jewelled ornament, known as a *sirpaish*, and, standing near the Queen, he bowed, presenting it with both hands lowered.

This time—as if she read his heart—there was no mere touch and remit. Her Majesty took the proffered gift and passed it on to the Duke of Connaught.

That evening, at the Royal dinner, to Sir Pratāp's delight, she wore the *sirpaish* on her breast.

' She was pleased to call me near her '—he wrote afterwards —' and to say that, as I had presented my *nazar* with my heart's esteem and affection, she was wearing it in the same spirit.'

As he had charmed the Queen-Empress with his magnetic personality, so he charmed all the Royal Family and the leaders of London society. Beneath his native chivalry, he was a shrewd and critical judge of women ; and a delightful story is told— among many—of his remark at a big Calcutta reception when the woman he was talking to said, ' Sir Pratāp, I want to introduce you to that lady over there.'

One comprehensive glance sufficed. Sir Pratāp shook his head.

' No, thank you, I not want. I think not very gentlemanly lady.'

Briefly, but decisively, the unknown was turned down by that quaint yet damning adjective.

He stayed in many great country houses and described them as ' unique of their kind in the whole world '. The grandeur of the Jubilee procession deeply impressed him ; and he records, with relish, how the other Indian Chiefs were ' mounted in carriages ' ; and he alone was proudly mounted on a horse. Those who knew him best could hardly picture him otherwise.

Famous already as a polo player, he had brought horses for his party. They rode in the Park. They won races and matches at Ranelagh. They saw a sham fight at Aldershot.

Five crowded months he spent in England—not merely in a social whirl. All that he saw and learnt of new ways and new countries struck deep. He returned to India, in his own phrase, ' with expanded head and heart ', his outlook widened, his brain alive with fresh ideas and plans for the better government and progress of his beloved Jōdhpur.

Among many schemes that thronged his brain the proudest was an ambition to create a regular body of horse : the which he did to such good purpose that it afterwards earned distinction as the famous Jōdhpur Lancers. The success of his cherished plan owed much to the services of Captain Beatson, afterwards Sir Stuart Beatson, a fine soldier and great gentleman, who became one of his closest friends. It was he who actively shared the inception of the hardly less famous polo team. Begun in 1889, when Sir Pratāp was well over forty, it became, in a few years, one of India's four leading teams, second only to that of the 7th Hussars. It defeated Central India, with three British officers and one Indian player. It followed on, the same year, with a victory of eight goals to love over the 7th Hussars, in the final round of the Challenge Cup tournament.

In later years, when his polo triumphs were over, he took delight in building up a young team to carry on the fame of Jōdhpur : and in 1922 he enjoyed the satisfaction of watching that young teąm beat Patiāla in the finals of the Prince of Wales' tournament, the Prince himself being present.

An eyewitness records that throughout the game he sat absolutely silent and motionless, intent on every stroke and counter-stroke. Only when a bugle-blast announced the end and he lifted his helmet, the beads of perspiration on his forehead revealed how excited and anxious he had been. Always he was silent at polo, his whole mind on the game, never missing a stroke, almost angry if some conversational outsider forced him to utter a word. In the polo world, beyond question, his name and fame will lastingly endure.

In 1895 he lost his devoted elder brother, the Maharaja of Jōdhpur, who had been almost a father to him, even as he became almost a father to that brother's son.

During a three-years minority he was appointed Regent ; and he brought not only ripe experience but pride and pleasure to the task.

Unhappily, in this difficult position, he was to suffer—as men of his type often do—from the defects of his own qualities. As Prime Minister, his strong likes and dislikes had stirred the hostility of many whose malpractices had been baulked by his wholesale reforms. Whatever changes had seemed to him necessary for the good of Jōdhpur, he had insisted on them ruthlessly, often to the disadvantage of those who hugged imaginary grievances or played a double game. Now was their chance to combine and harass him at every turn, to manœuvre for secret influence, and discredit him with his beloved nephew.

Sardar Singh, neither strong nor sturdy, may have been irked at times by his uncle's extremely Spartan training—an uncle who favoured stone beds for ' making boy hard ', who encouraged pluck and manliness by the drastic means of making boys wrestle with a full-grown panther, securely muzzled, his four feet cased in strong leather ' gloves '. The young Prince, now secure on his throne, could follow his own very different inclinations. Surrounded by parasites and sycophants, entangled in a network of intrigue, he was alienated gradually from the finer influence of his uncle, whose devotion and care had alone pulled him through a delicate boyhood. Leaving the home they had shared, he set up his own establishment, and fell so fatally under evil influences that Government thought it advisable to remove him for a time elsewhere. The new Imperial Cadet Corps founded by Lord Curzon provided a healthy change of atmosphere and occupation. That period was followed by a visit to Europe : and his brief reign ended in 1911, without any legacy of reform and improvements such as his father had left to Jōdhpur.

During those years of private disappointment Sir Pratāp was very much engaged elsewhere. In 1897 he was in England again for Queen Victoria's Diamond Jubilee. Inevitably he went to visit Her Majesty at Windsor Castle ; and Sir Walter Lawrence tells how, on the return journey, he sat apart in the train silent and depressed.

' What happened at Windsor ? ' Sir Walter asked him at last. ' Did Her Majesty say anything to disappoint you ? '

Sir Pratāp shook his head, his noble face sad and grave.

' No—not that. But I seeing Queen ten years ago. I seeing Queen to-day. I not seeing her again. So—not talking.'

His personal devotion could hardly have been more profoundly, yet more simply expressed.

That same year he was on the Frontier for the Tirah Campaign, where his Lancers were lauded as ' an honour to the Empire '.

And inevitably he must be in Delhi for the great Curzon Durbar in 1902, to celebrate the crowning of King Edward the Seventh, a display of India's manifold splendours only to be excelled by the Royal Durbar of 1911, that will be dealt with in a later chapter.

The first one marked an end of the Victorian era : an unforgettable revealing of barbaric mediaeval India. ' For sheer spectacular magnificence,' wrote Lovat Fraser, the distinguished journalist, ' no sight I have seen can compare with the elephant procession at the State entry.

' No picture can convey that marvellous moment when the Viceroy, on a gigantic elephant, with all the greatest Princes of India, entered Delhi, slowly, impressively, the central figure in a vision so resplendent that at first the awestruck people forgot to cheer. For those who saw it, nothing will ever dim the memory of that solemn, irresistible march of elephants, the swaying howdahs of burnished gold and silver, the proud Maharajas seated on high, the clanging bells and martial music, the motionless enveloping troops, uncountable crowds in radiant clothing, and the majestic setting of the mighty Jumma Musjid, the vast red fort with an umbrageous park between. The Durbar can be repeated ; but not that unforgettable scene.'

In the midst of so much collective glory individuals were dwarfed to insignificant items ; but, even in a crowd so vast and various, the individual counts for more than its outward seeming. No insignificant item, on that superb occasion, was Colonel His Highness Sir Pratāp Singh, Commanding Officer of his own Imperial Cadet Corps, that formed a contingent in the Viceroy's escort and filled him with pride at the applause it won from all.

A brief word picture of the man himself brings him vividly before the mind's eye : ' Every inch a Rajput and a soldier looked Sir Pratāp, with flashing eyes that no detail escaped, clear-cut profile and proudly curved nostril, the stern mouth, with its touch of humour lurking at the corners. As he rode by the side of his Commandant, at the head of his corps in the beautiful white uniform with facings of sky-blue and gold—the crowd acclaimed him, as well they might. " They are calling my name," he whispered happily to the Colonel as he rode along ; a splendid figure on his black charger.'

He had lately been installed as His Highness the Maharaja of Idar, a small Rajput State whose ruler had died without an heir. Offered the Regency, he had flatly refused to tread that thorny path again, after his experience at Jōdhpur. But later, when the adopted boy died suddenly, he had found himself standing first among claimants for the throne, owing to his kinship and his fitness for the high task of lifting the State out of its deplorable condition. He could only wish that this late honour had befallen him as a younger man ; and, for all his gratified ambition, he left Jōdhpur with genuine regret, not foreseeing the manner of his return.

On the 12th of February 1902 he was installed, in full Durbar, as Maharaja Diraj Colonel Sir Pratāp Singh, with a dozen letters after his name. Speeches were exchanged that struck a note of more than the usual sincerity common to such occasions.

The Political Agent might well express his conviction that all things wise and kind, foreseeing and statesmanlike would be done for Idar by its new Maharaja, whose simple straightforward speech revealed the modesty that was not least among his shining qualities.

Mention of his own ' humble services ' rendered ' by good luck ' to the Empire, led him on to a final touch, eminently characteristic of the man.

Gratified by the honours and distinctions bestowed on him, he added, ' I covet nothing more in that direction. I do not mean, however, to convey that I have no ambition left. There is but one ungratified desire, which still continues uppermost in my mind ; that desire being to have a little lead deposited in my head while fighting under the British flag.'

Such words from such a man were no mere flattering figure of speech. For him, with the blood of warriors in his veins, there could be only one way of life, one dignity, one purpose. For him, no man worthy of the name could desire a greater gift, a finer end than death in battle. That soldierly ambition was not destined to be realised, though higher honours and more strenuous work in the service of his loved King-Emperor yet lay before him.

At the time he could only see his last years devoted to the rescue of Idar from the ill results of slack rule and financial chaos : and into the demand of the moment he, as usual, flung the whole of himself. Convinced that Indian Rulers should keep State administration in their own hands, he offered them, on the subject, words of practical wisdom worth recording.

' One great lesson, taken from the experience of my life, I wish to place before my brother Princes, is this : Give up love of ease and luxury : make yourselves, in every respect, *fit* to rule ; and take personal interest in the work of your State.'

Only three years later his loyal heart was gladdened by an honour even dearer to him than the title of Maharaj. It arose from the Indian tour of King George the Fifth, as Prince of Wales, with his Princess—the first Royal lady to visit that land of high-born, veiled women. Sir Pratāp, to his frank delight, was chosen as Chief of their Indian Staff by the express wish of King Edward the Seventh.

Filled with natural pride and uplifted in spirit, he saw the appointment as a sacred charge, saw himself as a deputy father to the Prince, who was then barely thirty.

' As from a distance ', he wrote, ' the royal ship came into view, my heart danced with joy ! '

To all who knew him well there was a peculiar charm in the simple-hearted affection and modesty of one whose will and Spartan life made him so ruthless in discipline that ' under the lash of his tongue strong men quailed and crept away like terrified children '.

No sign appeared of that iron streak in his complex nature,

while he kept devoted watch over his Royal charges. Only at times he would venture on a quaintly phrased remonstrance when the tireless young English Prince looked like overtaxing his strength or getting too little sleep, largely on account of his consideration for others. No end to the *levées* and the social functions that often kept him on his feet till 3 A.M., meeting fresh people and talking to them without end.

Sir Pratāp himself strongly disapproved of late hours. To bed between nine and ten ; up at 4 A.M., fresh for the day's work, was his own sane rule of life at Jōdhpur. Realising the demands on royalty, he helped where he could and refrained from remonstrance. But when it came to hard days out shooting or pig-sticking, followed by late nights of talk, and the Prince went down with an attack of fever, Sir Pratāp's distress moved him to a fatherly protest, recorded by himself.

' That night it grew very late in talking after dinner, and the Prince had got fever on account of fatigue. That day he had exerted himself too hard. It was not proper for him to sit so late. Accordingly I stepped up to him and said, in my choice English, " Now is a must-be sleep ", meaning it was time he should retire. After this, whenever it was late, after a tedious day's programme, I would rise from my seat ; and the Prince would at once rise also, coming to me, and say with laughter, " Now is a must-be sleep ? " Then he would retire.'

Another time, at Amritsar, when a Sikh ' armed with all sorts of weapons ' came too close, in his opinion, to the Prince, he wrote : ' Not deeming it right that anyone armed should come so near his Royal Highness, I quietly stepped forward to put myself between him and the Prince. No one, I think, saw the incident : but the Prince took my meaning and smiled at me.'

A different episode is worth recording as a sample of his characteristic shrewdness and devotion to England. One day out pig-sticking at Bikanir, he noticed that a German officer among the guests had been mounted on a very fine horse : and he bluntly remarked to the Prince, ' It were better if that man were given a horse that would have tumbled him into some pit '.

The Prince expressed surprise at so frank an expression of hostility to an unknown man.

But Sir Pratāp had his answer pat : ' I consider these Germans as the greatest enemies of the British Empire : and as such they deserve that kind of treatment '.

In 1905 there were many who might have considered him unduly vengeful : but in 1914 King George himself—receiving his old friend after the funeral of Lord Roberts—recalled the

Bikanir episode and commended Sir Pratāp for his correct view of the proven enemy. During the tour he kept unceasing watch lest any harm might befall their Royal Highnesses ; and his admiration of the Prince as sportsman—whether shooting grouse at Bikanir or tigers at Gwalior—knew no bounds.

Their visit to Delhi—six years before it became India's capital —moved Sir Pratāp to comments that prove the far-seeing mind of one who was more than the mere sportsman and soldier that he seemed to the world at large.

' Delhi, ancient and historic, was the capital of India for centuries : and the whole history of India is, as it were, entwined with the history of Delhi—rightly named Imperial City. . . . It is my belief that the British Government of India should also have its capital at Delhi. Firstly, this city is a central spot in India : secondly, it is so strongly associated with the tradition of Empire that hardly a better means could be conceived of strengthening the idea of the British Empire in the minds of our Indian people. . . . When the Prince went through the city, before the eyes of his subjects, it struck everybody's mind—whether Hindu or Moslem—as if there was a re-ascension of the throne of Delhi before their very eyes.'

Too soon for the Royal pair, and for Sir Pratāp himself, came the day of departure, the end of five crowded months that would never be forgotten by India or by the two who had taken the whole country—its Princes and people—to their hearts.

Sir Pratāp, in his sincere sorrow, wrote : ' All of us, who had been with the Prince for those few months, felt the approaching separation most keenly : for his truly Royal soul had won the hearts of all. When I was making my farewell salute to him, the blue feathers fixed to my turban stuck in the Prince's G.C.S.I. medal and were left there. The Princess at once took them and put them in her button-hole, saying to me, " Now I have your turban feathers with me. I will keep them always for a memory."

' In bidding good-bye to their Royal Highnesses I could not hold my heart ; and tears of grief came from my eyes. Others also had their eyes filled with tears. . . . When the ship had embarked, cries of " Hurrah " were raised by those on shore. To me this appeared unseemly ; for it was not an occasion of joy, but of regret and sorrow.'

None of them could then foresee how soon the beloved pair would royally revisit India as King and Queen ; nor did Sir Pratāp dream of the greater services that would be required of him by that same King in the years of the First Great War.

2

No living picture of the man would be complete without some revealing of his deeper personality—his ideas on religion and marriage, two vital matters more closely linked in the East than in the West. For years, as a young man, he accepted the orthodox Hindu faith and ceremonies, while rejecting the grosser element of idol worship ; his own practical religion taking on the form of love for his country and his fellows, strict self-discipline and living up to the soldierly ideal of his race. ' From the very beginning ', he records, ' it has been a habit of mine to sift carefully all matters pertaining to religion.' But his developing brain soon discarded the ' fanciful ideas and mischievous customs ' that had obviously been grafted by Brahmins on to the spiritual truths embodied in the Védas and Upanisháds, initial sources of religious belief. Perceiving how many of those fabricated passages gave currency to wrong customs and ideas, his innate honesty forbade him to accept so insidiously falsified a religion.

Still seeking true truth, he studied the scriptures of Islam ; but the Koran, in spite of much that was fine and true, failed to meet his need. He kept company with staunch Moslems, probing the influence of their faith on their activities : but he still remained unsatisfied, unconvinced. Then he turned to the Christian Bible, reading it with earnest care. He admits that ' its fables and stories attracted my fancy, but neither head nor heart could honestly accept it altogether as the word of God. " Jesus begotten of God and born of a Virgin " were things I could never understand. To my mind religion has to do with the spirit and very little with the body. It lies in right principles, upright character and purity of soul ! '

While still troubled by inner uncertainty, he found himself laid up for two months with a broken leg. Here was his chance to study the Védas and have the deeper passages expounded to him ' in the hope of removing that struggle from my heart '.

Here, it seemed, he had found pure gold in the most ancient of all Aryan books : gold, free from alloy of ' truth and fiction mixed up in confusion '.

He was further convinced, years later, by the famous Swami Dynanda, a man of deep religious inspiration and vast learning ; one whom he finally accepted as his Guru—the Master and disciple relation still prevalent in the East. Thus did his questioning soul find anchorage at last.

In regard to the externals of religion, customs and taboos, he remained unorthodox always ; and again it is Sir Walter Lawrence who relates how one day he saw Sir Pratāp very skilfully shooting pigeons as they flew up out of a well. ' I'm surprised, Sir Pratāp,' he said, ' to see you doing that. I thought it was contrary to your religion.' ' Yes, Sahib,' the Rajput agreed with his twinkle. ' Not good religion ; but making very good pie ! ' A many-sided man under his stern soldierly aspect.

As to marriage, like so many of his kind he was baulked of his natural desire for an heir to carry on his name and title ; a disappointment that struck deeper than he would openly admit. His first wife died in giving birth to a daughter—afterwards reared by a childless second wife almost as her own.

To that wife—a woman of exceedingly fine character—he became so genuinely devoted that, although she could give him no son, he married no other lady of his own rank. She was a deep thinker, well educated and well read ; and in her quiet way she was a very real help to her husband. Like him, she was an early riser, all her religious reading and devotions done before breakfast, to keep the day clear for her many practical duties.

When Jōdhpur was smitten by the most terrible famine within the memory of man, it was Lady Pratāp who had a large camp of grass huts put up for the women and children some miles away from the city. Out there she herself lived in simplest fashion. Cows and grain were collected, milk distributed, all under her personal supervision. Long before sunrise she would be up and doing. Then she would drive home to see after the day's arrangements for her own house and husband, giving special care to preparation of food. Back to the camp at night, finding much to be done before she could go to bed. She herself kept all accounts for that city of huts ; gave out personally every pint of milk, every *chupatti*, every rag of clothing, while the hot-weather sun of Rajputana blazed on the glaring sand—and she no longer young in years, though ageless in spirit like her lord.

It was a task that the strongest man might have shunned ; the kind of work that must have called forth her husband's unbounded admiration.

In youth she had enjoyed a good deal of liberty, and she fully shared Sir Pratāp's views as to the freer mingling of men and women ; yet her exclusive, aristocratic spirit inclined her to mix only with chosen friends. For, on the whole, it is class rather than sex considerations that make many advanced Indian women still chary of complete exit from purdah.

It was an ill fate indeed, for themselves and for the next generation, that no children were born to carry on the blended qualities of that large-hearted, wide-minded man and wife, while folk of little or no merit assiduously people the earth.

They were privileged who met Sir Pratāp and his Lady in their own home : he in his familiar old clothes, stained and shabby *topi*, frayed jodhpur breeches, threatening to descend at any moment ; his legs curiously bent, both broken by a daring jump, as a boy, and again several times since. Nowhere else shone out more clearly the ingrained simplicity of the man, and the modesty with which he accepted his world-wide reputation.

There is a story, dating from the last war, of an Englishman who saw an Indian officer, in khaki great-coat, standing near Buckingham Palace, and spoke to him, thinking he might need help or direction.

After brief talk, impressed by the look of him, the Englishman said : ' May I ask what is your name ? '

' Pratāp Singh,' was the answer.

' What ?   *The* Pratāp Singh ? '

' Yes, I *the* Pratāp Singh,' the Maharaja of Idar and far-famed polo player, stated simply, but with quiet assurance.

The Great War added lustre to his name and to the fame of his Lancers, though it denied him the coveted honour of death in battle, leading them against the enemies of his King-Emperor. Under one of his nobles, Thakur Dalpat Singh, they did indeed cover themselves with glory, capturing the fortified town of Haifa at the gallop. The Thakur himself was killed in the hour of victory ; and Sir Pratāp's reply to General Allenby's cabled congratulations on the exploit was characteristic of the man.

After pondering the news for some time, he remarked, ' I thinking you send this : Dalpat Singh's great day has arrived.'

If his own great day eluded him, it was not through lack of zeal, but fortune of war and advancing years.

When the news of war declared reached India, he was nearly seventy, but still on the polo ground, as usual, surrounded by friends. Waving his arm, he shouted ' Hurray, Sahib, hurray ! I going knocking over one German ; dying for my King-Emperor.'

And to King George he sent a cable that was genuine Pratāp :

' Ever looking to your Majesty as my second God, I, as your Majesty's A.D.C., consider it my sacred duty to serve your Majesty personally at this time. I will deem it a special mark

of royal favour and a great honour, if allowed to serve on your
Majesty's staff. Your Majesty's old Rajput soldier will eagerly
await royal command to be present at your gracious feet.—
MAHARAJA PRATĀP SINGH.'
Promptly he put at the King's disposal his Lancers and all
resources of his State. Fearing, naturally, that Imperial Service
troops would be destined for Egypt or Palestine, he wrote a
personal letter to King George, in the name of old friendship,
begging for a transfer to France ; no lesser theatre of war. The
young Jōdhpur Maharaja—his great-nephew—also wrote to the
Viceroy asking for leave to serve on his great-uncle's staff : a
request that was granted, to the satisfaction of both.

When Sir Pratāp discovered that the Lancers were bound for
Egypt, he flatly refused to disembark them at Suez. No orders
could shake his faith in the King's response to his personal appeal ;
and he triumphed when a cable arrived from England ordering
him and his men on to Marseilles.

At the front he was attached to the Staff of General French ;
and in November 1914 his troops had a taste of the trenches, of
German bombs and hand grenades that they were powerless to
return in kind.

At Christmas-time the ' old Rajput soldier ' wrote to the King
and Queen—Eastern fashion—that they were his *mā-bāp* (mother
and father). The troops were their children. Would they
graciously send them some ginger and peppermint and brandy.
To his huge delight, these were given to him by the Prince of
Wales in person.

Vainly his doughty spirit craved that promised cavalry charge.
Generals, pressed to say when it would take place, could only
put him off with a vague assurance that it would come about
soon.

But it never came about as he wished. Instead he experienced
the battle of Cambrai, bivouacked with his men near the Hindenburg Line, and wrote of being in action from daybreak to nightfall,
as if these were normal doings for a man of seventy-two.

Early in 1918 all Indian troops were transferred to Egypt,
where General Allenby was working wonders and the country
was better suited for Indian forms of warfare. Here it was that
Major Dalpat Singh won his M.C. by a gallant exploit. Supported
only by his trumpet-major, he galloped on to an enemy machine-gun, killed the gunners, captured the gun and the Turkish C.O.
with his own hand. Here also Sir Pratāp found his old friend
Sir Harry Watson in command at Cairo, and joined his Lancers
in the Imperial Cavalry Brigade. Refusing the five tents des-

patched for his private use, he returned four, much to the relief of a Staff already over-burdened with transport.

His last achievement—no light matter at seventy-four—was a long march on horseback with Allenby's great advance into Palestine. Starting at 6 A.M., they rode eighteen miles and halted till dark ; then on again all night, reaching their goal next morning. Sir Pratāp, with legs broken many times, had some difficulty in mounting and dismounting ; but he solved his problem by remaining continuously in the saddle for thirty hours on end, only the brief halt at Liktera giving him five hours of rest.

That was real warfare, as he understood the word, and he enjoyed it to the top of his bent ; but, in disregard of age, he had driven his body too hard.

Soon after, he went down with a bout of fever ; and before he recovered there came news from India that the young Maharaja —having returned for his marriage ceremony—had suddenly died.

Personal grief apart, he must at once return, being urgently needed to act, for the third time, as Regent of Jōdhpur. Sorrowfully he took leave of Allenby's Victorious Command—never to return.

' I have always looked upon him ', wrote Lt.-Colonel Harvey, Brigade Staff to the Imperial Service Cavalry, ' as the finest Indian I have ever had the honour to know : loyal to the core, a sportsman to his finger-tips, a gallant soldier and a real gentleman.'

It is worth recording that the Armistice terms did not win his approval.

' Good, from a humane aspect,' was his sagacious verdict, ' but to my mind, politically, a mistake ; for I am quite sure the Germans will not rest without taking revenge some day. Most probably they will join hands with Russia.'

At that time, on a surface view, nothing looked less probable than any form of accord between Germany and Bolshevik Russia ; yet how correct the forecast proved for a time. Well might it be said, by those who knew him best, that Sir Pratāp Singh was more than a soldier.

Only four years of life remained to him ; years into which he packed much useful service for Jōdhpur and the Empire. At close on eighty he still lived mainly in riding-boots and breeches, still slept on his plank bed in a place like a saddle room, and could still be described as ' the hardest nut one could ever wish to meet '. Still he believed in ' making boy hard ', insisting on the disciplined life for all the young Sirdars and Princes ; turning

JŌDHPUR: LIEUT.-GENERAL HIS HIGHNESS SIR PRATĀP SINGH, K.C.S.I.

(From *The Life of Sir Pratāp Singh*)

JŌDHPUR : THE FAMOUS FORT. BIRTHPLACE OF MAHARAJA SIR PRATÁP SINGH

them out at dawn on to the polo ground or pig-sticking field, discouraging all tendency to softness and luxury, as unworthy of a great fighting race.

One likes to picture the old soldier on a night of sudden illness —that he believed to be his last on earth—bidding them dress him in full uniform and seat him in a chair, sword in hand, that he might face death in true Rathore fashion.

But even that gallant gesture was denied him. In a few days he was himself again, though obviously failing and suffering much from fever. To the last he kept open house ; and best of all he loved Englishmen ; summing up their manners, in his odd fashion of speech : ' I thinking they very good gentlemen ; plenty more "thank-you" say '. But above all he loved a soldier and a sportsman.

When the actual end came it was sudden and swift, the best that he could have wished. No weary dragging-out of life for that valiant spirit. No long procession of mourners or piteous wailing of women when the last of him journeyed to the cenotaph on the hill near the Fort, his outward and visible memorial for ever. In his practical fashion he left clear instructions for his exit from the world he had loved and served so well. All was to be of the simplest : a few men from his beloved Lancers ; a few relations and Indian friends ; and not least a small band of Englishmen who sincerely loved him. These could only stand aside, with bowed uncovered heads, as he was carried past by white-clad mourners, their hearts heavy within them, unable to believe that he was gone beyond recall. From the depth of their knowledge and friendship they could say, ' Devotee of an older chivalry, he kept the single-hearted vision of his ancestors. A nobler Rajput never lived and died.'

3

Modern Jōdhpur, under his great-nephew Sir Ummaid Singh, is in a condition as flourishing as even its famous Regent could wish, administered by a Council with the Maharaja for President. He employs several British officers ; and his revenue is equal to all needs. He himself is as fine a horseman and polo player as it behoves a Rajput Prince to be ; but like most of the adventurous youth of this generation he has taken to the air, having learnt to fly as an expert and possessing one of the fastest planes in India.

He will set out in the early morning, cover eight hundred miles or so before tiffin, visit some distant State, and return to Jōdhpur in time for dinner. He is a true Rathore, fit descendant of Sir Pratāp in his simplicity of life. The Spartan activity within and around his Palace refutes the libels perpetrated by political-minded Indians on their own Princes. Besides being an all-round sportsman, he is a serious-minded, rather shy young man, giving much time and thought to affairs of State ; and his people, on every count, are rightly proud of their Maharāj. His five sons are being reared to carry on the Rathore tradition of a soldierly life and personal service to the Empire.

His Maharani curiously remains in strictest purdah, associating only with her actual family. Indeed it has been said of her that she knows the sky better than the earth. In her car, with darkened windows—that enable her to see out, while none can see in—she drives to the aerodrome, climbs into her husband's newest, fastest plane, and alone with him she explores the skies ; looking down thence upon their desert State and all its wonders of improvement, in which she takes a keen practical interest ; looking down also on vast spaces of India beyond her ken.

Only in England she goes about freely, unveiled, enjoys London shopping and amuses herself in Woolworth's many stores. But she gives the palm to Harrod's for quality of merchandise, for comfort and beauty of arrangement. Her gems, very seldom displayed, are of exceptional beauty. The pendant worn on her forehead encircles a blue diamond worth some £12,000 : and her expanding cap is a glittering casque of diamond solitaires. When does she wear these marvels ? And who sees a strictly purdah Princess in all her jewelled array ?, are questions that dangle unanswered in mid-air. She probably wears them as seldom as her husband wears his ropes and collars of pearls.

Though he keeps up the tradition of Rajput hospitality, he prefers his own simple strenuous life of work and sport and scouring the skies.

On to his famous air-field British, French and Dutch liners descend with the regularity of mail steamers, linking up Europe and Asia. All his young officers learn to fly under a skilled English pilot : and the life of modern Jōdhpur centres in its polo ground, its flying club and fine State-owned hotel.

Even his British Prime Minister has taken to the air ; and in spite of many earthly tasks, he fairly rivals His Highness in the prevailing interest of Jōdhpur.

Forty years ago an isolated desert State, lacking all outward and visible means of progress, it has overridden every obstacle and literally out-soared most of its fellows. So that to-day it may fairly be said that Jōdhpur leads all India in the sky.

While Udaipur remains a land of legend, jealously guarding its beauty and tradition from the disfiguring touch of a mechanical age, Jōdhpur—the Warrior State, in its wilder setting—has gone boldly forward to the credit of its Prince and the benefit of his people.

JAIPUR:
CITY OF VICTORY

JAIPUR, the walled City of Victory, backed by reddish-grey spurs of the Aravāli range, has one point only in common with unbelievable Udaipur. There is no place in India quite like it. A supremely well-ordered oasis, half hidden by tree-tops of banyan, acacia and neem, it has held its own for more than two hundred years against the stealthy seeping in of the great Indian desert. Like its fellow cities, Jōdhpur and Bikanir, it has the air of an island set in waves of dust-coloured sand-dunes, broken by outcrops of rock, and crowned with tussocks of feathery grass, where parrots chatter and swing. There no other live thing grows except camel thorn and giant cactus bushes, like spectres stricken motionless in weird gestures for all time. North and east runs the irregular range of Aravāli hills, with their creeping lines of fortified masonry : and from south and west the desert filters in through Jaipur's many gates, powdering leaves and lamp-posts and lattices with the grey-white dust of death. But man, on the whole, is master of his conditions : and in Jaipur it may safely be predicted that the desert will not have the last word.

The streets of that spacious oleander-pink city are models of all the municipal virtues, drains, water supply, electric lighting ; a town as unlike mediaeval Udaipur as two cities in the same region could well be : streets thirty-seven yards wide and desolatingly straight, designed by a mathematical-minded Raja in the early eighteenth century ; adorned with wrought-iron lamp-posts by a Victorian Maharaja of the nineteenth century. For the Spirit of Progress has been, through the ages, a tutelary goddess of Jaipur, rivalling almost the ancient gods, who hold their immutable sway over the hearts and lives of its people.

The tangle of incongruities that is modern India, reflects the Hindu mind in all its bewildering variety. So Jaipur's vast main street is enclosed by inconsequent pink houses on irregular terraces, each one fretted with balconies, and the smallest of latticed windows to keep out sun and dust ; the whole scene tinged with an air of theatrical unreality ; an effect not lessened by the traffic that flows between at an average rate of two miles an hour.

From dawn to dusk it flows in a casual stream of shifting

58

colours : the full, swinging daffodil skirts of the women, veiled or unveiled, according to rank ; the unveiled, winnowing grain on open shop fronts, or crowned with baskets of cow-dung moving like queens. In and out among them move the gay muslins, the small turbans and inimitable swagger of the Rajput, Sun-descended. And there go the perpetual elephants, docile, intelligent, sensitive monsters ; camels roped nose to tail, great bells under their chins making full-toned music ; bullock-carts for omnibuses, shamefully overloaded ; and for taxis, bright little pagodas on wheels, hung with cream-coloured curtains, drawn by graceful trotting zebus—India's Brahminy bulls—their horns painted red and green.

In the wide open space that is the heart of the city, architectural exuberance runs riot in a nine-storey building, one of the strangest that even India has produced. Oddly named Hall of the Winds, the bewildering façade has suggested ' Hall of Windows ' as nearer the mark. One above another they rise, in countless numbers, curved outwards, giving the whole frontage a tubular effect, more curious than beautiful ; its colour the prevailing pink of Jaipur, its roof decked with metal flags, unmoved by any breeze.

Over the Palace waves the royal Rajput standard, orange and yellow, blue, green and white, blazoned on cloth of gold ; a thing of grace and beauty, floating wide or falling limp against the passionate blue beyond. And hard by the Palace looms a group of rose-red temples, elaborately carved from plinth to summit ; their monolithic forms rising through flights of crows and iridescent pigeons ; their shallow steps flanked with marble elephants, splashed with the orange-yellow robes of holy men and rainbow tints of brightly veiled women.

Palace and many-coloured shop-fronts throw into darker relief the human rag-and-bone heaps, half buried in drifts of sand ; beggars and cripples and starveling villagers, who come crawling to the city in the pathetic belief that the Mahārāj has plenty and will surely fill their emptiness. But access to a Mahārāj is beset by those who have their price, full-fed men to whom these skeleton folk seem like flies. If their *karma* [1] is propitious, they may get a few handfuls of food—and live ; if evil—they die.

So much for the vast main thoroughfare ; but another Jaipur, less brilliant to the eye, more fascinating to the mind, dwells and works in narrow side streets, where each craftsman sits absorbed in his own fine art, either of brass or ivory, inlay or sculptured

[1] Fate.

stone. These last have a street of their own where sculptors, old and young, sit chiselling marble in cupboard-like studios let into lower storeys of the houses ; and elsewhere in this wonder-city are workers in gold and silver and enamel, who ply their delicate craft squatting on flat roof-tops under the blue arch of heaven. ' Something living ', they say, ' must watch a man at work if he wants to come near perfection : and, in a crowded city, if you cannot get near enough to the Earth Mother, you must get a little nearer to the sky.'

Such is the composite rose-pink Jaipur, created by Raja Jai Singh in the year 1728, embellished incongruously by his early Victorian successor, Rām Singh, with water-works, cotton press, wrought-iron gas lamps and carriage drives of hewn stone, the work of a British Superintending Engineer who—according to Kipling—' converted the city of Jai Singh into a big bewildering practical joke '.

And beyond that pink city—on the shores of its blue Mān Sagar Lake—run the low red hills encrusted with battlements, culminating in the Tiger Fort that kept watch over Jaipur's original capital, Amber, Queen of the Pass, when it was counted among the glories of Rajasthān.

But glory departed when Jai Singh II, philosopher and astronomer—decades ahead of his age—found the marble city among the hills too restricted for his taste, and built him a new capital six miles off on the open plain : a spacious capital boldly planned ; and perfectly designed—though he knew it not—for the motor traffic that would speed through its wide thoroughfares in two hundred years' time.

While he fought and intrigued, like any true Rajput of his day, he found leisure to read and think deeply, to collect a vast library, to study the stars and become an astronomer of European reputation ; no light achievement, with never a newsmonger to assist the process. Like a royal Omar Khayyám, he probed the mysteries of ' that inverted bowl we call the sky ' ; re-formed the calendar, built a Prince of Dials with a gnomon ninety feet high ; and another based on the Zodiac—twelve dials on one platform—to find the moment of true noon at any season of the year. He made cups to calculate eclipses, a mural quadrant, and other strange astronomical devices, of which none but he knew the meaning. With all that, he was a skilled General—an essential item in an era when fighting was the sport of Kings. He died in 1715 : and he was, without question, the greatest ruler that his line has given to Jaipur.

The landscape of history reveals many such isolated peaks of greatness rising abruptly from the dead levels of human medio-crity : and Jai Singh—who won battles, who planned a capital and aspired to the stars—was followed by a line of poor Rulers, who brought discredit on the State that had been his pride. In 1820 it was reduced to the verge of ruin by Raja Jaggat Singh—unworthy of his heritage—who lived a dishonoured life, enthralled by the charms of a Moslem dancing girl. On her he squandered his wealth and possessions, even to Jai Singh's famous library that could be of no earthly use to such as she. Yet it was this debauched Prince who claimed as bride the lovely and high-born Udaipur Princess, Kishna Kumari, heroine of the tragic and heroic tale that has already been told.

But kingdoms, like cats, have nine lives ; and Jaipur, though impoverished and dismembered, found salvation under her en-lightened Maharaja Rām Singh—he of the lamp-posts and the water-works, and the invaluable Engineer, who did more for the State all round than will ever be known. For Colonel Jacob came of a race that finds it easier to do things than to talk about them. He and the few Englishmen under him, with an army of coolies at command and a lavish Maharaja backing them, became lesser lords of creation, making themselves one with Jaipur and its best interests as only Englishmen seem able to do. No doubt they enjoyed getting a free hand over fifteen thousand miles of Indian desert, and being invited to leave their mark on it—as they un-doubtedly did. Under the modest title ' Servants of the Rāj ', they served him in their practical fashion, not only on municipal lines. Between them and Rām Singh, a school of art, a museum and a hospital were added to Jaipur.

And the Maharaja himself was a finer personality than his great forerunner. Something of his quality, as a man and a Prince, has been shown in the story of Jōdhpur. His wisdom, simplicity and charm made him an influence for good throughout all Rajputana ; and Sir Pratāp Singh admittedly owed much to his lifelong friendship with his sister's husband, whom he loved as a brother. His death was a loss to more than his friends and his people. It was a loss to Rajputana.

After Rām Singh—Sir Madho Singh, very much a personality, on quite other lines : a strictly orthodox Hindu, not over-burdening himself with cares of States and leaving the indefatigable Englishmen free to carry on Rām Singh's work. A loyal devotee of the British Crown, he was eager to attend King Edward's Coronation, only fearful of the damage to caste incurred by crossing the ' black water '. Yet go he must, duly safe-guarded, in a special ship chartered for himself and his suite, with enough purifying

Ganges water in his luggage to last him six months. Armoured
thus against defilement, he braved the great adventure ; and met
his King-Emperor face to face, laying his unsheathed sword at
the Royal feet in token of homage. But because his ancestors
had to stand before Mogul Emperors, he would never sit in King
Edward's presence. He made many valued friends among British
officers and would sometimes give his favourites the Rajput
embrace ! In his latter years he was dominated over-much by
priests and women ; but Sir William Barton, who knew him well,
found him ' with all his faults, a great Rajput and a friend worth
having '.

There in brief we have the record of comparatively modern
Jaipur. For the tale of an Indian State is mainly the tale of its
Rulers.

And what of Amber—deserted by order ?

No Ruler ; no history. But the Solomon of Jaipur, in pursuing progress and space for his large ideals, left undying romance
behind him at Amber, Sleeping Beauty of Rajasthān, the most
spectacular ruin in all India. Desolate and forsaken, she still
seems to keep watch over the old road to Delhi and the Pass
beyond, that none need now defend.

Yet Amber, even to-day, is no mere city of ghosts and ruined
marble halls. Though Kings have deserted her, the gods remain.
There is life still in her temples and the blood of sacrifice on her
altar stones, within the second gate, where Kali the Terrible,
blackened with age and evil, dances in petrified gestures, with
serpents for waist-belt and necklace of skulls.

To see and feel, in every nerve, the all-pervading silence
of Amber, choose a night of full moon or the first hour of
dawn.

Out from the many-arched gateway of modern Jaipur the road
runs by the wide Mān Sagar Lake, among tumbled ruins and
broken pillars, where vultures brood and water-birds nest, and
the demoiselle crane stands knee-deep, seemingly absorbed in
meditation, actually intent on the next meal ; so still, so graceful,
every line and curve reflected in the quiet water.

Beyond the lake an uphill road runs beside the remnants of a
huge stone causeway that could tell many tales of heroic battle
and death. Above it, on the heights, three walls enclose the city,
guarding it from the invader, who will never now violate the
sanctuary of its temples and palaces, its houses cleft from roof to
roadway, its one-time streets choked with cactus and brushwood.
Three gateways in three walls ; and within the third wall a rough

descent leads to the valley, where temples and terraces and houses cluster round the sacred lake, like Queens and handmaidens round the shield of a dead King.

Pause there, first looking down into depths of desolation; then upward, where the hillside climbs past creeping battlements to the little temple of Shiva printed darkly upon a glowing sky. Silence and emptiness, not of years but of centuries, haunt the valley like a brooding presence. There is an emptiness of the desert, of an untrodden snowfield, that stirs imagination and approaches the sublime; but the emptiness of a city forsaken is akin to a body with the spark of life extinct—' the silver cord loosed, the golden bowl broken '.

Such is the emptiness of Amber; peculiarly so in the ruined Palace on its pedestal of jutting cliff, overlooking all things except the great red fort that was guardian of Amber—once upon a time. Lives that crammed it full—Princes and intriguing courtiers, soldiers, priests and women—have gone out like blown candles, leaving the Palace an empty shell of dusky rooms, winding passages and stairs that seemingly lead from nowhere to nowhere, screens of marble tracery, cloistered hanging gardens, baths for Princesses and their companions, chiselled out of rock; rooms that are mere cells opening on to a courtyard prisoned between towering cliffs of wall.

Glancing into those windowless, damp-encrusted cells, standing in that empty courtyard with its vivid patch of sky, one recalls the zenana Queen of Kipling's tale, ' What have women to do with thinking? They love and they suffer.' They also worship; and that innate Eastern faculty no doubt went far to halo conditions inconceivable to Western minds.

I have said there is life still in the temples of Amber; and at sunset every evening the ghostly silence is dispelled by a throbbing vibration of drums, when the Brahmins beat the great tom-tom before Kali's shrine. That is but the signal, awakening the dead city to discordant life. Howlings and clashings as of fiends in torment echo and re-echo from every temple and shrine, blurred by the mutter of drums, pierced now and then by the undulating wail of rams' horns, wandering like lost souls through the blare of cymbals and bagpipes and all kinds of music.

Sudden and clear from the height comes a ringing peal of bells —as if angel voices answered the wail of devils—from the little shrine of Shiva up against the sky. And the last word is aptly with the angels, with the throbbing undernote of drums.

Then silence descends again on Amber, like folded wings, for the space of twenty-four hours: silence deepened by the comfortable cooing of pigeons, the scream of peacocks and the chittering of squirrels ; normal voices of earth.

And less than seven miles away in the very new Jaipur, outside the last gate of the rose-pink city, life and movement and the spirit of progress go their ways unmindful of sleeping beauties, or of cities forsaken : a spirit that is transforming the face of India. It must be admitted that the architects of modern Jaipur have succeeded in combining splendour with comfort—no light achievement. Here the present Prince, Sir Mān Singh, has his country Palace and State Guest House, a Lady Willingdon hospital and a fine museum : in effect a suburb, with no taint of the suburban to mar its quality.

And for the last word in clash of contrasts, here we find a club as entirely English in appointments and atmosphere as any in London ; its members, Rajputs all, as true to type as if they had been familiar with club life for generations : drinks, cigars and bridge ; the manner, the very mannerisms of their Western prototypes.

Here also we find Boy Scouts, incongruously clad, leaping with queer cries, and chirruping songs about good deeds and the perpetual smile. As a fair imitation of the original article they are well enough : but will lads, so reared, imbibe or embody the Rajput ideal of manhood ? The answer lies with another generation.

And at sunset, when ' the stars rush out, at one stride comes the dark '. From desert and desolate ruins, the eerie cry of jackals—voice of immemorial India—can still fling over modernised city and temple and palace a kind of sorcery that outshines the charm of many lands as the full moon outshines the stars.

The young Maharaja, Sir Mān Singh,—adopted son of Sir Madho Singh—is a veritable Prince Charming, dowered with all the gifts by some fairy godmother at his birth. Supremely good-looking, with delightful manners, brains, character and horse-manship—one of the best polo players in the world—he has captured the imagination of India, much as our own Prince of Wales captured the hearts of England. His looks, his polished manners and cultivated drawl, might well make him a cynosure of London society. Many have tried to spoil him, happily without success. For his quality as a man goes deeper than his fairy-godmother gifts. He combines the finest attributes of Rajput character with a natural modesty as genuine as that of Sir Pratāp Singh.

A superb horseman, like his uncle, he also rides the skies and pilots the fastest modern planes with equal courage, zest and skill. A broken arm at polo gave him leisure from riding to perfect his prowess in the air. But he is happiest with his horses, over two hundred of them, chiefly English thoroughbreds, housed in regally appointed stables, with electric fans for coolness and shower baths for refreshment in the heat.

Perhaps a year at Woolwich, leading to friendships and pleasant associations, has given him his leaning towards things English, not only in the matter of horses, but in ways of thought and life. He thoroughly enjoys collecting congenial people in his comfortable modern country Palace, English in its furniture and food ; and his personal staff compares favourably with that of any British Government House. He and his A.D.C.s wear English dress, and his Prime Minister has introduced English herbaceous borders into Jaipur.

He himself—though a complete autocrat—wisely rules his State through a strong executive council that contains three British Members with the Prince as President : and he decrees a fixed sum for his ' privy purse '. Like most Indian Rulers, he has had to contend with the independent retrogressive spirit of powerful barons, lesser autocrats, dwelling in their fortified castles among the hills ; men whose idea of privilege does not always coincide with that of their civilised and right-minded young Maharaja.

But, for all his modern outlook, he retains a ceremony unique even in a land overrun with ceremonies ; not to be seen elsewhere.

Jaipur's white Durbar is held once a year, at full moon, on the roofs of an old Palace. A white carpet covers the marble ; and on a silver-plated chair, in white brocade, sits the Maharaja. All the rest are seated on the carpet, or lean on crutch-handled sticks. White everywhere, even to the jewels ; its purity enhanced by the moon's unearthly light. Cascades of pearls gleam through silver embroideries, and drip from diamond aigrettes on turbans. Pearls rain like drops of light over silver tissues and white velvet scabbards. Diamonds glitter on the borders of coats cut out of silver brocade. No touch of colour anywhere, in a country more addicted to colour than any other on earth.

The nearest approach to this exquisite conception is the yellow spring festival at Udaipur, where all is yellow even to the saffron-tinted food. But there we have colour—the sun-colour of Rajasthān.

And inevitably we arrive at jewels, without which no true picture can be given of any Indian State. Like most of his kind, the Jaipur Prince is lord of jewels and treasure beyond price, hidden from human ken in vaults of the great Tiger Fort that stands high above the city in a wilderness of battlemented hills ; treasure that is reputed to be Royal loot from Afghanistan ; its value enhanced by the curious instinctive worth attached to all things hidden. The mighty fort is guarded, strangely enough, by a criminal tribe. Robbers, plunderers, murderers, they obey no code except their own ; yet always they have been faithful to their trust — the Tiger Fort ; and every man of them would defend it to the death.

Only once in his lifetime is the Ruler allowed to enter that strong-room of natural rock ; blindfolded so that even he may not locate its exact position. When he has seen all, he can choose for himself one jewel or jewelled memento of his great possessions. The present Prince has yet to see his hidden treasure and make his own choice : but on one of his mantelpieces there stands a parrot—a very Fire Bird—encrusted with rubies, chosen by Sir Mahdo Singh. He himself owns a necklace of spinel rubies, each as large as a bantam's egg. They are said to have been collected by the great Mogul Emperors, Babar and Akbar ; and there are none others like them in the world.

But this fortunate and widely esteemed young man possesses, in his heritage of Rajput character and tradition, jewels that are above rubies. His time of testing is yet to come ; but already he has shown judgment in dealing with difficulties and readiness to follow sound advice, British or Indian.

According to one who can speak with personal knowledge, ' he should have before him a great career as Ruler and statesman in Imperial India '.

BIKANIR :

THE SOLDIER-STATESMAN

I

THE story of modern Bikanir, like that of Jōdhpur, is largely the story of one man : not an immortal memory, but a Prince in the full vigour of life, who has achieved much for his own State and his fellow Princes, with every prospect—in the new era—of greater things to be.

Without undue exaggeration, it may be said that his record of achievement as Ruler and statesman has hardly been equalled by any Indian Prince of his generation. In twenty years he transformed a desert kingdom, without roads, railways or water, into a land of gardens, canals and noble buildings : one of the most prosperous States of modern India.

He and his people, like those of Jōdhpur, belong to the Rathore clan ; Bikanir is, in fact, an offshoot of the parent State of Jōdhpur.

It was in the fifteenth century that Rāo Bikaji, a son of the Royal house, went forth into the surrounding desert, inhabited by colonies of Jāts, a warlike clan not easily subdued. But an alliance through marriage gave Bikaji a foothold in the land he coveted ; and in 1486 he laid the foundations of a fort that was to become the home of his descendants. Three years later he founded the city of Bika—Bikanir.

Five miles of battlements and five great gateways were held by a fort prepared to resist all invaders ; but none could have foreseen, even as a wild possibility, the fair city it would become in four hundred years' time.

Solitary it stood in the centre of the Indian desert : an endless vista of sand-dune and scrub, unrelieved by a tree or a ploughed field; all surface water brackish, as the pools of Sahara ; here and there a deceptive mirage increasing the sense of human helplessness : the kind of landscape—or rather sand-scape—that dwellers in a temperate zone can hardly conceive. But Rāo Bikaji and his Rathores were desert bred. A fight with Nature in her least responsive mood merely hardened their bodies, sharpened their wits and strengthened their devotion to the lone city that proudly challenged the elements; a monument to the hardihood of their race.

From that self-made dynasty, founded by enterprise and courage, came all the Rulers of Bikanir, His Highness Major-

General Sir Ganga Singh, G.C.S.I. etc., being the twenty-first of his line. In character and attainments he stands undeniably first. His independent spirit and resolute will distinguish him as one of the strongest men among present-day Indian Rulers. He began his career with an unusually long minority. Coming into his heritage as a boy of seven, he could not assume full powers till he turned eighteen. This involved a Council of Regency under a British Political Officer ; a difficult and responsible dual rôle. In effect, the young Maharaja is Ruler without practical power ; while the Political Officer has practical power, without the prestige of being Ruler ; an anomaly too often adverse to the State, while it works to the advantage of powerful Thākurs and court intriguers, leaving the Prince, when he ' takes over ', a legacy of dangerous internal unrest.

Eleven years of it sowed a harvest of tares for young Bikanir, more especially among his turbulent nobles ; but his manner of dealing with them at once revealed the fibre of his character and proved him bone-bred Rathore. For, besides a fine heritage, he had been fortunate in his education. Five years at Ajmir in the Chiefs' College grounded him in discipline, book learning and the team spirit of school life. It also revealed his natural ability and application. But since it involved much separation from his people and State, he returned, at fourteen, to Bikanir and completed his studies under a British tutor, a man who afterwards became well known in the Political Service as Sir Brian Egerton.

No happier choice could have been made either for pupil or tutor. Sir Brian liked and understood Indians to a rare degree. He combined sympathy and tact with a measure of wholesome discipline, essential to one who could not—because of his position —receive it in later life. Above all, he identified his own interests with those of his charge to an extent that captured the sensitive heart of the Rajput Prince, and made him early familiar with all that is best in an English gentleman.

In the words of his biographer, ' During those happy years with Sir Brian Egerton, the Maharaja gained a thorough insight into English character and learnt to appreciate the fine qualities of the British race '. He came to be perfectly at home in their company ; thus acquiring a first-hand knowledge of Western thoughts and ways that proved invaluable to him in later years. At the same time, he was encouraged by his wise tutor to remain an embodiment of Indian culture and tradition, a Rajput Prince with a genuine pride in his own race and country.

The relation so happily begun lasted for life, as such friendships are apt to do. As links between race and race, they have a more than personal value ; especially so in these days of too frequent political friction, misunderstanding and misrepresentation. The tale of India's Princes in contact with England is, in many cases, a tale of such friendships ; and of their incalculable effect on the personal and political relations between the Throne and its most loyal allies. It cannot be too constantly emphasised that only the best of Britain's manhood is good enough for India, above all for India of the Princes.

It was a year before he came of age that the Maharaja's first wife was chosen for him with all the formalities—priests and astrologers in conference : horoscopes compared, deputations flitting hither and thither ; all under the guidance of the bridegroom's mother. Behind most remarkable men you will find a hardly less remarkable mother : and the Dowager Maharani of Bikanir was no exception to the rule. Her keen, intelligent interest in all matters that affected her son never tempted her to interfere in any plans for his education or welfare, even if these clashed with her own accepted ideas ; nor would she countenance the back-stairs influence and intrigues that are a byword of Indian Palace life. Supreme in her own sphere, she never caused trouble, as do so many queen-mothers, in matters beyond their scope. But in this woman-affair of choosing her son's bride she could and did play a leading part.

That first wedding was brilliantly celebrated ; and of the three children it gave them, the eldest, Sadul Singh, is the Maharaja's heir. The young Maharani died only nine years later. A second wife gave him no children, which allowed him as a Hindu to marry again : and his third Maharani, mother of two sons, became his life companion.

At eighteen, after eleven years of minority and careful training, he was formally entrusted with full ruling powers : a proud moment of high hopes and secret anxieties. India loves a visible monarch ; and the young Prince, thrust into the limelight, is aware that those who have reared and trained him are watching to see how he will rise to his new and exacting opportunities.

Already this promising young man had shown himself to be ahead of his years in character and grasp of State affairs ; a talent that has distinguished him through life.

At his own first Durbar of Chiefs and nobles, he spoke with the voice of one who brought to his high office a serious purpose backed by a resolute will ; and his first statement had the informal ring of sincerity.

' I am saying what I really mean, not what other people have told me to say. I want you to understand that whatever I do in future, I shall do it because I think it is the right and just thing to do, not by favour. You must not expect me to show favour to anyone. It will be useless for you to send messages through my Sirdars, or through zenana Sirdars. Whatever you want to say, come and say it direct . . . and I will do my best. By coming straight to me you will save yourselves and me time and trouble. I hope this will put a stop to bribery, because you now know that the people with me cannot use their influence. I strongly disapprove of bribery. I mean to put a stop to it. God help the man who gives and takes bribes : for I certainly will not.'

Perhaps only those who have experienced the secret workings of Indian Palace life can fully appreciate the boldness of those forthright words spoken by a young Ruler of eighteen to powerful barons and courtiers for whom intrigue, seasoned with bribery, was the breath of life.

In the matter of zenana influence, a potent factor, he had his mother behind him. Wisely she had set her face against the interested approach of Sirdars through their wives : an immemorial custom not easily defeated even by an autocratic young Prince, who openly aimed at ' making an end of the bad old days of intrigue, faction and corruption ' ; weeds that had grown apace during his years of ruling in name, but not in fact.

And if his human material proved at times intractable, his barren State—23,000 square miles of desert, with a climate veering from fierce heat to bitter cold—was enough to discourage any but a desert-bred Rajput.

At that time, nearly fifty years ago, wave on wave of sand-dunes, from the rim of the horizon, surged right up to the city walls ; no trees, no verdure, but the sapless grey-green bushes of thorn and scrub ; no railway ; no roads worthy of the name ; the only form of transport either by horse or camel. From the last of the railway, the traveller journeyed in a camel carriage, behind two strange-looking beasts, padding all night through the sand ; the conveyance itself no luxury coach ; more like riding in a hearse with the disadvantage of being alive.

The scanty water supply was drawn from four wells, and willingly paid for at a regular charge per cup. To the Palace, visitors were driven in a carriage-and-four through massive gates with iron spikes, over steep stone ramps, through deep twining alleys : up and up till they reached the highest storey ; the four horses galloping at top speed : the visitor quailing at thought of the downward return journey.

But discomfort and dangers were offset by the Maharaja's

JAIPUR : HIS HIGHNESS MAHARAJA SAWAI MĀN SINGH II, BAHADUR,
RULER OF JAIPUR

BIKANIR : HIS HIGHNESS SIR GANGA SINGH, G.C.S.I., ETC.,
TWENTY-FIRST RULER OF BIKANIR

(From *Great Men of India*)

noble Hall of Audience. Not large but ' perfect in design and glorious in colour ' ; its sumptuous walls, centuries old, looking as fresh as any modern work in the fine Saracenic Lāllgarh Palace, built during the present Maharaja's minority.

His heritage in those early years was a desert kingdom, bankrupt in revenue, torn by factions, intrigue and discontent ; rich only in men and camels, tireless beasts who mainly carried on the work of the State. If any prophet had foretold the transformation that would be wrought in less than fifty years—largely through the vision and enterprise of one man—he would have been scouted as a weaver of fairy tales.

Yet even fairy tales have been known to come true ; and among these may be reckoned modern Bikanir.

But here was no case of the magic wand. The miracle came to pass only through years of toil, initiative and driving force, backed by the will and authority to carry through schemes that must have looked impossible at first sight : schemes for bringing water of life to many thousand miles of sterile sand ; for laying down railway lines, for the wonders of building achieved by a master builder of his time.

That transformation scene could only have been wrought by a Ruler who combined character with capacity added to a rare blend of wisdom and intrepidity. Always Sir Ganga Singh's major concern has been with the difficulties and triumphs of irrigation. Not a single river runs through Bikanir : and the worst that may come for lack of it was tragically brought home to him, eight months after his installation, by one of the direst famines ever known, even in Rajputana.

Not soon would Bikanir forget the great famine of 1899 : delayed monsoon, failure of crops, that were scanty at best : water and food reduced to a bare minimum. The unfortunate people—hardly recovered from the last infliction—were at a low ebb ; disease taking a terrible toll of bodies weakened by starvation. Whole despairing villages trekked northward, to the slightly less arid Punjab. By August, the worst was upon them : total failure of the rains ; blazing sun and burning sand ; no fodder, no water ; cholera and dysentery killing them all like flies : a calamity to wring the heart of their eighteen-year-old Prince— eager, enthusiastic, dreaming of future greatness for Bikanir.

It was the first big demand on the new power vested in him and admirably he rose to the occasion.

Day and night he spent all his energies on a practical famine-fighting scheme : converted his army Camel Corps into an emergency relief force ; put all his State resources into a battle against odds.

F

And he did not merely sit in his capital issuing orders. To the stricken villages he went in person to see that the people were given real relief. Officials are seldom over-burdened with sympathy ; least of all in the East. Undaunted by an attack of cholera, or by the problem of transport, he resolved to tour his suffering kingdom on camel and horseback. With the hot season at its height, with only three small tents for himself and his staff, he scoured Bikanir. No attendants to shout ' Make way for the Maharaj ! ' No cheering crowds to greet him ; only wan faces and skeleton bodies ravaged by disease, wailing children clutching at their mother's empty breasts. Without thought or attempt at impressing his people, he probably impressed them more profoundly by his personal concern for their well-being than he would have done by any triumphal procession.

In the words of Lord Curzon, who afterwards paid him a glowing tribute, ' He was his own famine officer throughout that fearful time ; and he conducted his campaign with indefatigable energy and skill '.

But the impression he made on others was of lesser significance for Bikanir than the after-effect on himself of that first tour through his famine- and disease-stricken State.

An indelible memory of the patient suffering, the uncountable corpses, became one of the great motive forces of his life. ' Never again, if human skill can prevent it ', was his registered resolve : and from that time forward his will was set on two great enterprises of the utmost difficulty : first, to provide his desert region with transport and water ; second, with a network of railways and canals. On that twofold achievement hung the making of a prosperous State ; and, between them, Prince and people have overcome all natural obstacles to the great end in view.

The network of railway lines has been translated from dream into reality. More than four hundred miles of permanent way serve the people and the growing State industries ; an achievement that pales before its life-giving network of canals.

' One of the miracles of India ', wrote a great traveller, ' is the concrete-lined Gang canal, which brings water from the Sutlej river at Ferōzpur, across eighty-five miles of sand, to the Bikanir frontier. Thence it branches into six distributory canals that irrigate an area of seven hundred thousand acres.

In another corner of the State—once watered by a tributary of the Indus—the canal system is patterned out like tapestry ; and here dead villages have come to life, fields have been ploughed, and emptiness transformed into fruitful earth. Coal mines are being successfully worked ; and the dread of famine is no more.

Only dust storms are unabated ; and locust swarms—primal curse of the East—still darken the air, strip the trees and pass like a blight over flourishing fields.

The city itself has been enlarged, but there remains the old battlemented wall ; the domes, among red and white roofs, bitten out of the passionate blue ; standards flaunting the colours of Rajputana—orange, yellow, blue, white and green. Within the city, its rose-coloured Lāllgarh Palace is built round a marble-paved courtyard ; and, above the open colonnade, trellised windows of the zenana give the royal ladies a view of all that passes below.

Even now, in spite of railways and motor cars, the supercilious camel holds his own ; policing the streets, lining the route on every high occasion, and drawing farm carts four in hand. Merchants still tramp, as of old, beside camels padding nose to tail in their unhurried, dust-coloured caravans.

But in the days of the great famine these wonders existed only as dreams in the mind of an ambitious young Ruler, dowered with the will and capacity to make dreams come true.

Conditions at the start were unfavourable. It was no easy matter for a boy of eighteen to assert his own decided personality after eleven years of nominal rule, under the Political Agent and Regency Council ; no easy matter to tackle barons of the feudal type, whose power and influence would be curtailed by the nature of his wholesale reforms. Their intrigues, amounting to conspiracy, required prompt and drastic handling, lest a passing ferment develop into armed revolt.

On this head there were differences between the Prince and his Political Agent, who was no longer dealing with a minor, but with a young autocrat, shrewd enough to see that this affair of the barons was a problem vitally affecting his future position in the realm. Rebel spirits among them were obviously prepared to oppose every reform, and thrust Bikanir back into the Middle Ages.

So he stiffened his own resistance ; while they, with Eastern subtlety, tried to play off the Political Agent against him. But behind the Political Agent was a Viceroy keenly interested in the Princes and their States, even if his methods were, at times, too authoritarian to suit their taste.

For many years they had been irked by a sense of losing ground in respect of their princely status and authority ; the last insidiously encroached upon by British officialdom, by restrictions and changes of procedure, even turns of phrase, galling to their pride and spirit of independence. For this very reason young Bikanir was the more determined to take a firm line with his own unruly barons ; to establish his own authority on the understanding that they should co-operate in his programme of reforms.

But the spirit of co-operation was not in them ; and when the Political Agent, to their dismay, backed up the Prince's authority, they boldly essayed an appeal to the Government of India. Even so, there was divided opinion between the Viceroy and his secretariat ; but the young Maharaja's blend of firmness and moderation won him the support of Lord Curzon, who had warmly appraised his famine campaign, and had accepted his offer of active service in China, as the first Indian Prince to fight abroad under the British flag. Moreover, recent birthday honours had given him a K.C.S.I.

So the word went forth that empowered the Prince to deal drastically with all rebel barons ; a diplomatic victory that revealed him to his people and foreshadowed the nature of his rule.

Very early he gave evidence of the shrewd political mind and combative temper that made him, for thirty years, the persistent champion of his fellow Princes in all matters relating to their interests and prestige : a position which brought him into close touch with more than one Viceroy.

Lord Curzon's departure marked the end of an era ; and in Lord Minto the Princes found a friend anxious to strengthen their position, to enhance their personal dignity. In Lord Hardinge, who followed him, they found a Viceroy far-sighted enough to perceive the great imperial value of closer association between the Government of India and the States.

Gifted with insight, understanding and sympathy, he speedily earned the confidence and goodwill of the Princes. Among his earliest guests at Government House were the Maharajas of Gwalior and Bikanir, who very soon became two of his most loyal and trusted friends. In his own words, they were men of the ' very highest character, models of what Indian Princes are and should be '. He marvelled at the extraordinary progress made by Bikanir during little more than thirteen years of personal rule : an achievement demanding high qualities of constructive imagination.

The Maharaja himself saluted Lord Hardinge as a true representative of his King-Emperor ; while the Viceroy saw in the younger man a far-sighted Ruler, ' staunch in devotion to the Empire, with noble ideals and a zeal rare in princes, a patriot and a statesman '.

Here was basis for friendship founded on a mutual esteem

very unusual between Ruler and Viceroy, cemented by a frequent interchange of visits, no less rare. Few Viceroys ever visit the major States more than once, though Lord Hardinge has voiced his conviction that friendship with India's ruling Princes provides the surest means of getting to know her people and acquiring insight into their mentality.

The fact remains that most Viceroys come to India as to a strange land ; and not many possess the un-English gift for making personal friends with men of a different race.

It was during Lord Hardinge's régime that Sir Ganga Singh celebrated his Silver Jubilee, though he had reigned, in person, for less than fourteen years. Even so, those years had been crowded with activity and achievement ; his desert State transformed ; its revenues doubled, its railway mileage quadrupled ; and the wonders of electricity revealed to an incredulous people.

A story is told of how the English engineer (knowing of their disbelief) made secret preparations for his first display of the marvel. Installing many powerful lights, he switched them all on at once with dramatic effect. At a touch, hundreds of constellations blazed forth to the confusion and amazement of the crowd.

The Maharaja's ambitious Canal scheme—hindered in a dozen ways, money not the least—still remained a dream that took fifteen years to realise ; but never for a moment was his mind deflected from that supreme purpose. Already his fifty new wells had brought life to barren land ; and, progress apart, his personal service to the State and to the Empire justified a note of pride in his Jubilee rejoicings. These were enhanced by a cable from King George, by salvoes of guns and the releasing of chosen prisoners to mark the auspicious event.

The Resident, in congratulating the Prince, could say with truth, ' There is probably no State in India where the culture and genius of the East, the traditions of the Ruler and his race are more happily blended with the science, energy and practical activity of the West than they are in Bikanir '.

That proud day for the State and its Ruler marked the beginning of a new period in his life : the beginning of wider political activities in the interests of his fellow Princes and in the changes foreshadowed for India at the close of the first World War.

2

The outbreak of that war, in 1914, gave the Princes of India —as we have seen—a golden opportunity for practical proof of their devotion to King and Emperor : an opportunity they turned to brave and generous account. Sir Ganga Singh, like Sir Pratāp, could be content with nothing less than personal active service in France. But, again like Sir Pratāp, he was disappointed of his hope. Even to be on the staff of Sir John French, Commander-in-Chief, was not the same thing at all. But whatever he was permitted to do he did with characteristic intelligence and zeal, refusing to let rank or position stand in his way, insisting on his full share of hardships and difficulties during that terrible first winter of war.

In his own country, he was out and out Maharaj. In France, he served his King-Emperor as a ' kindly, simple, self-effacing English gentleman ', and it was Sir James Willcocks, commanding the Indian troops, who wrote to him afterwards : ' You and I can fairly say that we saw the Great War in its most trying stage. I shall always recall your good work in those terrible days ; never afraid of mud or discomfort or anything else. You showed a fine spirit, Maharaja, worthy of your great race and name.'

But always his heart and mind were with his troops in the field ; and their transfer to Egypt, where they could be more effectively used, brought about his own transfer to Headquarters in that country—not for long.

Early in 1915, grave news of his eldest daughter's ill health forced him, reluctantly, to leave the scene of action ; hoping, if all went well, to return before long.· But hope was defeated by his own ill health and the insistence of Lord Hardinge—his most understanding friend—that duty to India and to Bikanir required him to remain in the country. A change of Viceroys was imminent, and Lord Hardinge urged that, at such a time, his political wisdom would make his presence in India peculiarly valuable. Though barely thirty-six, he had already won a unique position in the councils of Empire.˙ Experience in Europe had enlarged his outlook and added more than a cubit to his stature.

For many years he had given much time and thought to political questions, in particular to the problems of his own Order. Even before the war, he had set his heart on a Council of Princes that would give them the recognised position in the Empire to which their war record now entitled them. The whole of his influence and prestige was henceforth concentrated on upholding their rights, from greatest to least.

It was he who urged on his tried friend the Viceroy that after the war there would surely be enhanced sympathy and goodwill ; therefore more intelligent co-operation between Government and the Princes, who had proved, in all ways, their loyalty to the Throne.

Again he pressed for a Princes' Conference that would give Rulers of States an opportunity of frankly discussing their difficulties in an informal manner for the good of all concerned. That prospect carried within itself the seed of a larger innovation—the Delhi Chamber of Princes, that came into being six years later with a view to strengthening Royal India against the rising threat of Congress domination ; the Maharaja himself being rightly chosen as its first Chancellor.

It was a proud day for him ; a tacit admission from his fellow Princes that they owed their political step forward largely to his personal vision, his persistence, tempered with a natural courtesy, even in opposition, that has always gained a hearing for his considered point of view.

The Chamber itself has no voting power. It consults and debates matters of interest to the Princes. It provides a common meeting-ground where they may take counsel and protect their own interests ; a necessary matter in view of open Congress hostility to the whole idea of autocratic rule.

The Maharaja, as liaison officer between the Chamber and the Viceroy, made no claim to leadership ; a claim that might have aroused jealousies already stirred by the prominent part he had played during and after the war. He was, in fact, the first Indian Prince to share the councils of Empire in the Imperial War Cabinet, and afterwards, with Lord Sinha, at the Peace Conference in Geneva. Of the Chamber itself, it is not too much to say that first and last it was virtually created by him. For six years he had worked towards it against every kind of difficulty actual and official ; till, at last, he had the satisfaction of personally launching his own scheme.

That same year, 1921, brought to India yet another Royal visitor—Edward, Prince of Wales ; a visitor welcome to the Maharaja as a personal friend, so intimately had he been associated with the British Royal Family for close on twenty years.

For both it was a happy occasion ; Sir Ganga Singh, at his banquet, paid a sincere tribute to ' the unfailing kindness and consideration of their Imperial Majesties for all around them ' ; to the human touch of true sympathy and kindness that ' cheer and encourage one, even under adverse circumstances, and secure for all time the devoted attachment of those brought under the spell of such magnetic charm '.

His boundless hospitable welcome to the Prince was so friendly and informal that the Prince himself—no lover of the formalities—relished it as a break in the official round, even to the extent of changing his programme that he might enjoy a few more days of such rare sport and congenial company.

For Bikanir, in addition to pig-sticking, buck-shooting and polo, provides yet another attraction peculiarly its own. Home of the imperial sandgrouse, it is famed for its great shooting parties at Gajner, where the bag runs to thousands of birds ; their pace calling for the skill of a marksman, though their number dooms them to mass extinction.

For several days beforehand they are not allowed to reach water in any neighbouring tank. The whole countryside conspires against them. Frenzied with thirst, when the ' shoot ' begins they come over in clouds, at desperate speed, to reach the the lake. And by instinct or design, they fly in military formation : scouts, vanguard, main body, rear-guard. For hours on end the unceasing rattle of guns goes on, suggesting a brisk engagement rather than a morning of sport. There is nothing like it elsewhere ; and Sir Ganga Singh, who enjoys it as much as any guest, has been dubbed by a wit ' King of Bikanir, by the grouse of God '.

Towards evening, the Prince's guests enjoy tea and talk and cocktails outside the flamingo-pink Palace with its fairy-tale air of having been transported complete—garden, lake and courtyard —from some far exotic land and set down on the unlikely desert. Every detail mirrored in its artificial lake, it abides remote from the disarray and disturbances of normal life ; remote even from the crowd of rough-coated sportsmen who from time to time profane its dreaming silence with talk and laughter, with rattle of guns and the whirr of small frantic wings.

They pass, they pass ; but Gajner's enchanted stillness remains, ' itself the dreamer and the dream '.

And the party, that dispelled the dream, drives back to Bikanir in the brief dusk ' through mile on mile of silent golden country, under the vast arch of a sky all purple and powder blue '.

Everywhere along the road, camels and more camels ; lion-tawny beasts indigenous to Bikanir ; camels four-in-hand transporting luggage and goods ; camels guarding the road, or laden with coarse grass and firewood ; camels at rest in camp. Almost they seem an emanation from the desert landscape that, without their broken stilts of legs and ungainly, untiring bodies, would be desert indeed.

A year after Prince Edward's happy, informal visit, Bikanir was entertaining yet another Viceroy—Lord Reading. He had met the Maharaja in England ; but he had little or no actual experience of India ; and he had arrived at a time of peculiar difficulty. Gandhi, with his creed of non-co-operation and non-violence, was engendering violent disturbance over a wide area. Political India was in a ferment, from causes too complex to be analysed in this brief study of one remarkable man. Like many other Rulers, he favoured, in principle, the proposed reforms that were giving no satisfaction, just then, to political-minded British India ; but the States were not blind to the likelihood of revolutionary developments that would undermine their independent rights, unless a move to safeguard them was made in good time.

For all that, his proposal to convene an informal Princes' Conference found no favour with Lord Reading, whose hands were full enough with the disturbances in British India. Probably neither he nor his advisers fully realised the alarm and anxiety of the major Princes, who must needs look to the future and tackle their own problems ahead of events. Whatever the reason, he remained unshaken by argument or persuasion ; and the Maharaja could say no more.

But, in spite of friction and acute disappointment, Sir Ganga Singh's courtesy prevented any rub between men who had worked together at the Imperial Conference ; and the official visit was carried through in the grand style : sport, banquet, review ; the Maharaja and his two sons resplendent on parade in full-dress uniform. The Prince himself, wearing a jewelled aigrette in his turban, galloped forward to meet the Viceroy, sword unsheathed for His Excellency to touch the blade, and wheeled round to take up his place for the Royal Salute ; while bands blared for the passing of Camel batteries and Camel Corps, Lancers and State infantry. Finally the Camel Corps went by at a trot, the favoured beasts looking bored and scornful as only a camel can do.

The day ended with a weirdly effective fire-dance in the sandstone courtyard after dinner : a Hindu sect working themselves into a frenzy round blazing wood and charcoal, dancing barefoot on live cinders, picking up red-hot fragments in their fingers or even between their teeth—and never a burn or a blister among them : a problem for sceptics, confounded by unbelievable fact.

And so to the station : the Viceregal pair escorted by the Prince and his Raj Kumar [1] ; the State band excelling itself, at the last, by an expressive rendering of ' Abide with me '.

Since then—after three conferences and endless deliberations that have exacerbated Indian nerves—the major States have come to feel less assured as to their own position in the kind of Federation

[1] Heir Apparent.

visualised by Congress leaders of to-day. It soon became clear to them that they could only accept ultimate Federation if it included a guarantee to keep inviolate their personal treaties with the Crown and the independence of their collective territories—two-fifths of the country and a quarter of its population. Equally clear was the need for a united front among themselves, so that none of them would ever have to stand alone without a solid backing from their fellow Princes ; a condition easier to propound than to achieve among six hundred-odd principalities of all sizes, and at all stages of development.

To begin with, among the Rajputs there was more than a little jealousy of Sir Ganga Singh ; not only on account of his personal eminence, but because the changes he had wrought in Bikanir placed it definitely among the greater States of Rajputana : a fact not very willingly recognised by the three Princes of premier rank —Udaipur, Jaipur and Jōdhpur. The Maharaja, proud of his country's fine record, would not rest till he had proved its claim to equal rank, in a documented historical volume—*The House of Bikanir*.

Thus honour was satisfied ; and the matter is only mentioned as an instance of the difficulty, among so many States, of presenting the united front essential to changed conditions in British India.

More relative to a personal study of Sir Ganga Singh was the celebration of his silver wedding in 1933. Simply and un-ostentatiously he and his Maharani gave thanks for a marriage that had given them twenty-five years of happiness, only clouded by the loss of two sons. The elder, Prince Bijey Singh, a young man of exceptional promise, had been killed by a gun accident only a year earlier ; a loss the more tragic because father and son, remarkably alike, had been constant companions for many years ; the son sharing his father's experiences in England and Europe. Only Sir Ganga Singh's ruling zest for work and the State served him as a stimulant and a refuge from personal grief.

The Maharani herself, though keeping strict purdah, has all her life taken a practical interest in the progress of Indian women ; and her exceptional position among wives of her rank has been marked by a coveted decoration, the Crown of India, only bestowed on women of notable distinction or achievement.

Her own special achievement has been a school for nobles' daughters. Named after her, it is housed, now, in a magnificent building, complete with playground, gymnasium and gardens ; and it has owed much of its success to her unflagging zeal. In spite of purdah restrictions, she has shared all her husband's cares, pleasures and responsibilities as fully as any free-faring wife could do. In his words, ' she has been the embodiment of all that a Rajput Princess and Consort should be. Cheering me in all times of difficulty, stress and anxiety, she has been a continual source of inspiration, encouragement and help to me in every way. A detailed enumeration of her unostentatious, valuable work and many-sided activities . . . would prove how wrong are the notions of ignorant people as regards purdah princesses and other Indian ladies who keep to the purdah.'

Their eldest granddaughter, married to the heir of Udaipur, has this year (1941) given them their first great-grandson. There are many deeply happy marriages among cultured Indians of a quality little realised in the West.

The Maharaja himself, at sixty-two, is still in vigorous and vital prime of life; his flair for politics and broad grasp of political issues—mellowed by experience—is every whit as notable as it has been throughout his career. More and more, of late years, he has devoted himself to the State that is his pride and will be his monument.

Combining in himself Ruler, Prime Minister and Foreign Minister, his work is never-ending. From 9.30 to 11.30 he dictates letters and minutes to his assembled stenographers, who vanish as their notebooks are filled, to be replaced by others. Follows a respite for religious observance and the midday meal. By 2.30 he is at work again; interviewing heads of departments, inspecting every plan for new buildings that are his favourite hobby. He is seldom free till late in the evening, when he dines with his family.

By way of holiday, he spends six weeks or a month in his Bombay house; and at Christmas he organises a ' shoot ' on the grand scale; his guests numbering anything from a hundred to a hundred and fifty; the whole affair so perfectly planned and carried out that he has been called a very Napoleon of hospitality. Sport and these famous parties are his chief recreations; for the rest, his time and thought and energies are spent on one main object—the advancement of Bikanir State; while he is never unmindful of the wider problems of his motherland, to which he has given so many years of his life.

From early days, he has seen India as a Federation in which all sovereign States would be united with self-governing Provinces, under the aegis of the British Crown; the States remaining free to develop along their own lines, in friendly accord with the more democratic Provinces; a vision that presupposes extinction of the present inimical attitude of Congress leaders to the whole policy of autocratic rule.

Of a possible move towards an All-India Princely Federation more will be said in a later chapter. Enough to add now that, in any developments affecting India's future within the Empire, the Maharaja of Bikanir may be counted on to play a leading part. Taken as a whole, he is one of the most remarkable personalities modern India has produced ; an asset to his own country and to the British Empire.

NÁWANAGAR:

THE IMMORTAL 'RANJI'

In Lt.-Colonel Sir Ranjitsinhji, Jām of Jamnagar, we have yet
another Rajput Prince though not ruling in Rajputana : a man of
many attainments and high character, known wherever cricket is
played as Ranji, a batsman of genius—and a good deal more than
that, as will be seen from the chequered story of his career. In
his own way, he was perhaps as widely known and loved as his
incomparable uncle, Sir Pratāp Singh, who did him good service
in the difficult days before he came at last into his own.

His State Jamnagar—more correctly Náwanagar—will be found
on the map in the coastal region of Káthiawar, where many smaller
States are scattered among fragments of British India. Yet here
you will meet Rulers of all types, from the splendid-looking
Maharāo of Cutch [1] and the Chief of Gondāl, an Edinburgh M.C.,
with the polished manner of Harley Street, to the old-style Thākur
(noble) who can barely read or write. Of these, Náwanagar is the
largest and has become the most important, mainly owing to the
name and fame of Sir Ranjitsinhji. Its ruling family, Jadéja
Rajputs, claim descent from Krishna, the Hindu Christ, an
incarnation of love idealised into deity. According to the *Gita*,
whenever religion wanes and irreligion prevails, he is born again
and again ; in fact, whenever a flame from the Sacred Fire is
needed to lighten the darkness of mankind.

The condition of the world to-day suggests that there is urgent
need for another coming of Krishna to revive the lamp of the
spirit. The Hindu idea has much to commend it ; and, among
all their deities, Krishna is reckoned the most human, merciful and
kindly, because he has experienced the limitations of life as man.

So it is no mean descent that they claim, these Jadéja Rajputs,
who were ruling Princes in Sindh at the time of the Arab invasion
in the seventh century. It was from the Arabs that they derived
the curious title of Jām—Prince—not used elsewhere in India.
From Sindh they migrated to the coastal region of Cutch; and
so, across the water, to Káthiawar. There, already established,
was an earlier community of high distinction : Nagars, who had
come south with Scythian hordes. Such was their quality that
almost at once they were raised to the rank of Brahmān. Such

[1] He has lately died.

was their innate pride that they seldom troubled to use the title. They would simply say ' I am Nagar ', as who should say ' I am the Prince '.

Outside Káthiawar they are chiefly famed for the beauty of their women : fair, with a vivid golden fairness like ripe wheat ; dark eyes that glow with passion or gleam with humour and innate intelligence ; finely rounded figures, graceful carriage and much conscious charm. A beautiful Nagar woman is a picture not easily forgotten ; and it need hardly be said that she and her kind have been extolled in countless ballads throughout the centuries.

But no race in that region could excel the Jadéja Rajputs, with their roots deep in history. And it was one of their most famous Chiefs, Jām Rawal, who descended on the bowl-shaped peninsula of Káthiawar in 1540, took possession of a great territory and built himself a capital worthy of it. Náwanagar—New Town— he called it, and placed it not far from the coast so that sea breezes tempered its climate, and two rivers provided fresh water. To-day, thanks to Sir Ranjitsinhji, it is indeed a New Town, such as its founder would barely recognise. But, in those days, it was a sufficient achievement of its kind ; and under Jām Rawal, Náwa-nagar became chief among the Káthiawar States, as it remains to-day.

Only in 1807 did the English become a factor in Náwanagar politics, not as conquerors, but in the wake of the Marathas, who had settled themselves firmly in Gujerát. It is some eighty years after that we come to Ranjitsinhji's immediate forerunner, Jām Vibhaji—to the curious tale of his many marriages and Palace intrigues, that so disastrously affected the early half of the younger man's life.

It is authentically recorded that, in order to ensure having a direct heir, he married no less than fourteen wives ; yet never a son did they give him : which may have some bearing on all that followed.

Driving one day past the great lake, his fancy was caught by a comely Sindhi peasant woman, known to be a prostitute. The Jām, powerfully attracted, sent a message inviting her into his zenana ; but the woman of much experience in men returned an answer that she could not accept the honour unless she came as a wife. Even so, she stipulated that her three sisters should come with her : a tall demand from a Moslem woman to a Hindu Chief, who could not legally marry her without changing his own religion.

Since that was out of the question, he consulted his priests, ever resourceful and astute in the matter of pleasing the Palace.

Between them they ferreted out an ancient form of marriage, long obsolete, whereby heroes, in Hindu epics, were united to their lady-loves. They could not deny that it was an obsolete rite, which had never, to their knowledge, united a Moslem to a Hindu. But the lady need not know these things. To satisfy her affected scruples, the ceremony was revived in the form of a few sacred verses solemnly recited by priests over the morganatically married pair.

A few months later that spurious Rani presented her Jām Sahib with a son, to the fury and jealousy of many true, sonless Queens, who whispered audibly that the illegal one had bargained for marriage, knowing that she would shortly become a mother.

The Jām Sahib, having at last secured an heir, did not worry unduly over the boy's doubtful paternity : and, as his Rajput Queens continued to fail him, he appealed to Government for recognition of the little Katōbha as his heir, should no other son be given him. The plea was granted ; but breeding, like murder, will out. Before the boy reached manhood Jām Vibhaji was urging his disinheritance, having discovered that the graceless youth—probably incited by his mother and aunts—was trying to poison the man he called father. That plea was also granted ; and arrangements were made to adopt a boy of Rajput lineage, without a thought of his probable fate, exposed to the wrath and jealousy of a thwarted, if unauthorised Queen.

Furious at the failure of her dishonoured son, she would see to it that the interloper should not live to supplant him. No lack, behind the curtain, of means to do ill deeds ; and her vengeance did not tarry. A secret dose of arsenic in the boy's evening meal, a few hours of agony, and there was an end of him.

The Jām Sahib—again left without an heir—was not to be thwarted by any Queen of them all ; though it apparently did not occur to him that he might well have repaid the murderess in her own coin. Instead, he looked hopefully round among the younger members of his own near connections ; and, in a good hour for Náwanagar, his choice fell upon the seven-year-old son of a man who was, in every way, the beau-ideal of a Rajput gentleman.

Young Ranjitsinhji bore a name of good omen—'Lion Victorious '; but if the lion were to live and conquer, he must imperatively be guarded from the jealous hate of a spurious Queen. For safety he was entrusted to the British Political Agent, Colonel Barton, with the significant words, ' Take the boy, Sahib, and bring him up yourself in the right way. There is danger here.

So it happened—as often in life—that the woman who wished him ill rendered him unwittingly a signal service.

The future Indian Prince, of unusual destiny, was reared apart from Palace influences and intrigues ; reared as the gentleman he was by birth. From Colonel Barton's home he was sent to the Rajkōt Chief's College, that is modelled on Eton ; then on to Cambridge, where he soon became a shining light in the world of sport, especially cricket; achieving—in the words of C. B. Fry— 'a fantastic success as batsman ' ; excelling even Englishmen at their own national game. His shooting parties were long remembered by those who enjoyed his hospitality and skilful planning of the whole affair.

'He was a beautiful shot, I never saw a quicker '—again I quote C. B. Fry—' but he spent more time in providing that his guests got the shooting than in occupying positions of vantage himself.' The last was eminently characteristic of the man who was later described by one who knew him well as ' the greatest man, physically, intellectually and morally—English or Indian— whom I have ever met '.

But neither distance nor his fine qualities, could guard him from the subtle poison of Palace intrigue, while the dishonoured Rani and her sisters could pull strings behind the curtain to his detriment and their own advantage.

One of the sisters, Jānbai, at last produced or procured a male child, named it Jaswant Sinhji, and pressed it on the distracted Jām Sahib as his lawful heir, who should by rights displace the adopted boy. Unfortunately a clause in the adoption document stated that it should not prejudice the rights of any son who might later be born of any rightful Queen. Therein lay the whole crux of the matter. For the shameless Jānbai was neither Rani nor Rajput, nor any true wife at all. Her so-called son had no backing to his claim beyond her own feminine wiles and guiles.

Jām Vibhaji, not deceived, resisted her pressure, till at last she cornered him with a deadly ultimatum ; either he must cancel the adoption, or he himself would suffer the fate of the earlier poisoned boy. So secret and skilled were zenana methods in that delicate art that the unhappy man knew he had no means of protection against them. Neither could he openly go and live elsewhere. In desperation, he decided to consult the Bombay Government as to his dilemma, though well he knew that a concubine's unscrupulous intrigue could not in any way disqualify his own adopted heir.

Inevitably the Bombay Government refused to recognise the spurious son of a low-born Sindhi woman. But her deadly ulti-

NÁWANAGAR : THE JĀM SAHIB AS MAHARAJA
(From *The Land of Ranji and Duleep*, published by Blackwoods)

NÁWANAGAR: 'RANJI', THE JĀM SAHIB OF JAMNAGAR,
A CRICKETER OF GENIUS

(From *The Land of Ranji and Duleep*, published by Blackwoods)

matum goaded the Prince into seeking a personal interview with the Viceroy of that day, one whose whole policy was based on advertising his friendship and sympathy with Indians, at a time when early symptoms of unrest were causing political friction and clash of opinion in Government circles.

Here then was a chance to court popularity by favouring a Prince who ruled the chief State of Káthiawar and had lately been decorated with a K.C.S.I. The fact that his flagrant request was not in order, nor backed by the Bombay Government, weighed lighter in the scale. Probably little thought, if any, was given to the legitimate heir—unseen, unknown—whose life and prospects would be ruined by this obvious intrigue against him.

Be that as it may, the near outweighed the far. Viceregal decision was given in favour of the bastard boy, and Jām Vibhaji enjoyed the triumph of having persuaded the ' Lord Sahib ' to grant his plea, in spite of all that the better-informed Bombay Government would argue against it. His so-called son was to be recognised by Supreme Authority ; and the true heir—in far-off England—was to receive the shock of his life.

Not all at once did he feel the full effect of that unjust decision. His adoptive father had sent him to Cambridge with a handsome allowance : and his own magnanimous nature was incapable of bearing ill-will. Only when the Jām Sahib died in 1894 did his real troubles begin. The allowance was promptly stopped ; and in distant Náwanagar his ' face was blackened ' unscrupulously by enemies who feared he might return and press his true claim to the throne. In the fine art of plausible, insidious defamation few can surpass the born intriguers and mischief-makers who infest the minor courts of the East. Drawn, in this case, from all the baser elements of the State, their flood of calumny seemed never to run dry.

But the man they vilified was of a stature, mental and moral, beyond their low conceiving. At that time England was his world. Ignoring evil tongues, he devoted himself to college life, to sport and his many friends. Very soon—as has been told— he achieved his fantastic success as a batsman of genius. His repeated centuries attracted widespread attention. He qualified for Cambridge, for Sussex—and more than Sussex. By 1895 he was recognised as the first batsman in England ; incidentally also as the first shot and first salmon fisherman of his time. In one season he made three centuries for Sussex, his county, ending with a grand total of 1760 runs. In the next year he totalled over 2000 ; in 1897 he published *The Jubilee Book of Cricket*, admittedly the best work on the game.

G

Cricketers will appreciate a brief tribute from C. B. Fry : ' At his best, Ranji was a miraculous batsman. He had no technical faults whatever. His distinctiveness was a combination of the perfect poise, the suppleness and quickness peculiar to the athletic Hindu. . . . It was almost impossible for the best of bowlers on a fast pitch to bowl him a ball on the wicket which he could not force for runs somewhere between square leg and fine leg. These strokes were outside the repertoire of any other batsman I have seen. He made them look like conjuring tricks, yet with an air of complete facility.'

That winter he played against Australia : and thence, at last, he paid his first visit to Káthiawar. His name and fame as a cricketer did not help to ease a delicate situation. Every British Political Agent was eager to meet him, while the Government of India was pledged, by the decree of an earlier Viceroy, to recognise his bastard supplanter.

He himself—head and shoulders above them all—was incapable of feeling embittered, though no doubt the hurt struck deep. He came of a kingly race. He could rule as ' to the manner born '. He could also—a rarer quality—take fortune's buffets and rewards with equal thanks. He had accepted the earlier Viceroy's decision as a blow of fate, not to be railed against, but endured ; even as he accepted his cricket successes with the modesty of his grand old uncle, Sir Pratāp Singh.

Taken by Mr. Kincaid, I.C.S., as guest to an officers' mess, he charmed all who met him ; and even moved the Colonel to wish that all his English guests had manners equal to those of the young Rajput Prince, deprived of his kingdom. Many among his fellow Princes felt the slur, the injustice, more keenly than he himself appeared to do, or allowed others to guess. In spite of all that could be done to right a flagrant wrong by the powerful Maharaja of Patiāla and the far-famed Sir Pratāp, he went back to England still the Disinherited ; back to cricket and shooting and fishing, to his countless friends in a land he had grown to love.

He was not married, then or afterwards. As a boy he had been betrothed to a Rajput girl who was quite illiterate, and on that account he refused to marry her. But a Hindu betrothal amounts to marriage ; and his fastidious Rajput sense of honour would not let him take another wife. There was no need for an heir to follow him ; and his devotion to sport made him very much a man's man. So he remained, throughout, that singular anomaly, a bachelor Hindu. His physical powers of endurance seemed to know no bounds. Once, when playing for Sussex and making a hundred in each innings, he went salmon fishing all night during the entire match. Asked if he did not feel fagged out, he replied : ' Not at all. I didn't even feel sleepy ! '

Another kind of story is told of a cricketing friend who asked Ranji how he could become qualified to play for Middlesex—a county then very lax about qualifications. Ranji answered gravely : ' My dear chap, that's quite a simple matter. All you need do is to meet a girl under the clock at Charing Cross.' The friend's face must have been a study : but Ranji—kindest of men—backed up his witticism with a note to the Middlesex captain : and the thing was done.

In 1903 the Náwanagar usurper was formally installed ; and it then seemed that Ranji's hopes of possible restitution had reached their lowest ebb. But it was the traditional dark hour before dawn.

The Prince, who was no Prince, had been allowed by an indulgent Administration to contract five marriages, that there might not again be a failure of an heir—a chronic trouble in the States. For all that, he had proved incapable of begetting a son : and within three years he succumbed to typhoid fever, leaving behind him an empty throne.

It was Ranji's moment. At once he renewed his claim, after more than twenty years of unjust banishment. But so potent was the effect of lies heaped on lies, blackening his character for years, that his chance of success even now looked poor indeed. To crown all, it was rumoured that the Indian Government might even be induced to authorise another adoption by one of the childless Ranis, without any regard for Ranji's rightful claim.

The rumour, true or false, roused such a storm of feeling among all who knew the facts, that it even strained the fine loyalty of Sir Pratāp Singh, whose devotion to the British and all their works was second to none. The then Governor of Bombay, like the earlier one, again took up the cudgels in favour of the rightful heir ; but it was the strong action of Sir Pratāp—to whom Authority could refuse nothing—that ultimately won the day.

So it came about that on March 7th, 1907, Ranjitsinhji—Victorious Lion—was installed as Maharaja in his own capital to the delight of all his subjects and the discomfiture of the corrupt clique, who had maligned him and battened on the ill management of the usurper.

Unhappily, his belated triumph was tempered by the legacy of a semi-ruined kingdom that must, by some means, be restored to prosperity. Large tracts of land had been alienated by the reckless generosity of his adoptive father, and what remained to him was little more than the size of three average English counties, reduced to the verge of bankruptcy.

At first there seemed no escape from that dire fate ; no port of his own ; no outlet for his products. The Baroda Maharaja, his near neighbour, had built a port on the Káthiawar coast ; but Ranji had no railway to reach it, no funds to build a port of his own. And there were English officials counselling impossible retrenchments, while the Government urged on him a higher standard of administration : a veritable case of the devil and the deep sea. Clearly nothing could save Náwanagar but a loan : and at last he came to an understanding with his neighbour, Sir Sayaji Gaekwar, Maharaja of Baroda, who agreed to supply money for the necessary railway if the British Government would guarantee to pay interest. But Government raised difficulties over a simple proposition ; and the scheme fell through.

Ranji might well have despaired : but with his astonishing gift of patience he set himself to do, unaided, what he could. He improved his valuable pearl fisheries in the Gulf of Cutch : an excellent investment ; and on the strength of it he began to improve his capital.

Old Náwanagar had long been an eyesore to one like himself, familiar with the fine towns of Europe. Its streets were narrow and ill-drained, full of strange smells ; and infected by mangy pariah dogs covered with sores or ravaged by disease. Rabies was endemic among dogs and humans. Cholera, malaria and plague took toll of thousands. Here was an Augean stable crying out to be cleansed : and Ranji—first cousin to Hercules—set to work on it with a will. Inevitable opposition could only be overcome by tact and patience and the great prestige he had gained among his people. Whole rows of decrepit houses were destroyed and rebuilt on healthier lines. Crooked streets were straightened out and tarred for motor traffic. A working system of drains helped to check the spread of disease. Only one reform—and that the wisest—moved his astonished people to a show of rebellion.

To save them from constant dread of hydrophobia and other maladies, he ordered a wholesale slaughter of pariah dogs, unwitting sinners against his recreated city. Here was a drastic measure undreamed of in the fatalistic East ; and a large number of his people belonged to the important Hindu sect known as Jains, to whom all life is sacred, even the most harmful, the most minute.

The true Jain is kin to Ingoldsby's ' Bishop of Blois ' :

A holy man was he ;
Though his cassock was swarming
With all sorts of vermin,
He'd ne'er take the life of a flea.

The most orthodox Jains wear a strip of gauze across the mouth to avoid any risk of swallowing unseen insects ; and in certain hermitages it is said that the monks keep a kind of ' bug refectory ', where charitable Jains will sleep once à month, ' so as to give the vermin a good meal '.

Imagine, then, how the Jains of Náwanagar received that startling decree. For them the life of a dog—diseased or no, dangerous or no—was a spark of the divine fire, sacred as their own : a logical conclusion that overlooks the patently unequal value of life. Even by order of their Maharaj, that sinful slaughter could not be.

Their revolt, in the name of religion, seemed to clinch matters ;' but Ranji knew when to yield a point, and his unfailing sense of humour gave him his cue. If the dogs must not be killed, let the people—he said—remove all pariahs themselves. By a fixed date they must undertake to clear the city and dispel the dread of hydrophobia. If they failed to carry out that reasonable order, all remaining dogs would be shot ; and their blood would be upon the heads of those who had failed to dispose of them by merciful means.

Here was a challenge in the right vein : and it worked.

The Jains—fearful of blood-guiltiness—were spurred to superhuman activity. Such a rounding up of dogs, in every degree, had never been known in the memory of man : and, by the appointed day, no vestige of a pariah was to be found in Náwanagar. Where the doomed creatures had been transferred to was the Jains' affair. History merely chronicles the fact and the triumph of a sane Ruler over a crippling prejudice that could not have been dealt with by force.

From that day, every ownerless dog was destroyed or removed by the police ; and Náwanagar itself, purged of pariahs, became almost the only city of India where Western eyes were not shocked by the sight of countless diseased and mangy dogs.

More : the Jâm Sahib, by his masterly tactics, had so converted his people to new thoughts and ways that they positively assailed him with petitions for fresh improvements in their purified city ; nor would they now tolerate the appearance of even a single stray pariah in their streets.

As for their unusual Maharaja, having cleansed and remade

Náwanagar, he set to work on the vital matter of irrigation; and in that direction also he worked wonders with his energy, patience and skill. Water was stored in vast tanks, one of them the largest of its kind in India. Wells without number were sunk all over the State. But he was still hampered by his major difficulty : no good railway line to the coast. Even that essential item his perseverance achieved at last, British Authority belatedly recognising his necessity and the excellence of his rule. The money was found partly by himself, partly by the Maharaja of Baroda : and the thing was done.

Exactly twenty years after the whole scheme had been turned down by the Bombay Government, a profitable railway was carrying goods and passengers from inland towns and villages to the open sea. It was Ranji's triumph : and it was typical of the man that he bore no ill-feeling towards those who had so short-sightedly hindered the development of his State ; though the long delay involved by that hindrance had trebled the cost of his railway to Náwanagar. He was incapable by nature of bearing a grudge or forgetting an act of kindness ; and his own acts of kindness were legion. Unchangeably he loved England and Englishmen, however strained, at times, were his relations with official British India.

A trivial episode at a Simla hotel has its bearing on this magnanimous spirit even in small matters, since it is often the trifle that reveals the man.

He was at lunch in the Cecil Hotel. The dining-room was crowded. A waiter asked if he would object to a stranger sharing his table.

On his agreement, a very young subaltern joined him ; and Ranji proceeded to make him feel at home, without revealing his own identity.

Presently the boy asked if he happened to know the Jām Sahib of Náwanagar.

' I know him well,' said Ranji with an innocent air. ' He's my best friend.'

The boy looked surprised. ' I've always heard that he was rather an extravagant rotter. Isn't he ? '

' I've heard it said so,' Ranji admitted ; and while the unwary youth dilated on his theme, an Englishman came up and clapped Ranji on the shoulder.

' Hullo, Jām Sahib—didn't know you were up here.'

Consternation of the subaltern, who reddened furiously, rose and offered humble apology.

' Not your fault, my dear fellow. You've simply given me a taste of the famous lines :

Oh wad some power the giftie gie us
To see oursels as others see us!

Sit down again and be my guest.'

The boy gratefully obeyed; and Ranji not merely paid for his dinner but plied him with good wine, coffee and costly cigars. The favoured subaltern departed a happier and—let us hope—a wiser young man.

Yet another episode, far from trivial, bears the stamp of his princely nature.

It happened during the Great War, when he served in France for two years on the staff of General Willcocks, commanding the Indian contingent. Through those years he passed unscathed; but he came over to England on two weeks' leave; went out shooting with a party near a Yorkshire village; and, through the carelessness of another man, he lost his right eye.

The vicar of the village chanced to be an old Cambridge friend, and Ranji had one of the daughters in the butt with him. A keen local sportsman, following a bird with his gun, shot down the line.

Ranji instantly jumped in front of the girl and covered his own face with his right arm.

The grouse escaped; but one shot came under the crook of his elbow and hit him in both eyes. The right one was destroyed; the other badly injured, but saved by medical skill.

The culprit, overcome with remorse, begged to be told how he could possibly atone. Ranji turned it off lightly; but moved by the other man's genuine distress, he said at last, ' Well, if it troubles you so much, you can endow two beds in the local hospital ': a curious form of reparation, that would please his friend the vicar.

' No one ', wrote C. B. Fry, ' ever made less fuss about a major accident ', that condemned him to a glass eye and spectacles for the rest of his life. Yet he saw more accurately with his one remaining eye than most people see with two; and he was almost as good a shot as before.

After the war, he earned fresh distinction as an Indian delegate to the Peace Conference at Geneva, where he set himself to enlighten Europe on the subject of Indians in general and Indian Princes in particular. By means of his social gifts and charm, he largely succeeded; and did good work all round for his country. ' No delegate was better known or liked ', is the verdict of one who was with him throughout.

Back again at Náwanagar, his devotion to sport—and the lack

of it in his own State—spurred him to attempt, and carry out, one of the most astonishing achievements in his astonishing career.

On Rozhe Island there stood a lighthouse, alone in four square miles of sand and coarse grass that was cut once a year and sold by auction. Ranji, with his one eye and alert mind, saw that desert island conjured into a flourishing game preserve for himself and the English guests whom he delighted to entertain. The thing looked sheerly impossible — a word that has never yet baulked any man of resource and resolute will. So Ranji opened his attack on the island by building roads in every direction, by sending men all over the State to snare partridges, quail and other small game. Those captured birds were settled on the island, whence they could hardly reach the mainland with their limited powers of flight; nor would they be likely to venture far along the connecting causeway for fear of hawks and kites.

As foreseen, they proceeded to settle where they found themselves : but they must needs be fed. So every evening Ranji himself drove in his car along the causeway, scattering grain right and left. Hungry birds came flocking to the feast, not having learnt to fear either motor or man : and very soon the sound of his horn became a call to food. Often, besieged by birds and hares, he would be forced to stop the car ; but at once they would flee, fearing capture. So he could only move forward slowly, with brief halts.

Keepers were trained to protect them from kites and kestrels, jackals and foxes, who would soon have exterminated his cleverly contrived colony. So the wonder progressed and prospered : a wonder that non-sporting readers may incline to see from the birds' point of view. Here was man—arch enemy of wild things —feeding, protecting and preserving them, only that they and their kind afterwards might fall in thousands to his invading army of guns : a view that assails the whole tradition of game preserving, in England or elsewhere.

Under his wise rule, Náwanagar prospered as never before. Its revenue rose from twenty-one to seventy-five Lakhs,[1] the largest in Rajputana. Though his State is among the smallest, it ranks, in importance and influence, far beyond its mere size : the man counts for more than the square miles.

Thus did Ranjitsinhji, the Disinherited, lift his late-acquired kingdom from bankruptcy to wealth, in defiance of all that his virulent local enemies could say or do against him. Docks and railways and motor roads had grown under his hand ; water had

[1] Lakh = £7500.

brought life and fertility to hundreds of square miles. His capital had been lit with electricity. There were fine houses for his officials, palaces for himself and his guests. There was an English hospital, a solarium, that ranks third in the world, and radium treatment that is the first in India. More : he had so completely won the hearts of his people that he could and did go into the villages unattended to hear their complaints. Never were calumnies more triumphantly refuted.

But increase of revenue and production involved the imperative need for a port on his own coast. Nothing daunted, he set to work, secured the services of a retired British naval officer, and between them they created the now flourishing port of Bedi—quay and railway sidings and large wet dock complete. The heavy outlay had been partly met from State revenues ; and there would be increase of trade with custom duties to cover the rest.

Events justified his hope. Trade increased ; his ports flourished exceedingly : too much so for the taste of Bombay merchants, who foresaw too many imports reaching India via the more northerly harbour of Káthiawar.

Jealousy reared its ugly head. The vexed question of customs brought him up against the Finance Department and the interests of the Indian tax-payer. By way of compromise a second customs line was imposed inland to prevent imports reaching British India, through Káthiawar, duty-free.

Now Ranji's treaty with Government gave him full control of his own ports ; and having foreseen that possible move, he had secured an assurance providing against it, in his favour. But the assurance apparently did not mean what he took it to mean. It merely multiplied official correspondence ; and the Bombay Port Trust kept up a ground-swell of complaints. There was talk of rebate allowed on goods going through Káthiawar ; of Bolshevism and the possible leakage into India of seditious literature.

Ranji protested that he had no concern with pamphlets. He wanted to import perambulators and umbrellas ! He argued that the ports belonged to his State, which was by treaty internally independent ; that he was entitled to untrammelled use of them, and ought not to be deprived of their geographical advantages. But if he were suspected of seditious literature or unfair methods, he requested an investigation of his port in order to refute the libel. Officialdom politely disowned any idea of investigation, while pointing out that Náwanagar ports would not be of much use without the Indian hinterland. Therefore the Maharaja ought not to demand too much profit.

Finally—after much to-ing and fro-ing—the customs line was

removed in favour of an arrangement not precisely welcome : British control of customs levied at the actual ports, the resulting sums to be shared between the Government and the States. But the Finance Department wanted all the customs profit ; a demand to which Ranji could not agree since it ran counter to the treaty and against the interests of his own State. Result : a long wearisome debate as to the amount he was willing to accept and the Department willing to pay.

For nearly twenty years the indecisive dispute dragged on : Ranji losing money on his port dues, yet unable—as trustee of his State—to accept the poor bargain offered him. Finally he appealed to the Secretary of State for India—without result, except to render himself extremely unpopular. But, knowing he had a case, and needing the revenue, he ventured to ask that the matter might be argued in England before the Judicial Committee of the Privy Council, which made him more unpopular than ever. His many friends in the House of Commons backed the appeal ; and in due course the Committee produced a verdict altogether in his favour ; all his demands were justified, all his rights reaffirmed.

Unhappily the proceedings had so dawdled on, as proceedings will, that before the verdict could reach India, Ranjitsinhji—disinherited in youth, embittered in middle age—fell ill and died, leaving at least to his nephew the satisfaction of a belated success and freedom to use his own ports for the benefit of Náwanagar.

The present Maharaja, Sir Digvijay Sinhji, K.C.S.I., possesses many of his uncle's fine qualities. Educated at Lancing, he played in the cricket eleven and afterwards held the rank of Captain in the British Army. He has seen active service in Egypt, Palestine and the North-West Frontier.

In that connection it is interesting to record that his cousin—also a soldier—son of Ranji's elder brother—was the first Indian officer to receive the honour of a D.S.O. for a gallant exploit near Tobruk in the spring of 1941 : an exploit in which he displayed ' initiative and leadership of the highest order '. The story is worth telling, not only for itself, but as proof that India possesses much fine officer material in the various branches of her princely families and her many nobles with warrior blood in their veins.

The officer in this case was Major Rajendra Sinhji of the 2nd Royal Lancers, Indian Army, leader of a squadron that distinguished itself in supporting and defending the 3rd Indian Motor Brigade.

The Brigade itself, holding the wells at Mekili, was encircled by vastly superior German and Italian forces ; yet they must hold those wells till the main British forces, retreating from Benghazi, had reached Tobruk in safety. Hard pressed, they were in dire straits ; faced eventually by two dread alternatives—to surrender or make a bold bid to break through. They made the more soldierly choice ; charged gallantly through the ring of enemies ; broke out into the desert ; and so, in small parties, worked their way back to Sollum or Tobruk. In that critical move, Major Rajendra Sinhji's Lancers acted as rearguard.

While waiting for Divisional Headquarters to go through, they were overwhelmed by a German tank attack. The Major, finding his squadron not seriously involved, led them off westward out of the *melée*. But he was forced back by heavy machine-gunning from the flanks. Nothing daunted, he charged with his squadron and fragments of other units straight at the enemy's position, the trucks roaring along at top speed over bumpy ground. Right through a battery they charged, the crews flinging up their hands. Unable to deal with prisoners, on they must go ; first west then north ; shaking off the pursuit among the hills. There it was possible to lie for the rest of the day, hiding in deep nullahs.

But as soon as night fell, they must move on southward, leaving behind them all kit, except food and water, arms and ammunition. So rough was the ground that many trucks had to be abandoned, men doubling up in those that remained. By five in the morning they had only covered forty miles.

Nothing for it but to press on till they encountered an Italian encampment with fifteen lorries. A flank attack proved so demoralising that 200 Italians rushed out with their hands up. But again nothing could be done about prisoners. Some thirty, including all the Germans, were picked out, stowed into lorries, and taken along. Sixty miles they covered swiftly ; encountered a German light patrol ; captured one of their cars, and still pushed on. Again they spotted fresh troops, and—tired though they were —Major Rajendra Sinhji decided on an attack.

No sooner had the word been given than they recognised, with immense relief, that the approaching troops were no Germans, but a force of British scouts : and the worst was over.

The gallant party got to sleep that night by about 2 A.M., having driven continuously for more than thirty hours, moved right round the enemy on the desert flanks and come back to their own troops.

It was a feat calling for the utmost courage and resolution, combined with brilliant navigation and a high order of leadership : a feat worthy of one so closely linked with Maharaja Ranjitsinhji— wise ruler, magnanimous friend and foe ; a great Prince and a great gentleman.

THREE MARATHA STATES

' Great personalities make great nations : and great personalities must be left measurably free to express themselves.'—GRAHAM SETON HUTCHISON.

GWALIOR
PREMIER MARATHA STATE

I

FROM Bombay, southward to Poona, runs a tract of mountain country as rugged and impressive as any in India—the Western Ghauts : a region less familiar to globe-wanderers than the hills and lakes of Rajputana or the Himalayan splendours of Kashmir. Its fierce hills were reckoned inaccessible, before the wonders of modern engineering banished the word. Now an electric train climbs the ridge, revealing at every turn a wider and wilder panorama of naked ranges flung out from the tableland of the Deccan : of peak and crag and castellated summit, like bastions of some ruined fortress ; twisted crest-line and straggling spurs gashed into gullies, where torrents foam in the monsoon : a fit country to breed one of India's finest fighting races.

The Maharastras, or Marathas, were originally a hard-working peasant folk trained to arms by Mogul rulers of the Deccan. Under Akbar the Great they lived in comparative peace ; but with the decline of a great dynasty, the fanatical Moslem spirit flared up again. Persecution, forcible conversion and the wanton destruction of Hindu temples evoked a resurgence of the Maratha spirit, inspired and led by the famous Shivaji—a robber baron, from the Ghauts near Poona. Fine soldier qualities, a spirit of independence and a dynamic personality proclaimed him the born leader, apt to emerge unheralded at some crucial hour. As champion of desecrated Hindu temples and gods, he drew all men after him, and soon became a terror to the country round.

Like most great men, he left no comparable successor ; but to this day he is worshipped by all true Marathas as their supreme hero.

In fifty years, the national impulse he awakened established Maratha dominion east, west and north. Their armies of light horse swept over India like a swarm of locusts, carrying all before them. They subdued even the Rajputs ; pushed on as far as Delhi ; and for a time, occupied the Punjab. Only the genius of Asaf Jah—ancestor to the Nizām of Hyderabad—prevented them from engulfing the whole of southern India ; while the Moslem adventurer, Hyder Ali, kept Mysore out of their clutches, till he himself was conquered by the rising power of British arms in alliance with Hyderabad.

Then the stage was set for a trial of strength between Great Britain and the Pirate Princes of Central India, who, by that time, had annexed, or laid under contribution, nearly half the country. Clearly there could be no settled peace in the land if their power were allowed to prevail.

In the years of clash and counter-clash that followed, three Maratha generals distinguished themselves as more than soldiers. Men of unusual character and ability, they secured fiefs from conquered lands and became founders of three Central Indian States—Gwalior, Baroda, Indore. Greatest of these was Madhāva Sindhia, who founded the house of Gwalior. A born leader, statesman and soldier, his whole life was a battle ; and he stands out against that stormy background as one of the most remarkable men that India has produced : one who dreamed of an Empire under Maratha rule. Boldly he attacked the Moguls, the Nizām, the Portuguese ; but he lost the Gwalior fortress ; and everywhere he found the road to Empire barred by Warren Hastings, and the whole disciplined might of the British Army.

Thus the two ablest men in the land confronted each other with equal resolve, if not with equal means, to compass victory. The contest was hard and long. Four times the Maratha hosts were defeated by the British and their allies. Four times they returned to the fray. Only the military genius of Wellesley and Lake saved India from wholesale Maratha dominion ; but not until 1818 was that powerful confederacy broken up, to the relief of lands they had conquered without attempting to rule, and of many great neighbouring States as well. But although their power was reduced, their grandiose plan frustrated, the Marathas remain one of the strongest groups of Indian Princes, a race whose prowess and fighting qualities brought the Hindus very near to regaining the lordship of India.

But our present concern is with the founder of Gwalior, Madhāva Rāo, whose invincible personality triumphed over defeat and the aftermath of treaties. Like his famous rival, Warren Hastings, he loomed greater in adversity than in success : and out of that long enmity sprang a friendship with the British honourable to both races. For close on a century, the house of Gwalior has been second to none in devotion to the Crown. But it remained for the father of the present Prince to give the State a second Madhāva Rāo—aptly so named ; for in character and capacity he came nearest to the founder of his line.

At ten years old he entered into his heritage : and the promising boy grew into a remarkable man. At eighteen he was invested with full ruling powers that gave ample scope for his immense energy and versatility of mind. He lost no time in mastering every detail of statecraft, that he might lift Gwalior towards modern standards and create an army worthy to do battle for the British Raj.

In both respects, he achieved his end through the double gifts of personality and vision. Whatever he expected of his officials, he set the example himself. To his people he was the embodiment of sympathetic interest, personal authority and untiring zeal. Under his rule Gwalior became one of the most ably administered States in all India ; and he himself played a fine part in the Great War.

Thickset and below middle height, there was little in his aspect to suggest unusual vitality of mind and body except the eager, interested eyes, quick to assess the value of men and things. In dealing with his subjects, he was as regally Eastern as any Raja of to-day is permitted to be ; but, for all his ropes of pearls and robes of state, his mind—with its prankish vein of humour—was as modern as that of any Oxford undergraduate. He abhorred ' long faces ', and never seemed to outgrow an almost schoolboy relish for practical jokes. He would even inflict them on his mother, whom he worshipped ; and at times they were extremely annoying.

Later he adopted ' April Fools' Day ', which became almost an unofficial State holiday. Not even distinguished guests were immune from his devices ; and Miss Fitzroy tells us of her own experience on one such occasion : how the ladies were treated to a brackish concoction for early tea ; how the men, returning hot and thirsty from their morning ride, calling for lemon squash, were served with iced bubbling glasses of Eno's Fruit Salt ! Their poached eggs were yellow stones, their matches duds, their cigarettes harmlessly exploded ; in the sandwiches, for the shooting party, pink flannel masqueraded as ham ; and at bridge, after dinner, their pencil points proved to be made of india-rubber. ' The Maharaja's chuckle ', she adds, ' rested like a benediction on the distracted company ; but he was himself caught at last, by some irreverent trap prepared in his bed by A.D.C.s driven to retaliation.' [1]

[1] Yvonne Fitzroy, *Courts and Camps in India*.

' I must have my joke,' he would excuse himself to the sedately minded. ' A little play is desirable in those who would not be guilty of stupidity ': and there lies a deeper truth in that simple statement than he himself may have recognised.

Never was Sindhia guilty of stupidity ; and, as a host, his vitality and love of laughter made him exceptionally popular with English guests. None was readier than he to discard formalities ; to become simply their friend and fellow sportsman. Only those who knew him well and worked with him could gauge the rare qualities of his mind and character, ' his mental breadth, capacity and variety, hardly to be matched even in England '. Innately a ruler, he was also a sound financier and practical philanthropist, a tireless worker, an experienced soldier and fine sportsman. He never went the way that young royal India was once prone to go, lavishing money in the pleasure haunts of Simla or Paris. He preferred to work for and among his own people.

His mastery of detail matched his energy and zest. Owning many hundred miles of railway and a garage filled with cars of every design, he could himself drive anyone of them or any railway engine. He could break up the works of car or engine and put them together again with the skill of a practised engineer. He was his own Prime Minister and Commander-in-Chief, devoting himself especially to the Army, which—in spite of ox and elephant batteries—he welded into the strongest and best-disciplined force of any Indian State, with the possible exception of Kashmir. To his energy and capacity there seemed no limit set.

It is, beyond question, a sign of good hope for India's future that, in such distinguished Princes as Gwalior and Bikanir, Mysore, Kolhapur and Bhopāl, the graft of Western training and ways of thought has not—as often—robbed the kingly Eastern stock of its racial virility and intelligence ; qualities that have left indelible marks on the history of that great land.

The State itself covers more than twenty-five thousand square miles of rocky plain, watered by the river Jumna, and rising in the west to a range of forest-mantled hills, the home of mediaeval barons who lived for fighting and plunder, like the reivers of old Scotland.

Its chief glory, the famous rock fortress of Gwalior, rises abruptly from the plain ; a mass of yellow sandstone, nearly two miles long, fit pedestal for the fort and Palace that seem almost to grow out of the hill into which they are built. Its heroic record of siege after siege, of stubborn resistance to the invader, is worthy of a race that claims Rajput blood in its veins. The pride of Gwalior, as of Udaipur, aptly centres in its rock-enthroned fortress that looms majestic above the comparatively modern city at its base. Northward, jagged cliffs, quarried for centuries, threateningly overhang the old town. Eastward, the summit is crowned by the fort and the superb Palace built for Raja Mān Singh, with its façade of three-hundred-foot battlements, tall towers, carved balconies and fretted domes ; a marvel of architectural inspiration and craft, almost equal to that work of demi-gods at Jōdhpur. Above the Dondha gate there still remain prison cells that could terrible tales unfold ; and the hill itself is crammed with ancient temples, honeycombed with caves and cells—a sinister foundation for so much grandeur ; but that is India. This formidable fort, ' pearl on the necklace of the castles of Hind ', has in fact been taken and retaken many times over from the dawn of history : held in turn by Rajput, Afghan, Moguls and finally by the British. After holding it for a year, they restored it to Sindhia, who is not likely to lose again that pearl more valuable than even the costliest among his crown jewels.

It was in 1905 that he enjoyed to the full one of the most memorable events of his reign—a visit from the heir to England's throne, Prince George (afterwards King George V), accompanied by Princess Mary ; the first Royal tour since King Edward's visit thirty years before. It was also the first time that a Royal Princess had come to India : an innovation that proved as successful as it was courageous.

Thirty years earlier the public appearance of a woman at Durbars and other functions would have seriously perturbed many Indians of high standing, especially in those States where purdah was strictly observed. Even at this later day there had been official qualms as to the wisdom of running counter to India's traditional custom. Many might object to seeing a woman set aloft on the State elephant—immemorial throne of kings.

But the Prince and Princess—with characteristic faith in the good feeling of India—had decided to take the risk ; and, long before the tour ended, their faith was justified beyond the most sanguine hopes, by India's enthusiastic greeting to England's loved Princess. Her sympathy, her patently sincere interest in the lives and personalities of India's women, moved them at first to an almost surprised regard. The success of her purdah parties, her desire to get in touch with her guests, as women like herself, charmed away their natural shyness and won all hearts. For them the fact of her royalty was but a reflected lustre. It was she, herself, who dispelled all lurking prejudices, and produced everywhere a complete change of attitude that amounted to a personal

GWALIOR: ENTRANCE TO PALACE OF MĀN SINGH IN GWALIOR FORT
(High Commissioner of India)

GWALIOR : THE FORT
(High Commissioner of India)

triumph. An old Chief, full of years and honours, spoke for thousands when he said, ' We loved the great Queen for her greatness and justice. But in your Princess we have most of all loved her love for us.' And her English subjects could, from their hearts, affirm his words.

So that favoured Royal pair came to Gwalior through a various yet curiously monotonous India, beflagged and cheering, as even the East can cheer when kings pass by ; an India zealously disfigured by stock decorations and trite sentiments repeated *ad nauseam*, crude flags and strips of bunting, aptly described as ' a pertinacity in disfigurement scarcely credible in anything so well meant '.

And through all the blaze of pageantry resounded the intermittent thunder of guns and more guns, and again guns : a monotonous yet stirring tribute to royalty. Thirty-one guns for greeting ; thirty-one on landing ; thirty-one boom-booming everywhere, on arrival and departure, with an added trifle of twenty-one or less for their princely hosts, according to status.

Everywhere, also, there was dust unlimited, from the Khyber to Central India ; for a devastating drought was on the land. Yet water—though crops withered and cattle pined for it—was splashed over miles and miles of unresponsive roadway by the patient, perpetual *bhisti*, human water-carrier of India, immortalised by Kipling's *Gunga Din*. Picture Gunga Din, with scores of his kind, ineffectually laying the dust for royalty ; his glistening brown body and dingy loin-cloth, the familiar wet goatskin slung across his back, his forward stoop and skilled turn of the wrist that sends fan after fan of water across the sun-smitten highway. Over and over, without ceasing, those *mussaks* ¹ were emptied and replenished. Because it was an order, men who had seen the torments of ' the great thirst ' must squander, on desert dust, veritable water of life.

When the Royal pair went by train, scores of galloping horses guarded the track : and at night sentinels were placed on either side of the line ; flaming torches held aloft by rigid bronze figures, white-robed with crimson turbans ; each erect and motionless in his own circle of light against the limitless dark of desert and star-powdered sky.

In Gwalior State, long beforehand, preparations for the event had overshadowed all else. The young Maharaja had organised and supervised every detail of every function in his elaborate programme, that could not quite escape the monotony of any Royal tour ; but his welcome to England's Prince and Princess

¹ Goatskins.

H

provided a pageant of Eastern splendour and glamour too often lacking in the modern Indian scene. No mere motor cars, but a solid phalanx of elephants, bearing golden howdahs, awaited the Royal guests : thirty dazzling monsters, in full panoply of gold, embroidered velvet and trappings, their solemn faces masked with paint and silken fringes, flanked by immense earrings, each a man's full burden. From their gold-*mohur* [1] necklaces hung silver gilt bells that tinkled, soft and clear, when they moved : and their huge feet were burdened with heavy gold anklets. Sixty wicked little eyes twinkled through paint and fringe, as if elephantine wisdom were privately amused at the childish folly of man.

It was on the backs of those untiring monsters that the Royal guests mainly lived through the crowded days that followed : elephants guarding their routes, saluting and trumpeting on parade ; elephants joggling them into the jungle and treading out wounded tigers ; elephants lifting them up the steep rocky face of the fort : an experience they were not likely to forget. There were also Great Occasions when Western eyes took their fill of colour and glitter and sparkle of gems : the tireless Maharaja being mainly concerned for the smooth working-out of his programme : driving off alone in his car to meet new-comers ; leading his own cavalry on parade ; presenting his own Chiefs at the Royal Durbar—a great gathering of nobles to meet the son of their King-Emperor.

Gwalior's fine, Italianate Durbar Hall, with orange and yellow hangings, fitly framed their many-coloured magnificence ; embroidered coats of every shade from purple to flame-colour and rose pink, steel cuffs fringed with gold ; and for headgear the small brick-red Maratha turban. Above them on a dais, the Maharaja sat resplendent, in cloth of gold and state jewels, collars and ropes of pearls ; and beside him the bearded young English Prince in his simple dark uniform and Royal decorations. The vast hall, in its panoply of colour, throbbed with the strange mutter of tomtoms, a blurred accompaniment to the high nasal voice of a girl singing.

Long and solemn were the formalities ; Western eyes almost surfeited with splendour. Prince George himself, the focal point of homage, would no doubt have preferred a smoke and drink in a comfortable armchair, an informal talk with this most informal of Maharajas. But traditional functions held the field ; a grand parade of the State army, a banquet in the pillared hall hung with arms and silks and spears ; plates and dishes of pure gold ; a dinner worthy of any famous London restaurant, in a setting such

[1] An Indian sovereign.

as only India could produce in these levelling days.

And when at last the table was cleared, the glasses set for dessert, there appeared at one end a small silver train run by electricity, the model engine followed by seven silver trucks containing port, liqueurs, brandy, cigars and cigarettes, nuts, chocolates and fancy sweets. A pressed button set the train in motion, each guest helping himself as it passed. Lift out the silver lining of a truck—and the train stopped automatically. Replace the lining—and on it went : the kind of engaging toy one could only find in the palace of an Indian Prince.

But all the splendours of Durbar and banquet were eclipsed by the experience of ascending the rock-fortress on elephants, and the many wonders that the ascent revealed.

At every turn a wider scene of hill and desert unfolded itself, as they passed in stately procession through a sequence of massive gateways arched and towered : Gate of the Cloud-Capped Fort ; Gate of Ganesh—the elephant-headed god—presiding deity of the rock ; the Lakshman Gate and the high *Hāwa Darwaza*—Gate of All the Winds. Beyond the last of these, the famous palace of Mān Singh reared its grey stone walls, beautified by tiles of blue and green and gold, exquisitely enamelled with flights of Brahminy geese. Impossible for pencil or camera to convey the mediaeval atmosphere, the mingled beauty and power and dignity of Gwalior fort : a very Gibraltar of the desert.

There were great days also for Prince George in the jungle, after tiger and lesser trophies, mainly on elephants who could tread the thickest jungle in darkness and track wounded tigers by their own unerring instinct.

Later, it was Princess Mary who had her personal triumph at the Christmas party for close on fifty English and Indian children : a real Christmas Tree, decorations and crackers and surprise parcels for all. Seeing that their programme would bring them to Gwalior for Christmas, she had planned the whole affair in advance, had brought out from England all the decorations and delights, including fifty presents chosen by her own children. And the happy idea proved an unqualified success, once she had dispelled the shyness of her little Indian guests, to whom she was giving the surprise of their young lives.

In a lofty room hung with chandeliers the Tree stood resplendent : candles and coloured balls and a glittering star on its topmost twig, mysterious parcels piled under its boughs. These were presented by a realistic Santa Claus in scarlet cap and snow-flakes and long beard ; whilst the children clung nervously together in groups, looking like dressed-up dolls, in their gaily-coloured silks and velvets and jewels, with pillbox caps and stiff little coats of gold brocade, their round eyes fixed on the Princess in mingled curiosity and awe.

The five English children clustered round her when she plucked a cracker from the tree and pulled it with one of them. Another and another flashed and crackled. Paper caps and toys appeared as if by magic. The small Indians looking on, startled and wide-eyed, were seized with sudden excitement. They, too, must pull crackers and have paper caps. Shyness gave place to a wild stampede, a general assault on the Tree. When the boys were getting the best of it, small girls were lifted on grown-up shoulders to give them a chance of snatching at treasures out of reach. Even the shyest joined in the fury. Boys began raiding unfairly favoured girls ; and one small creature intelligently kept very near the Princess, to whom she confided all her treasures for safety.

At last excitement subsided. Reluctantly, they were all removed from that hall of delight. Trooping up the wide staircase, they turned again and again to look back at the dishevelled Tree that had given them probably the most exciting hour they had ever known.

On Sindhia himself that gracious and genuinely interested pair left a lasting impression that not only deepened his devotion as an ally, but captured the heart of the man.

Richly endowed as to heritage and personality, he still lacked the one thing needful—a son to follow him. As an orthodox Hindu he had married early, a bride of his mother's choosing. But no child had come to them ; and the young Maharani—saddened by that unkindest blow to an Indian wife—must accept the man's right to choose another bride. This time the choice was to be entirely his own.

Spending the season in London, he met and feel deeply in love with the Princess Indira Raja, only daughter of his friend the Maharaja Gaekwar of Baroda—a beautiful girl of twenty, irresistibly attractive to men. Her father, a Prince with modern ideas, had refused to let the orthodox marriage-makers decide her destiny. She must think for herself, choose for herself, in a matter so vital to a woman's happiness. So their pearl of a girl had been educated first at a college in Baroda, then at a ' finishing ' school in Eastbourne. Later on she had appeared with them in London society and travelled round the world. Outside India, both mother and daughter discarded the restrictions of purdah ; and Princess Indira's early love affairs had been left more or less in her own hands, her parents accepting the risk that all freedom involves. But when the Maharaja of Gwalior fell a victim to her charms, they could not conceal their urgent wish for so brilliant an alliance between the two leading Maratha kingdoms. It was natural, in such a case, that they should be readier than she to overlook the fifteen years' disparity in age and the domestic drawbacks involved. The Princess, a modern-minded, high-spirited girl, would have to take her place in the Palace household as second wife. She would have to revere and obey an orthodox mother-in-law, to accept all the complex conventions of Hindu home life, including the strictest purdah—she, who had freely enjoyed the society of men and must have realised fully her own powers of attraction. And Sindhia himself, for all his informal ways, was pure Hindu in unquestioned worship of his mother, whose word must be law to the household.

So dire a prospect of retrogression justified Indira's reluctance to accept her ardent lover ; but in the end she assented as a matter of duty to her parents. Shutting her eyes to the future, she took her fill of the brilliant present : the stir of interest among their London friends, the choosing of lovely garments and fine linen ; the garden party he gave at Ranelagh in her honour ; and a young girl's natural pleasure in the homage of a lover completely subjugated by her charm.

For six months all went well to outward seeming, the princely suitor secure in his hope of the love-marriage he so desired ; but those who knew the Princess intimately felt far from certain of the wedding fixed for late January 1912. To discerning eyes it was evident that she still shrank from a marriage that involved strict purdah and the rôle of dutiful daughter-in-law ; a marriage of one-sided devotion. No more dancing ; no more rides across country in tailored breeches and skirted coat ; and she as fine a rider as any Irish girl. But one great coming event in December promised her chafed spirit a taste of festivity and freedom ; an experience that was to prove the turning-point in her life.

That Royal event brought most of India and much of England to Delhi for the great Coronation Durbar of 1911, when the former Prince and Princess came back as newly-crowned King and Queen, having seen enough in that earlier visit to make India a living reality to their minds and hearts.

The King-Emperor himself had chosen Delhi—not yet named as capital—for its poignant and glorious associations ; the royal city that, for nearly three thousand years, has witnessed the fate of empires.

But the Delhi prepared for their welcome was by no means the shabby old Civil Station where they had briefly stayed in 1905. From the most unpromising material on earth a transformation must be wrought that looked, on the face of it, impossible. True, the miracle had been worked once by Lord Curzon, in a white heat of creative energy. It could therefore be repeated, on a greater scale, to welcome the Royalties in person.

So the word went forth : and things happened.

Only those who saw them happen could have any conception of the unremitting thought and forethought and labour, the immense cost involved in creating a mushroom city for 250,000 people, to say nothing of putting a new face on Delhi itself, too long neglected and fallen into decay. Roads must be widened and straightened ; unsightly buildings removed, dingy ones whitewashed till they hardly knew themselves. And beyond the sandstone walls that city of tents, elaborate past belief, must be conjured out of an undrained swamp, flooded every year by the river Jumna, and frequented by garrisons of officers in pursuit of duck or snipe.

All must be prepared, designed and achieved in the space of eleven months that included one of Delhi's most malignant hot weathers and an unusual failure of the monsoon. Hindrances were legion ; distractions only known to the men who wrestled with them. Important cargoes were wrecked ; the whole main encampment was flooded by torrents of belated rain, and part of the railway washed away : gorgeous pavilions set up in the Fort were completely destroyed by fire, less than a week before the event. Yet all was repaired, every detail punctually completed, thanks to the zest and skill of a few tireless British officers with their veritable army of coolies and all the resources of the land.

Eleven months of labour—of money dispersed like water—and all for one short week. But that week was crowded with colour and movement and music—massed bands a hundred and fifty strong ; East and West met together in a fervour of loyal enthusiasm, not merely for their Imperial Majesties, but for the widely loved man and woman, returning in triumph to the land where they had won all hearts only six years before. ' Never '—it has been said—' was welcome more magnificent given by a people to its King : never a greeting more sincere and cordial on both sides.'

And in that mushroom city—twenty-eight square miles of canvas—there were State camps for every Indian ruler of note ; each camp complete with roads, arched gateways, lamp-posts, pot-plant gardens and flags of many colours : at night a fairy scene, outlined by electric bulbs.

Here was a majestic setting for scores of human tragedies and comedies, for the petty jealousies and scandals that flourish like weeds in social and official British India. And here, in this crowded hour of ceremonial and festivity, the romance of Maharaja Sindhia suffered a set-back unlooked for by all, perhaps even by the Princess herself.

Outwardly resigned, inwardly rebellious, her fretted spirit found relief in the prevailing gaiety and the companionship of three Cooch Behar Princesses, former school friends at East-bourne; lively modern girls with whom she had interests in common. Her parents, fearing their influence, had bidden her keep away from the Cooch Behar camp; but the attraction proved too strong. For there she met not only her school friends but their brother, heir to the throne of Cooch Behar. They danced together again and again. The spell of instantaneous attraction was upon them. He would marry no other girl, nor she any other man; and yet—there loomed, beyond the bright circle of their rapture, her imminent wedding, her duty to the parents, who would back Sindhia through thick and thin.

Here came the pull between two sides of her heart; a call for independent action. Without a word to her parents, before their special train left Delhi, she posted a letter to the Prince breaking off the engagement.

But between Hindu royalties the affair was not so simple as that. The coming marriage was more than a personal affair. It was an alliance between the leading Maratha Prince and the premier Hindu Princess of India :—Hindu still in name, though Western education, as so often happens, had robbed her of one faith without giving her another.

A telegram from Sindhia to her father—' What does the Princess mean ? '—brought the love-smitten girl up against the rock of parental authority. It was the prelude to months of strain and stress, of open antagonism between her and her devoted yet disapproving parents, of alternations between hope and despair for her betrothed, who, from the Hindu standpoint, was virtually her husband. The marriage was not cancelled ; it was deferred. But the heart, like the tongue, ' can no man tame '. And the Prince, for all his orthodox Hinduism, wanted more than a mere obedient wife to be the mother of his son.

When the driven Princess at last told him frankly that she would marry him to please her parents, though she could not pretend to love him, he sent answer—deeply wounded in pride and heart—that on such terms he would not accept her. He had taken one orthodox wife. He wanted not only herself but her love : and that, with the best will on earth, she could not give him to order.

It was a cruel position for a high-spirited girl, resolved to make a stand for freedom to shape her own life : but the record of her struggle belongs to the story of Baroda. Sindhia himself —resolute, even in discouragement—could only beg his enchanting Princess to think again : and it was not till August that he received the final blow—his ring, his presents and her definite refusal, taking the full blame on herself, since her parents had always favoured the match. Even so, he could not at once give up his secret hope that by some means his dreams might yet come true.

Months passed ; hope wilted ; and in the summer of 1913 it was killed outright by an announcement in *The Times* that a marriage was about to take place between Prince Jitendra, Maharaj Kumar of Cooch Behar, and the Princess Indira of Baroda.

Whether or no he could banish her image from his heart, he could no longer defer his obvious duty—to take another wife who might give him a son. The professional marriage-makers had long been on the alert ; and between them a suitable bride was found. Within the year she presented the Prince with a girl child in place of the desired heir to the throne.

Disappointed he must have been ; but profound reverence for his mother and the memory of his lost love, evoked the surprising decree that his new-born daughter should be acclaimed and fêted, in every way, as if she were a boy. By way of added lustre he christened her ' Mary '—a personal tribute to the First Lady of England, whom he had entertained as Princess and saluted as Queen.

A year later came the long-awaited son : and although ' Mary ' had in a measure stolen his birthright, he was welcomed as Raj Kumar and given the royal name of George, thus completing a princely tribute as unique as it was sincere.

Both children were born when the Great War, at its worst, was demanding from England and her Empire the utmost they could give. The war record of Gwalior—most renowned among Maratha fighting clans—was second to none. His own personal gifts amounted to nearly forty lakhs of rupees : and his practical good feeling showed itself, in countless ways : free feeding for all passing troops, British and Indian ; his own State Guest House reserved for British officers or their wives who might need it. This last was praised by Lord Hardinge as ' the kindest act of any Indian Prince ; one that deeply touched the hearts of all concerned '. His restless energy at that time was abnormal. Though incipient disease prevented him from offering personal service, sheer vitality kept him going ; so that he seemed almost his old self again at twenty, dashing round and getting things done. And the years that followed heightened his reputation as a man and a Ruler. Recognised by all as one of the ablest and most powerful of Indian Princes, he remained in himself, completely unassuming, a generous loyal friend, unshakably devoted to the British Crown. Yet this fortune-favoured Prince who lost his heart's desire, lost also the satisfaction of seeing his son grow to manhood. Cut off in early middle age, he bequeathed to that son a heritage greatly enhanced ; left also an explicit decree in his will that the boy should be educated in Gwalior by carefully chosen British officers. He had given much thought to the vexed question of Eastern or Western training ; and he deemed it better, in every way, that the heir to an Indian throne should be trained for kingship among his own people. He saw it as a fact worth noting that many of India's wisest rulers had been so trained, including the father of his own adored Princess.

For the years of minority he appointed a Regency Council of distinguished State officers : a council in which Hindus, Moslems and Marathas worked together under their President, the Junior Maharani, mother of George Jivaji : a council handicapped, in a measure, by his own peculiar success.

During his last years of life diabetes reduced him physically to a shadow of his former self ; yet, to the last, he remained the liveliest, most vibrant of men ; suffering hardships gladly, though his mental grasp and quick temper made it less easy for him to suffer fools gladly. At one time he could be relentless ; at another overflowing with tenderness and emotion ; at all times a magnetic personality hard to resist. Most of his failings were due to a certain lack of moral elasticity. Angular and enigmatic, his strong prejudices and stubborn belief in his own point of view made him, in later life, over-emphatic and impatient of contradiction. Taken all round he was a curious mixture of mental breadth and narrowness, of shrewdness and surprising simplicity, of hard elements mingled with tenderness ; rigidly stern in public relations, kindly in all private ones ; in every way a singularly original if composite personality. With truth it may be said that for every one man who understood him, there were ten who did not ; yet, for every one who did not like him, there were twenty who did. So ingrained was his personal magnetism that he compelled affection even from those who criticised him ; yet he failed to win the one woman who captured his heart.

No saint himself, he expected no high standards from the world at large ; and, in spite of a deep, religious faith, he shrewdly asserted that ' nothing is so firmly believed in as what we least know '. The one sin he could not forgive was disloyalty. Above everything, a man must be ' true to salt ' ; a creed he lived up to in great things and small. He would have liked nothing better than to be remembered—and he surely will be—as a ' damned good fellow '. To the end he believed in the divine right of kings, which did not imply a divine right to indulge in irresponsible government. An autocrat who exercised his own authority through Ministers and a Council, he frankly detested the arid plane of democracy, ' where every molehill is a mountain and every thistle a tree '.

There is no tendency, in Gwalior, towards any form of popular government—' a will-o'-the-wisp that India is blindly pursuing '. The masterful spirit of Sindhia still pervades the State he so ably ruled and served ; and to his son he has passed on a large measure of his own ability and foresight, his taste for supervising every detail of State business. The young Prince—a godson of King George the Fifth—is as keenly addicted to sport and games as any English boy, and was as little inclined to take over too soon his active State responsibilities. But having entered into his kingdom, he has proved himself very much his father's son.

Wrapped up in the welfare of Gwalior, he is immensely popular with his people, though they accept his reforms rather because he is their Maharaj, than because they set any store by that doubtful blessing, the vote, or by new-fangled designs for improving their social, economic and physical conditions of life. Preferring to live as their fathers lived, they are bewildered rather than enchanted by schemes for ' rural uplift ' on which he proposes to spend some ten million rupees. His own light railway covers 250 miles. Motor buses run everywhere, hindered only by the perpetual bullock-cart, overloaded with every conceivable item, animal, vegetable and human, liberally powdered with dust ; past and present rubbing elbows, as they do all over India and the East.

The young Prince himself is very much of the present. Though his wife was chosen for him, in approved Hindu fashion, he knew her personally and had more contact with her before marriage than custom normally allows. She and the dowager Maharani, his mother, though not publicly discarding purdah, can and do receive friends in their charming club-house and gardens. Here they give parties for tennis, badminton and bridge, like any free-faring wives of the West ; both perfectly mannered, both intelligently interested in the strange world outside their charmed enclosure. Only at times they lament their difficulty in persuading the young Maharaja to take sufficient care of himself.

His own chief care is for the State. His whole interest centred in Gwalior, he cares little for the turmoil of modern Indian politics ; but he is lucky in possessing a friend and neighbour many years older than himself—the Maharaj Rāna of Dhōlpur, a man of subtle intellect and a philosophic turn of mind. The frequent and friendly intercourse between them must tend to enlarge the vision of young Sindhia, who promises to be in every way worthy of his fine heritage. He will do well if he can preserve undimmed the brightest features in the rule of Gwalior's ' Mādho Maharaj '.

BARODA :

THE ROYAL SAGE

I

In the clear gold of an early autumn morning, bugles heralding the dawn, Baroda's Raj Mahāl—Palace of the King—has an almost fairy-tale aspect ; the risen sun, gilding its domes and towers, the pools of purple shadow, under its many arches ; the whole elaborate façade mirrored in a circular tank, where swans, black and white, sail among reflections with their lordly air of owning the waters they deign to adorn. One tall Italianate tower, bitten out of the blue, serves as a landmark for miles around.

The Palace itself, Lakshmi Vilās—Abode of Wealth—has neither the dream-beauty of Udaipur nor the heroic associations of Jōdhpur and Bikanir. Its chief claim to interest lies in its long association with two distinguished personalities : the late Maharaja Sir Sayaji Rāo Gaekwar, and his Maharani, proud and beautiful : a woman of character, courage and intellect, ' most simply and with utmost assurance—a Queen '.

From the great centre portico, steps lead into a vast hall ringed with a gallery of carved cedarwood and paved with green marble, only to be found in Baroda. From a second hall, four life-like stuffed tigers glare at all comers, and the walls are hung with trophies of shikar. Beyond the marble staircase, an incongruous lift ascends to higher storeys where each member of the family has his or her suite of rooms. The central block—drawing-room, library and Durbar Hall—was occupied by the Maharaja ; the Maharani's side of the Palace having its own entry, reception and private rooms.

The Maharaja, Sir Sayaji Rāo Gaekwar III, Sena Khās Khēl, Samsher Bahádur, Farzand-i-Khas-i-Dowlat-i-Inglishia, G.C.S.I., G.C.I.E., was, in early middle age, a shortish thickset man ; his fine eyes and thoughtful face index to a mind at once philosophic and practical ; a mind that mellowed and broadened with age. From earliest days the State was his watchword. Later, that ruling passion became his master. Travel where he would, his mind was always seeking for new ways to improve and enrich the lives of his people. And his interest, his influence, reached far beyond Baroda. Everywhere, unceasingly, he worked for better understanding and co-operation between the two conflicting creeds—Hindu and Moslem—whose age-old feuds have caused more friction and bloodshed throughout India than almost any other factor in her troubled history. His taste for simple living, economy and hard work was a heritage from his yeoman stock. For this Prince was not born royal. He was adopted, like many of his Order. When his predecessor was deposed for flagrant misrule, records were searched for a boy of Gaekwar lineage : Gaekwar being the Baroda family name, not a title, as is commonly supposed. One might as reasonably call Napoleon the Buonaparte of France as call Sir Sayaji Rāo ' the Gaekwar of Baroda '.

The needful kinship was discovered in a yeoman family of three brothers ; and the dowager Maharani, with unconscious discernment, chose ' the serious one ' ; a boy of twelve, who little relished his transfer to the vast Palace. Missing his father and his simple home, he lived lonely among strangers who made much of him.

At twelve years old he was practically illiterate ; but his eagerness to learn was turned to good account by a Scottish tutor, Mr. Elliot, I.C.S., whose inestimable services he repaid by a lifelong affection. These lonely years—that drove him in on himself—may have made him the finer man and ruler, caring less for pleasure and more for work than most of his kind ; though the purely pleasure-loving Maharaja is a rarity in these days.

At the age of seventeen he was formally installed ; and afterwards married, by arrangement, to a delicate girl from South India, who lived only five years : leaving the young Ruler with one son, who should have succeeded to the throne. But he died early ; and it is his son who rules Baroda to-day.

The Maharaja's second wife, chosen from a Deccan noble family, was illiterate at fourteen ; but her mental capacity, like his own, triumphed over all hindrances, so that eventually she became one of the most distinguished women of India. Of her four children, three sons and one daughter, it was the girl, Indira Raja, who achieved distinction, with her blend of beauty, brains and character. Possessing all an Indian woman's grace and rhythm of movement, her added intelligence and sparkling wit made her irresistibly attractive to men. Both she and her mother on their travels discarded purdah ; and the girl very early developed a distinctive personality not always in accord with the ideas and wishes of her parents. For modernised India is already being troubled by the clash between two generations that is a common-place of home life in the West.

In this connection, both mother and daughter owed much to their friendship with a young Englishwoman of brains and character ; young enough to feel with the daughter, old enough to understand the mother. Introduced by a friend to the Baroda family, it was her good hap to spend eight years with them, as companion to the premier Maharani of Hindu India, then in the prime of early middle life. The delightful book that Miss Tottenham afterwards wrote,[1] gives a vivid impression of Her Highness in those days—a figure of gracious dignity and charm : the broad forehead with its scarlet marriage-mark ; the finely-pencilled eyebrows above dark eyes that could flash in scorn or melt to a liquid softness ; the smooth head veiled by a sari of gold tissue ' that seemed to give the wearer a halo of apartness, accentuated by her queenly manners '.

Attraction was mutual. The two women soon became close and permanent friends.

The Maharani's two eldest sons were then mainly out of India : one at Harvard University, the other at Christ Church, Oxford. The youngest, with his sister, Indira Raja, was still at home : a fine and stately home, dominated by the notable person-alities of husband and wife.

The Maharaja himself, simple-hearted and serious-minded, had, from his youth, one urgent desire, ' to be a good Ruler and under nobody's thumb '. A good Ruler he proved beyond question ; lifting his scattered kingdom—impaired by half a century of bad government—from its nadir to its zenith. At the time of his accession in 1875, the State was only just emerging from years of chaos. Its finances were in hopeless disorder ; its highways unsafe, its nobles unruly. There existed hardly a track that could be called a road ; State railways were unknown. How-ever, the young Ruler had been fortunate in the Indian Minister appointed to remodel Baroda during his seven years of minority. Thus the foundations of a progressive State had been well and truly laid by a man who frankly admired British works and ways. But it is to the Maharaja's glory alone that he built so well on those foundations.

He it was who inaugurated railways, hospitals, schools and a first-rate water supply. Through wise expenditure, through per-sistence in well-doing and his own financial ability, he had by then become one of India's wealthiest Princes.

Yet, in all personal ways, he remained abstemious to a degree ; drinking no wine, and wearing no jewels except on high occasions. Such kingly items as his golden howdah and silver carriage, gold bedsteads, dinner services of gold and silver, must be reckoned as matters of course for any Maharaja. But in all his vast Palace,

[1] *Highnesses of Hindostan.*

with its regal appointments, he permitted neither extravagance nor waste. His spirit and his personal touch were all-pervading. He would lavish money only on public works, and on education, so that his subjects could in time become fitted to take part in their own government : a boon they might or might not appreciate. Certainly not one in a thousand could comprehend his high aim and steadfast purpose. Human and ignorant, they took for granted all that he did to improve or enliven them. The spirit that prompted him was simply not understood. These be the high lights and shadows of modern kingship in the East.

From early days his wide-flung interests and pursuit of knowledge induced an insatiable taste for travel that was shared to the full by his beautiful and cultured wife. Together they visited England, Europe, Japan, and—in 1906—America, where they were right royally entertained. Very keenly they appreciated American vitality, directness and hospitable spirit. The Maharaja himself took an active interest in Western forms of education, his favourite study ; with the result that, later on, he sent his own son to Harvard University ; and on his return a successful library scheme was started by an American in Baroda.

His taste for reading was wide and varied : history, philosophy and comparative religions, with excursions into fiction and lighter themes. It was a young English cleric—an Oxford friend of his second son—who introduced him to *Alice in Wonderland*, when *Anna Karenina* had proved rather heavy going. Success was immediate. The Little Man (as his admirers called him) was charmed with that immortal phantasy. His own rendering of ' *You're old, Father William* ' was—in Mr. Weedon's phrase— ' worth going ten miles to hear '. The Maharaja even commanded a translation of the book into Marathi ; but there remains no record as to how, if ever, any man achieved that formidable feat.

Throughout all India, especially in the greater States, one finds the eternal fascination of sharp contrasts and incongruities, arising from the frequent clash between civilised ways in the Palace, and city life with its ancient traditions, its festivals and processions that must be shared, even by the most advanced Prince, if he would keep in touch with his people. Not least among these are the elaborate ceremonies and feastings incidental to any Hindu wedding, more especially that of a Raj Kumar, heir to the throne.

In this case, young Jayasinh Rāo, fresh from Harvard and anxious to acquire a wife, had inspected and approved a girl of thirteen, carefully chosen by his mother. Court astrologers had named an auspicious day. The Maharajas of Mysore and Indore, with their families, were among the distinguished guests, Indian and English. It was to be a brilliant affair : ceremonies and festivities to last for several days. Flags waved from roof-tops over decorated streets. At night the great tank was ringed with rainbow lights, its waters reflecting illumined barges and rafts.

On the actual day, British guests were invited into the wedding pavilion, where the girl bride, gorgeously arrayed, was set upon a dais beside the bridegroom in sheer muslin and brocaded coat : a curtain held up between them till the actual moment of ' giving in marriage '. That done, the symbolic thread must be tied round each wrist. Together they must tread the Seven Steps, that made their union irrevocable, while priests chanted appropriate texts from the Védas.

Now, once more, they were seated ; the curtain down between them for life. Yet even then they could see little of each other, so garlanded and festooned they were with flowers and pearls ; so demurely the bride pulled her sari across her face.

None but those who knew would suppose that here was a Harrow-cum-Harvard young man of twenty-three taking to wife a wisp of womanhood who, in Western eyes, appeared little more than a child.

Followed a five-day programme of family meetings and feastings : public fêtes, a cheetah hunt, fireworks and elephants wrestling—a form of sport peculiar to Royal India.

Two monsters, heavily chained, entered the arena from opposite sides. Men armed with spears, creeping through passages made for them, cautiously unshackled the combatants.

Instantly they charged at one another like run-away engines in collision : head against head, trunks entwined above tusks closely jammed. Trumpeting with strange squeals, they rocked their huge bodies to and fro like vessels in a storm : a fearful yet impressive sight, the crowd yelling encouragement.

At last one great tusk snapped like a rifle shot. An order was shouted to pull them apart : a much stiffer task than getting them together.

Again the men creep up behind, armed with steel springs cruelly spiked, and clap the horrid anklets round a hind leg of each. With a squeal of pain the swaying beasts stop dead, each pathetically lifting an injured leg. Yet, even so, they would assault each other again, but that men with ropes and chains manage to haul them apart, still waving wild tusks and trumpeting defiance.

On that occasion, it needed more than a hundred men to propel and persuade the madly excited beasts out of the arena.

Next day, after a brilliant State banquet, Baroda was emptied

BARODA: HIS HIGHNESS SIR SAYAJI RĀO GAEKWAR III:
LATE MAHARAJA OF BARODA

(Bassano)

BARODA : HER HIGHNESS THE MAHARANI OF BARODA (WITH HER FIRST TIGER)

(From *A Year with the Gaekwar of Baroda*, by E. and Clare Weeden, published by Hutchinson & Co.)

of wedding guests ; only the Mysore and Indore families remaining for a purdah party and the queer Hindu finale described by Miss Tottenham, who came upon it, unawares, driving from the English camp at one in the morning. Just beyond the Palace gates high curtain-walls, guarded by soldiers, enclosed the road. Within the enclosure, flags waved and women stood like statues, bearing on their heads great acetylene lamps. The far end was all lit up with a strange lurid glow. ' Could it be the Palace people that I saw ? ' she writes. ' Yes. It was.' They were enjoying a riotous carnival, men and women hurling red dust at each other, looking miles removed from London and Harvard. In the midst were Baroda's Maharani and Indira, the Maharaja of Indore with his very modern young wife and a score of others : all mad. ' Crackle of fireworks mingled with wild laughter as from red devils. Shrieks rent the air.'

At half-past nine the bride's party had challenged the bridegroom's to a mock battle ; the red powder their harmless weapon of assault. And they kept it up till four of the morning ; the bridegroom's people victorious, as of custom.

When the dawn came—red as their haze of dust—the ladies of that midsummer madness retired to take cleansing baths ; to reappear as Queen or Princess, clothed in their normal dignity and grace, as if the mimic battle was no more than a crazy dream. But very real it was while it lasted, releasing primitive emotions even in the cultured Maharani and her daughter and in the modern young pair from Indore.

So much for the incongruous : but this land of sharp contrasts can give us another night scene, revealing a different facet of the various-minded East, equally prone to orgies of religious fervour and to the spiritual appeal of music more intricate in its half-tones, rhythms and subtle harmonies than any straightforward melody of the West.

In Baroda, Hindu music was profoundly understood by its gifted Ruler ; and on the eve of his fiftieth birthday he commanded a competition among players and singers at the Palace.

The chosen hour and the setting were eminently of the East. Indians know that music's mysterious influence is enhanced by the pervading mystery of night and stars—and, if possible, a moon ; the body at ease, the mind undistracted by irrelevant intrusions.

Again it is Miss Tottenham who gives us the companion picture to those midnight revels :

I

' A marvellous scene one looked down upon from the balcony
over the main porch of the Palace. Under the dark dome of
night arc lamps flared. Sheets on the wide lawn showed up the
picturesque groupings of musicians. Eye and ear revelled in
beauty of sound and colour : strange dividings and unions of
musical tones ; pipes and flutes, stringed instruments and drums
and the vibrant notes of a woman's voice. The musicians im-
provised, giving rein to pent-up emotions and spiritual feelings ;
pouring out a continuous stream of golden melancholy.'

To Western ears Indian music may sound unmelodious and
monotonous ; but listened to hour after hour it becomes insidiously intoxicating, attuning the ear to finer shades of sound.

Only through such contrasting scenes, as I have chosen, can
Western minds gain even an approximate idea of India's manifold
interpretation of life.

2

And what of the Princess Indira, throughout those weeks of
wedding and spring festivities ?

None perceived more clearly than her English friend the dark
undercurrent of trouble and strain caused by the breaking of her
engagement to the Maharaja of Gwalior, her resolute refusal to
accept any other prospective bridegroom than Prince Jitendra of
Cooch Behar, who had so swiftly and completely captured her
heart. The girl's beautiful eyes were dulled with worry, her
whole being disturbed by primitive emotions, her inner resolve
merely hardened by opposition. Since the Delhi episode, she
and her parents had been openly estranged. The Maharani's
pride and impatience made her seem hard, at times, to the beloved
daughter, who was paying the price of her English education, of
her father's wise decision against early marriage.

To the older generation it was a serious matter—the difference
in caste and religion ; for the Cooch Behar family had broken with
Hinduism and become Theists, members of an influential sect
known as the Brahmo Samāj. So Jitendra's wife must needs
accept initiation into their tenets, a proviso that did not trouble
the Princess at all. Heart and will were set on marrying her
' Jit ' [1] ; and in pursuit of that aim she was proving herself to be
very much her father's daughter, revealing a strength and tenacity
of purpose hardly less than his own.

The story of her dramatic declaration of independence is worth
recording for more than its personal interest. Definitely it was a
sign of the times. Such cases are bound to multiply as purdah is

[1] Pronounced ' Jeet '.

more widely discarded among high-caste girls educated on Western lines. In many ways the change will be all to the good ; but during the process individuals are bound to suffer.

For several months, a virtual deadlock left the Maharaja of Gwalior still hoping, and Indira straining at the leash, while Palace life pursued its normal round.

In April there was the move to Ootacamund, among the Nilgiri Hills, where the Barodas had their summer home—a gabled, English-looking house set high above the Lake. Here the Princess could ride to hounds or scour the rolling uplands to her heart's content : and here the Maharani, encouraged by Miss Tottenham, must learn to play tennis—she who was turned forty, and had never run a step since her marriage. Excelling in all sports, she proved an apt pupil and eventually became a past mistress at that delightful game.

Later in the summer they all returned to Baroda ; and there the Princess, in a white heat of determination, wrote definitely to her betrothed, returning his ring and gifts, taking all blame on herself, and begging forgiveness for the sorrow she had caused through her inability to return his love. Gwalior's answer was addressed to her father : a generous letter, thanking him for all past kindness, wishing prosperity and happiness to his lost Princess in her marriage with his friend Cooch Behar, who had had the good fortune to win her heart.

But to such a marriage the Maharaja of Baroda refused sanction : and here he had to reckon with his daughter's Gaekwar heritage of will and character.

Not until the spring following her brother's wedding did Indira make the first decisive move by writing to her father, since she could not speak to him on the subject. With parental permission if possible—without it if denied—she wished to leave Baroda on March 15th, to be married in Calcutta on the 18th.

Her father, acutely distressed, sent word that he could not give his consent to her plan. If she flouted his refusal, she would get no money from him. She had none of her own. Her very jewels were State property. Vainly she raged against the sordid obstruction ; but even for love of her parents she could not bring herself to wreck the happiness of two lives.

' After all, it is Father's own doing,' was her not unnatural view of the situation. ' I could have married at sixteen, but he said I should wait till I was old enough to have some voice in the matter. Now I make my own choice—and here I am a prisoner.'

Blinded by strong feeling, she could not see that her parents also were paying for their courageous attempt to enlarge her life.

Intent on her own moral struggle for freedom, opposition only goaded her to decisive action. And an impending visit to Europe on account of her father's constant ill-health, gave her the opportunity she craved. Secret arrangements were made for a party from Cooch Behar to arrive in Bombay, while the Barodas were staying there, and to carry off a willing Princess before she should sail for England.

All went smoothly : success seemed assured. But, at the critical moment, by design or mischance, the plan was discovered. It was her parents who carried off a rebellious daughter, in the belief that six thousand miles of sea would effectually separate that persistent pair of lovers.

It need hardly be said that Prince Jitendra promptly followed the Baroda party to Europe ; his elder brother, the Maharaja, being there already, very ill in a London nursing-home, and quite agreeable to ' Jit's ' marriage, as were all his family.

Followed weeks of secret correspondence and manœuvres : the Baroda Highnesses, even in Swiss hotels, aware of being shadowed by friends of Cooch Behar, if not by the Prince himself, probably planning another elopement. Troubled and angered, fearing an open scandal, they were at last reluctantly persuaded to countenance the marriage they deplored. But there would be no marriage portion ; and they would not attend the wedding. It was to take place in London, where friends of the family could be trusted to see that proper provision was made by the bridegroom to support a Princess who was giving up all for his sake. Miss Tottenham was chosen to escort her and see her safely through the great adventure of her life.

There remained only one fear for her, and hope for her parents. So seriously ill was the Maharaja of Cooch Behar that it seemed possible he might die before the wedding could take place. In that case Prince Jitendra would succeed him ; and it was an unwritten law that no actual Maharaja might marry the daughter of another without full consent from the father of the bride. But Fate itself seemed partial to this constant pair. Not until they had been three weeks married, and were enjoying their honeymoon at Maidenhead, came the news that transformed them into Maharaja and Maharani of Cooch Behar.

On Indira's wedding day her father sent her a pair of diamond earrings and a telegram wishing her happiness. From her deeply wounded mother came no word : and in October the young people sailed for India, still unforgiven.

The bereaved parents also sailed not long after ; the Maharani's mind distracted from her ' lost ' daughter by the active interest of choosing brides for her two younger sons on her return to India.

It was a voyage of mixed feelings ; for although she dearly loved her Indian home and people, she also loved the social life of Europe and England, free from even mild purdah restrictions. For six months she had enjoyed a round of theatres and parties, entertaining and being entertained in hotels and restaurants. On her return home, how would it be ?

There was much talk, at the time, of changing Indian views on the subject of purdah ; the men as a whole being readier to dispense with even semi-seclusion than the women, who cherished it often as a mark of aristocracy, of feminine modesty. Yet the idea was gaining ground that, for health of mind and body, women should go about more freely ; and many younger Indian husbands insisted on it. The Maharani—always a keen advocate of the freer life for women—was deeply concerned as to whether she would be permitted to act on her conviction when she returned to India. A step involving so many changes, public and private, could not be taken without her husband's full accord. He himself had little good to say of purdah ; but how far would conviction carry him in respect of his own wife ?

Arrived in Bombay, she awaited his lead.

When their special train halted at Baroda Station—the platform red-carpeted, officials lined up in his honour—he turned to the Maharani.

' You just come with me,' was all he said ; and, smiling in her heart, she followed him, shared his reception and drove home with him in an open carriage-and-four, escorted by outriders in front and cavalry behind.

That victory, without flourish of trumpets, over the major godling of *dastur*,[1] opened the door to a new era of activity and usefulness in her own life, which had hitherto been hampered by the clash between Eastern tradition and her own desire for personal freedom. Even she, at first, found it not so easy to break with accepted custom ; but, from now onward, she could and did turn to fuller account her fine capacities of mind and character, her clear conviction that only India's women—working on lines at once practical and exalted—could create a new spirit in themselves and in their country. Crushed between the millstones of priest and *dastur*, they yet remained the core of her stability and strength. In the Maharani's own words : ' If only the right spirit could stir Indian women to-day, what wonderful things would be done ! '

That was in 1915. In 1941 we can say with truth that the

[1] Custom.

right spirit *is* stirring India's women and wonderful things *have been* done. It is safe to prophesy that in the near future still more wonders may yet come to pass.

3

In the spring of 1914 the Maharaja Gaekwar celebrated his Silver Jubilee ; and, to honour the event, his people commissioned a mounted statue of him—symbolising the spirit of progress—to be erected in the public park, at the cost of Rs.60,000.

On the day of its unveiling, the Maharaja of Indore spoke with sincere admiration of the Rulers who had greatly dared in persuading his people to give up so many obsolete ideas and customs ; had risen high above his surroundings and pursued the good of all without prejudice of caste or creed.

A great day for Baroda ; a landmark for the Prince ; a day of pride for the Maharani, whose life was bound up in his success. With truth she could say to her English friend, ' He is my glory. His life is very precious. He is no ordinary man ! ' And all who really knew him would affirm the words of one who, from first to last, was a help-meet for him.

More and more, outside her family cares and anxieties, her mind was centred on the progress and right education of her countrywomen, the importance of their influence on the new India they were, consciously or unconsciously, helping to create. Too clearly her shrewd mind could foresee the harm that might arise from over-free intercourse between men and women, unless the women were educated on lines that would make their freedom a blessing rather than a danger. It was a matter she could only discuss with her, now, intimate English friend, who had come for a few months and had been persuaded to stay for many years.

' European life ', she frankly declared, ' spoils our men for life in their Indian homes. The kind of women they meet over there, they do not find on their return. It is sad. Trouble and worry will increase for Indian women until they are reared to be fit companions for their men. Then the Indian home would become ideal. For our women love their husbands. And love is the strongest force. By that I do not mean passion. It is my belief that the Indian wife is never passionate. She does not know what it means, as Western people do. If I marry at fourteen how can I know what it is to be passionate ? Man is superior ; and woman knows it. But she does not know what is meant by passion. We have to see '—the Maharani concluded—' what we can do to prevent this coming unhappiness.'

That talk reveals but one facet of this many-sided great lady who, in her prime, had an almost masculine zest for salmon fishing and big-game shooting. The tale of her first tiger is worth telling, not only for her achievement, but for the way in which India does these things.

Their host was a Raja of the old school, who would spare neither pains nor money in planning a royal shikar.

The road to their first camp ran through rocky jungle varied by steep hills that even cars could not climb. But the word went forth ; and elephants, harnessed to the cars with stout ropes, hauled them over impossible places. At the camp itself two bungalows awaited them, standing in pot-plant gardens that had been tiger-jungle only a few weeks before ; and there, in the wild, they enjoyed sumptuous hospitality—the kind of entertainment that only India could plan or achieve : endless time, endless money lavished on a mere halt of three days.

In the second camp they spent a week of daily outings into the jungle, partly tamed by a hundred miles of new road laid down for the cars to carry them within reasonable range of their *machāns* —rough platforms, built into branches of trees, ten or fifteen feet above the ground. Towards these the doomed tigers were driven by beaters, practised in detecting their presence, aided by the modern device of telephone lines laid through the jungle. At the first indication of ' tiger ', a message sped along the wires, a bugle sounded ; and the beat began.

Every half-hour or so an accommodating victim would saunter into the open. Then shots rang out. If merely wounded, he must be followed up at any risk ; for a wounded tiger may become a man-eater.

On this occasion the tigers were accommodating to a marvel. Seven fell to the Maharaj Gaekwar, three to his host, and five to the Maharani, whose wish to shoot *a* tiger was royally fulfilled : a costly slaughter of fifteen jungle lords.

But the Maharani, no fancy sportswoman, could enjoy in her own State rougher conditions of that great game ; could sit up all night over a kill sooner than lose her coveted prize. Almost equally she enjoyed the milder diversion of her own grand tennis tournament that drew the best of Indian players to Baroda ; she herself — by now a skilled player — presiding at her own ' Wimbledon '.

There were many visits, also, from other Princes—Mysore and Indore, Kashmir and Kolhapur. Between the Mysore and Baroda families there was intimate friendship and yearly meetings in their

summer homes at ' Ooty '. The two Rulers, unlike in temperament and far apart in age, were linked by a mutual devotion to
their State and people. Baroda many years older, rich in the
wisdom of experience, won the admiration and affection of the
younger Prince. Many letters passed between them that might
almost have been those of father and son. Both achieved high
distinction as Rulers. Both had the proud satisfaction of knowing
that their States shone out with almost equal lustre, as two of the
best governed in all India.

The visit to Baroda from Kashmir's Maharaja—Major-General
His Highness Sir Pratāb Singh, G.C.S.I., G.C.I.E.—was a more
formal affair.

A Rajput Prince of rigid orthodoxy, he had never crossed ' the
black water ' to England. He could eat with none but his own
people ; and that only after more than two hours of elaborate
pujah,[1] which sometimes deferred his evening meal to 1 A.M. As
for his retinue—a horde of servants vied with each other in doing
nothing on earth beyond upholding his princely dignity. On the
day before his departure he was respectfully requested to send
most of them by an early train, keeping with him only those who
were essential to his needs for one night and morning. This he
agreed to do ; retaining, as essential, a mere trifle of thirty men :
five to help him to dress and undress, eight to help him dine, the
rest to wait upon that privileged thirteen !

In this, and many other ways, he belonged to the older type
of Indian Raja, now almost extinct. Baroda's Ruler had long
since reduced his travelling staff to five or six men.

The Baroda return visit to Sir Pratāb was fixed for April, high
tide of spring in the valley of Kashmir : silver lakes fringed with
Persian lilac, fields of palest mauve iris crowding to the water's
edge ; cherry, plum and apple in full bloom ; and everywhere the
rose-flush of wild peach trees ; everywhere green and purple hills
rising to a frieze of eternal snow.

The princely guests were housed in a châlet near the Nishāt
Lake. From a porch smothered in honeysuckle and early roses,
they looked out upon mirrored mountains, blue sky and drifting
cloud. At a large gathering in Jehangir's Garden of Delight they
were guests-in-chief. There were also visits of ceremony, and
more congenial expeditions among the near hills ; a mingling of
East and West followed by a purely Eastern trek into higher,
wilder mountains.

As pilgrims they joined in the great procession to Amarnāth—
Shrine of Shiva, Creator and Destroyer—the most impressive

[1] Worship.

natural temple in northern India : a fissure in the great barren range, 17,000 ft. up. Its vast arch is formed by an inner curve of the hill ; its altar, a slab of sinister-looking green ice, is strewn with humble gifts of the devout, who throng in thousands, once a year, to that remote and solitary shrine, mysteriously informed with a Presence higher and holier than Shiva, Lord of Mountains —unseen and omnipresent, the God beyond all gods.

There the Maharaja of Baroda, with his few attendants, became a man as other men ; pilgrims all, in those days of high summer and nights of full moon.

Thence their small party descended from barren heights to radiant valleys ; and so, by an unfamiliar route, back to the familiar levels of their own incomparable land.

And what news, in those days, of the young Cooch Behar Maharani ? Banished from their lives, she was yet not entirely unforgiven, though four years were to pass before the mother could bring herself to meet her beloved daughter in open friendship. Both parents were hampered in that respect by priestly refusal to condone the outrage done to their religion through the defection from Hinduism of their own Princess.

But, from the Calcutta side, came word of the valuable work she was doing for her husband and his debt-crippled State ; pulling things together and cutting down expenses ; so that, in little more than a year, State debts had been wiped out, and personal debts reduced by her careful management. It was even said that she locked up the whisky, and knew precisely how much butter and sugar were used in the kitchen.

' Takes after her Daddy ! ' was the laughing comment of the Maharani, whose personal expenses were severely restricted by the ' frugal mind ' of her lord.

The arrival of a Cooch Behar daughter induced an exchange of telegrams and letters ; and later on the Maharaja met Indira with her husband at Delhi ; but not till 1917 did the mother and daughter meet at last, in Bombay, and banish the memory of that unnatural estrangement.

Only her youngest brother, Dhairyashil Rāo, had from the first ranged himself on her side, had openly gone about with her in London after the wedding ; and eventually, growing restless at home, had became attached to the court of Cooch Behar.

Out of four sons, he was the only one who survived early manhood. All had been given the best that England and America could do for them in the way of education. All had shown signs of good capacity, but little or no taste for serious work : in each case it was the record of a promising boy gone astray, partly from the dangers inherent in the grafting of Western school and college training on to Eastern temperament and tradition : a sad conclusion for a Ruler whose faith in education was the mainspring of his passion for social reform ; one that, in his own phrase, was ' a glutton for work '. So much so that, in after years, he positively came to suffer from his own incapacity for true relaxation.

In this connection, it may be well to recall that he himself was not subjected to the unfamiliar influence of English public school or university. He was educated to fulfil his high calling by the first-rate Scottish tutor who inspired his pupil with a zest for knowledge, a deep sense of duty and a taste for simple personal habits that went far to make him the remarkable man he was. The comparison between father and sons, between method and results, goes far to uphold those who advocate education in India for Indian young men, more especially if they be heirs to a throne.

To the mother, whose love and pride centred in her sons, the loss of two within a few years did, for a time, bend—though it could not break—the fine steel of her spirit. Her Maratha courage enabled her to surmount even the sharpest personal grief, while her Eastern soul was upheld by a philosophy hardly known to her sisters in the West.

And there still remained much that, in her position as consort, she was peculiarly fitted to achieve for the cause she had most at heart—the awakening of India's women. In her own sphere she resolved, with Miss Tottenham's help, to make the ladies of Baroda fitter mental companions for husbands, who were admittedly unhappy in their homes, increasingly drawn towards outside interest in the progress of modern thought and life ; while their wives remained immersed in past and present, fearful of plucking dangerous fruit from the Tree of Knowledge. Now they were made welcome in the English atmosphere of Miss Tottenham's house ; their minds awakened to new interests, enlarged by the spirit of questioning, source of all mental growth. No work could be more rewarding to all concerned ; and it prospered, as it deserved to do.

But the Maharani's influence—like that of her husband—has radiated far beyond Baroda. A born leader, gifted with a fine perception of affairs, political and diplomatic, she holds clear-cut opinions on almost every subject, expressing them in fluent English, with a frankness as rare as it is admirable in a woman of her race and status ; and Indian women everywhere have responded increasingly to the stimulus of her faith in them.

In 1926 she definitely gave the lead to India's Princesses, as

Honorary President of the National Council of Women ; and in 1927 she presided at the first ' All India Women's Conference '. In her seventy years of life she has accomplished much and suffered much. She believes in the future of India, but with no blind faith. ' Soon ', she has said, ' there will be only two real things left to us here. The Indian State and the Indian village council.'

It is hardly too much to assert that she and her beautiful daughter—well known in London society—are two of the most distinguished Indian women of their day. The Maharaja had every reason to be proud of them ; and he must have been so in the depths of his hidden Eastern heart.

4

The last twenty years of his remarkable reign set the crown on his life's achievement—the virtual creation of modern Baroda, for which he spent himself all his days. Fifty years of his guidance, wisdom and vision had changed it out of all recognition. On every form of progress he had left his mark. Above all, he had combated the less desirable elements and hindrances of caste ; so that men might live together in freer intercourse and women be offered a wider sphere of life and work. Under his rule, for the first time, they were admitted to State appointments ; and they exercised the vote ten years before the women of England. The list of his many achievements makes dull reading to-day, when progressive State government has become almost a matter of course among India's major principalities. But in those early years of his reign, to-day's matter of course looked more like reaching for the moon. Undaunted by inevitable mistakes, misunderstandings and opposition, he possessed in full measure the eye of imagination to foresee, the patience and wisdom to await the day of fulfilment.

Long since he had tempered his benevolent autocracy with a Cabinet, a form of Parliament and many Departments under carefully chosen Ministers ; but, from earliest days, he had been so intrinsically Maharaja that, in later years, he could not at will dispense with the burden of its cares and formalities. In England and Europe he could enjoy life simply as a distinguished private gentleman. In India he could never forget—or be allowed to forget—his princely state. Even to his own wife and daughter he was ' Maharaj ', to be saluted as such and implicitly obeyed, except when the daughter, of his own fibre, rebelled against a marriage that offered her neither a husband she could love nor personal freedom. The apartness engendered by these formalities was not of his own choosing. Of necessity he must conform to the standards and traditions of his people.

That very necessity and his own mental fibre tended to make him a lonely figure, cut off from those around him by their lack of larger views and wider knowledge ; cut off from the stimulus of contact with his intellectual equals ; his own alert mind not always able to make allowance for the slower brains of his fellows.

Withdrawn thus behind the invisible barrier of etiquette and temperament, he was not by any means an easy man to know. He lacked Sindhia's genial humour and the affability of the popular ' Ranji '. Only by degrees one came under the spell of his magnetic personality, and discovered behind the aloofness of the Maharaja the genuine warm-hearted simplicity of the man. When he did feel able to discard tiresome formalities, it was as much a relief to him as to his companions. ' Let us go for a walk,' he would urge, ' and be ordinary mortals for a change.'

His biographer, Stanley Rice—for years in close ministerial and personal touch with the Maharaja—admits that he was never elated by a summons to the Palace ; but he significantly adds : ' I have never left His Highness, after a private talk, without wanting to stay longer. The charm, whatever it may be, is undefinable.'

None the less one may hazard a suggestion that it sprang mainly from the sincerity and simplicity emphasised by all who knew him. It was not merely in himself, but in his way of life, his manner of dress, his un-Eastern distaste for adornment that increased as he grew older. The crown jewels of Baroda, housed in an older palace, are said to be worth millions. Arranged and displayed under glass, they would be one of the sights of India. Yet, like the uncountable treasures of Hyderabad, they remain hidden in a strong-room, shown occasionally to a favoured few.

Here, supreme among many wonders, may be seen the famous pearl necklace, its seven strings valued at a crore of rupees (= £750,000); a diamond necklace, worth £500,000, its magnificent centre stone, the seventh largest diamond in the world, christened ' Star of the South ' ; a black pearl of untold value, and diamond aigrettes so delicately set on springs that every movement makes them shimmer like sunlit water. On one wall of this Palace hangs a carpet made entirely of gems. On its groundwork of pearls is wrought a lovely design in rubies, emeralds, diamonds and turquoise.

Yet the owner of all that jewelled wealth seldom wore any adornment with his plain brocaded coat, except his glittering orders and a priceless string of pearls, or a favourite necklace of large single emeralds. His overdress of finest muslin was patterned all over with an intricate lace-like design, executed always by one Baroda family, who trained their thumb-nails to a point especially for that purpose, often taking three months to perfect one single coat.

And his Maharani's taste in the matter of jewellery matched his own. At no festivity did she choose to vie with other Princesses, in the Eastern fashion of loading neck and arms with precious stones ; not even for the supreme occasion of Queen Mary's Purdah Gathering at the Coronation Delhi Durbar. Well aware that her restraint might be misconstrued by Indian ladies of rank, the Maharani still chose to honour the Queen-Empress by wearing simple jewellery of rare value. From the seven strings of the famous Baroda pearls she chose two only ; and, though many of her sister Princesses looked askance at her lack of adornment, the Maharani of Baroda had her reward. Long after, in Simla, she was told by a great lady, who had been present, how the Queen-Empress had noticed her simplicity and the beauty of her pearls ; had appraised her as a woman of good taste, widely travelled enough to break away from the old Indian idea of massed jewellery for festal occasions.

That courage to break away from old customs and ideas was one among many virtues that she and her Maharaj owed to their taste for travel, not merely in pursuit of change and pleasure, but quite as often in pursuit of knowledge and health. The last was not always fully recognised by the Simla Foreign Office ; partly, no doubt, because several younger Princes were being tempted, by cheap and easy transit, to spend too much State money on trips to Europe or elsewhere. In the best interests of Ruler and people, it was the business of Paramount Authority to discourage any absentee tendency : but a Ruler so devoted as the Maharaja Gaekwar could not endure the least implication of putting self before State ; and his sense of dignity, his independent spirit, inclined him to resent any hint of interference with his liberty of movement.

He knew very well—and his people also came to know—that his trips to Europe had been as fruitful for Baroda as for himself. Early in 1887 he was writing to Lord Dufferin, most friendly and understanding of Viceroys : ' I hate the idea of an absentee Ruler . . . and the people do not like to see me run about so much. Though they do not know the reason that compels me to go, I cannot, all in all, say they are wrong.'

It was true that, in those early days, his long absences ' across the black water ' filled his people with alarm for his safety. England, to them, was a mysterious land full of unimaginable dangers. In Hindustan these strange white folk had more or less to ' behave themselves '. What might they not do in their own land, without temples or restraining Brahmins ? . . . But perceiving that no harm came to him, fear gave place to curiosity. Others also wished to see England for themselves. There is a call of the West quite as strong as the overworked ' call of the East '.

All his life the Maharaja's restless, eager spirit constantly overtaxed his body. All his life he strove to follow the highest ideals : an invitation to disappointment in a far from ideal world. Small wonder if there were times of depression, aggravated by a sense of futility, of making little headway with his great designs, and being at times misunderstood in high places.

' You English people have no imagination,' is the oft-repeated Indian indictment ; a sweeping statement as inaccurate as most generalising ; but, admittedly, there has been, in some cases, a dearth of imaginative understanding in Government dealing with Indian Rulers ; an apparent lack of any real attempt or capacity to see the other side.

In the Maharaja Gaekwar, a Maratha spirit of independence, an uncompromising sincerity, a sensitive pride and lack of diplomatic flair, caused much of his unpopularity and friction in high quarters ; the defects of his qualities often tending to make him his own enemy. His devotion to the British Royal Family dated from a personal meeting with Queen Victoria, when he and his Maharani were Her Majesty's honoured guests at Windsor Castle. There she invested him with his G.C.S.I. and was herself so attracted by his personality that she called him henceforth her ' favourite son '. But, for all his pride in the title and his unshakable loyalty to the Throne, he has admittedly ' not always been treated as his title deserves on such matters as opium, salt, seaports and military defence '. There are two sides to every argument ; and if, at times, the Maharaja may have been difficult, it was seldom altogether without reason.

He was fortunate in that the gods gave him length of days to live down the stress and strain of his difficult middle years. In spite of passing disappointments and personal sorrows, these were ultimately crowned by the triumph of his Golden Jubilee in 1925 amid spontaneous rejoicings of a devoted people.

' The Maharaja ', wrote Stanley Rice, ' was greeted throughout his kingdom with fervent exclamations. This is not a figure of speech. . . . The Indian is a past master in the art of discrimination : and no one who heard the hearty shouts of " *Maharaj*

Ki jai! " [1] could possibly mistake them for anything but what they were—expressions of genuine attachment.'

Few, if any, Eastern Rulers have done more to deserve that crowning reward. For fifty years he had successfully kept the balance between the benevolent autocrat and the ardent reformer, whose insight and judgment had warned him against forcing the pace. The new light was not always acceptable to a people embedded in custom ; and although wisdom restrained him from reforming in a hurry, no priestly, or other, opposition would turn him from his championship of the Depressed Classes, known as Untouchables.

Across fifty years he could look back to that very Imperial Delhi Durbar of 1877 when King Edward VII, as Prince of Wales, wrote home to Lord Granville, ' The little Gaekwar of Baroda, as old as our eldest boy, seems really a very intelligent youth ; though but six months ago he was running about the street adorned with the most limited wardrobe '—delightfully Victorian phrase.

Now he rode aloft on his elephant in his golden State howdah, the size of a small motor car, that took twenty-four men to lift it ; yet the great beast, already heavy laden, bore it as though it were made of basket-work. From leg to leg he swung along as if proudly aware of his own worth and that of his Royal rider ; his wicked little eyes twinkling through a mask of blue and yellow paint ; his neck hung with a massive chain of gold *mohurs* ; tusks cased in gold, the huge flapping ears weighed down with earrings the size of breastplates ; anklets hung with golden bells : gold everywhere for this golden festival ; the saddle-cloth of gold hanging almost to the ground : the worth of him as he stood amounting to about £200,000.

The Maharaja himself, on his gilded throne, seemed scarcely one with the simply clad Prince in his habit as he lived. Above his small Maratha turban waved a diamond plume. Round his neck gleamed a wide collar of pearls. On his breast blazed the jewelled Star of India ; and more jewels flashed on his fingers when he returned the salutes of his people. For all his love of simplicity in daily life, he was truly Maharaj in his response to the emotional appeal, the instinctive Eastern demand for regal display at fitting seasons. For escort, his infantry and cavalry were drilled and equipped on Western lines ; but his gold and silver artillery drawn by white oxen struck the Eastern note more in keeping with the whole memorable scene.

For days the festivities lasted, in true Indian fashion : banquets

[1] ' To the Maharaj be victory ! '

and speeches and the laying of a foundation stone for the Temple of Fame : a long-cherished plan to keep in fresh remembrance the names of men who had greatly served the State.

' Greatness ', he told his people, ' is fundamentally of character. Sincerity, unselfishness and far-seeing wisdom are its never-failing qualities. With these, the great man stands unbroken and undaunted in the face of all physical misfortunes.'

In those few words, many must have recognised an undesigned portrait of the man who uttered them.

Followed a cordial viceregal visit from Lord Reading. The political sky was clear. Dark clouds of misunderstanding and his ' bruised sense of dignity ' had long since rolled away. The Great War, among its few blessings, had drawn the States closer to the Paramount Power. Nor was that happy celebration to be the last of its kind for this man of delicate health and unquenchable vitality. In 1935 a Diamond Jubilee—like that of his admired Queen Victoria—was added to his unique record of rule. By then, he had proved over and over the benefit that had accrued to Baroda from his far-ranging journeys and study of other lands, other ways.

Like most modern Rulers, he had to combat the prevalent curse of intrigue and the undercurrent threat of Communism fostered by the ranker politics of the West. Ahead of his people and his time, he came into conflict with Brahmin priests, and many cherished schemes went agley ; nor was his personal view of patriotism always understood by the official mind. He saw it as a persistent effort to make the highest type of life available to the greatest number of his fellow men : and through every phase of disappointment and discouragement, he kept the eye of his inner vision always on a horizon of greater things to be ; the ideal of an ultimate Indian Nation, self-sufficing, strong in the added strength of spiritual unity ; one with the Empire and the Crown.

Most widely travelled and deeply read of India's Princes, he was sought after, as guide and teacher, above all in the sphere of world religions, to which he had given the study of a lifetime. His philosophic mind led him to take a vital interest in man's highest aspirations, his desire to ' have sight beyond the smoke '.

' Truth is Truth,' he rightly insisted, ' wherever we find it— in Athens or Jerusalem, in Benares or Mecca, in the literature, language or thought of centuries. All religions are the common wealth and common property of men. Freely and frankly we should seek inspiration from them all.'

In view of his influence and mental breadth it is not surprising to learn that he became first President to the World Fellowship

BARODA : THE PRINCESS INDIRA OF BARODA AT SEVENTEEN

(From *A Year with the Gaekwar of Baroda*, by E. and Clare Weeden, published by Hutchinson & Co.)

BARODA : HER HIGHNESS THE MAHARANI OF COOCH BEHAR
(PRINCESS INDIRA OF BARODA)
(Portrait—Dorothy Wilding, London)

of Faiths, a movement inspired by Sir Francis Younghusband. At the Baroda College he early established a Chair for Comparative Religions ; and his Hall of Fame was intended to become a centre where men of all creeds could meet in unity, ' to seek truth and apply it as best they might to the service of humanity '.

The writer of a recent paper on ' The Spiritual Basis of International Order ' recalls how ardently the Maharaja Gaekwar anticipated an end ' that will have to be seriously considered, as more than a visionary's dream, when the nations face their one hope of lasting renewal after the war '. Too few have realised the extraordinary amount of work done in this direction by the late Maharaja of Baroda, one of the most shining examples among those who added strength and prestige to a great movement. He furnished its philosophic background. He practised what he preached in the land that he ruled with so much wisdom and vision. He was indeed *Raja-rishi*—Royal Sage. Always he sought out the best men to hold office in the State, whatever their race or creed—Bengali, Madrassi, Parsi, English ; and by all he was well served.

It was a direct inspiration from him that his Moslem subjects should join in Hindu festivities and invite their Hindu friends to their own annual celebration of the Prophet's Birthday and their great religious festival, the Mohurrum. In these matters the Maharaja gave the lead himself, and year by year more and more Hindus attend both feasts. ' Tolerance ', he maintained, ' is not enough. . . . Without understanding, it is a blind alley. Only from working together is understanding born.'

If ever the eternal feud between Hindu and Moslem should be resolved, without arbitrary change of creed, it may safely be said that much of the credit will be due to Baroda's Maharaja.

Only a few years remained to him after the acclamation of his Diamond Jubilee. He was then well over seventy; but he retained to the last his versatile activity of mind, his restless pursuit of new knowledge, new scenes and human types. At an age when he was hardly fit for the pursuit of big game, he actually adventured on a shooting trip in East and Central Africa—the last of his many journeyings.

Late in 1938 he returned to India so ill that it seemed clear he would never leave it again. They moved him from Bombay to Baroda ; and there, in his Raj Mahāl, the over-driven body found rest at last ; the free-faring spirit set forth on its greatest journey of all.

The passing of Maharaja Sir Sayaji Rāo Gaekwar left a gap hard to fill in the State he so loved and in the hearts of his people.

K

They give willing allegiance to his grandson; but Indians, once their loyalty and affection have been won, do not forget. They may at times have been slow in perceiving the wisdom of his many reforms; but, before he passed from them, he could claim with truth that a changed spirit had come over Baroda as a direct result of his travels, an awakening to interests far beyond its narrow horizon. The whole State had been transformed mentally and materially, so far as any Ruler can achieve that end.

Work was his hobby; administration his passion; and the fruits of both will live while India endures. Posterity may wrangle over this or that incident, in the middle years of his reign; but he has builded himself a monument that will outlast all strife of tongues—the modern Baroda State.

His funeral rites were an impressive mingling of Eastern ceremonial with Western reverence for the departed. When the pyre had been prepared, the Last Post was sounded and two salutes were fired by State artillery—the first time that such an honour has been paid to a Ruler of his House. Then were the ashes taken to Allahabad; and after a further salute of twenty-one guns, by British troops, they were carried in procession to the confluence of India's two holy rivers, the Jumna and the Ganges.

The mantle of him who has gone falls upon the shoulders of his grandson, Pratāp Singh: and the best that Baroda can wish the young Ruler is that he may consistently carry on the work and high aims of Sir Sayaji Rāo Gaekwar, greatest of Maharajas, since the Gaekwar line came into possession.

KOLHAPUR

I

KOLHAPUR—How many outside India know even the name of this comparatively small yet distinguished Maratha State ? Its claims to distinction, racial and spiritual, bear no relation to its size. They are claims that count for much in the mind of India ; and of late years Kolhapur has earned a higher distinction, through the unusual character and attainments of its great reformer-Prince, Sir Shahu Chhatrapati, champion of the aptly named Depressed Classes, and maker of modern Kolhapur.

The original State and its ruling family were founded in the seventeenth century by Shivaji, the Maratha national hero, who has already appeared in the story of Gwalior. Its present rulers cherish the distinction of direct descent from that famous fighter of whom it was said that ' He met every emergency or peril with instant discernment and unshakable fortitude '.

A fighter in a different field, but of equal courage and resource, was his descendant, Sir Shahu Chhatrapati, whose unique personality must dominate any sketch of Kolhapur, though he died in 1922 and is grandfather to the present Prince. The courage required of him, in his lifelong fight against the tyranny of priest and caste, was moral rather than physical ; and he excelled in both, as will presently be seen.

Only those who have known at first hand the rigid restrictions of that spiritual bondage can realise the seeming impossibility for even a Maharaja to set his face against it. Yet, according to Max Müller, there is no authority whatever in the Hymns of the Védas for the complicated system of castes on which the Brahmins take their stand ; nor for the offensive privileges they claim at the expense of the merchant and peasant class.

For those who are unfamiliar with the caste basis of Hinduism, a brief statement of its divisions and implications will better enable them to understand a measure of all that was achieved by Sir Shahu, finest and most original among Indian Princes of his own or any other period.

I have already written of the Hindu social system evolved by invading Aryans in a thousand years of peace. That system divided their world into four classes, or castes :

(1) The learned, literary or priestly orders—Brahmins.
(2) The soldier and kingly order—Kshattriya.

(3) The landowners and merchants—Vaisyas.
(4) The peasants, artisans and all humble folk—Sudras.

Of these the Brahmins monopolised the whole province of
knowledge, spiritual and mental, as priests have done everywhere
ever since. But nowhere, perhaps, have they attained and maintained a spiritual autocracy so potent and permanent as that of
the Brahmins among orthodox Hindus. They permeate every
phase of life. They hold the monopoly of education. They
dominate the lives of Indian women, whose minds are saturated
with religion and superstition.

In Central and Southern India, where Hinduism chiefly prevails, the Brahmins largely exercised political power, enhanced by
their sacred authority ; nowhere more so than in the Maratha
region. Hence their jealousy of Shivaji, all-powerful warrior,
their antagonism to the State and rule of the family founded by
him. For that reason they have tried again and again to crush
Kolhapur without success. They even set themselves to degrade
all warrior Marathas to the status of Sudra or peasant ; refusing
them the special Hindu rite, Vedokta, reserved for the two highest
castes ; themselves monopolising all State offices and enrolments,
with a view to becoming virtual rulers of the land. More especially they aimed at degrading the Chhatrapati family ; an evil
design forwarded by Maratha intrigues and by an unlucky
succession of minority Princes, which increased their power. In
Sir Shahu's time, owing to an earlier, unfortunate appointment,
the State was overrun with Konkán Brahmins, his deadliest
enemies. Either they or he must prevail.

He himself was an adopted Prince, wisely chosen, like the
Maharaja of Baroda, and was equally fortunate in the Government
choice of a tutor, then Mr. Stuart Fraser of the Indian Civil
Service. Now, as Sir Stuart Fraser, K.C.S.I., he can look back
on the rare experience of having educated three princely pupils
for their high calling. Of these, the first was Sir Shahu of
Kolhapur, with whom he established a close friendship of lasting
value both to the State and its Ruler.

The young Prince very early gave proof of his courage and
independent character. Pressed on all sides to finish his education in England, he steadily refused, for the sound reason that,
after a long minority, his people must surely need and desire his
presence among them. In a personal interview with the British
Governor of Bombay Presidency, he so forcibly stated his case
that the English University plan was wisely given up.

At eighteen he assumed full powers and full authority to

combat Brahmin influence and intrigue. Shy and diffident with British officials, there was no uncertainty in him, of aim or will, to be master in his own house. A giant of a man in body and mind, he relished the prospect of a fight against forms of tyranny peculiarly alien to his temperament and his deeply-rooted sympathy with the oppressed.

Love of sport took him far afield after big game and also gave him chances to cultivate kindly, informal relations with the humblest of his subjects, to hear at first hand the tales of tyranny and hardship that fired him to decisive action, such as no ruling Prince had ever undertaken against the only power comparable to his own.

From first to last, he used his high position to champion not only Kolhapur ' Untouchables ', but millions of the oppressed throughout India. That the fight must be hard and long he knew very well when he set his hand to the mighty task of freeing his non-Brahmin subjects from the thraldom of a caste system that has its merits, if not too rigidly enforced.

Justly it has been said of him that ' few, if any, Indian reformers have made an effort more courageous, more unselfish, more practical and inspiring than that consistent crusade against a rule of life based on religion and hallowed by tradition '.

He ' opened fire ', so to speak, by taking into his own service well-chosen, educated non-Brahmins : an unheard-of innovation. Tenaciously, in defiance of intrigue and opposition, he held his own against spiritual forces unchallenged through the ages : and by the time he was twenty-five, he had changed his whole State personnel and largely strengthened his hand, though his antagonists, who controlled the Brahmin Press, warned him that his unorthodox doings would bring disaster on himself and his people.

Undeterred by spiritual thunder and lightning, he went his own way. He made many reforms, mixed freely with all castes and classes, arranged loans for peasants, built an asylum for lepers, and took an active interest in all that concerned Marathas, even in British India, where they are stronger in numbers, and in national spirit, than in their own States.

At twenty-three the birth of a son was hailed by his people as proof that the wrath of God had been removed from their ruling house, which had for so long failed of a direct heir ; though well they knew that Kolhapur had been no loser in the person of its present adopted Prince.

Two years later he pulled his little kingdom through famine and the horrors of plague ; offering himself at once for inoculation by way of example to superstitious and fearful folk who would rather let the body perish in agony than risk spiritual defilement. He visited plague hospitals, directed famine relief works and reduced taxation to ease the burden of living.

In six years of honest and courageous rule he had completely won the heart of his people and established his own personal power : vital assets in his fight to free the Depressed Classes and give them a fair share in the offices of State.

In this semi-religious matter of caste, it should be recognised that there is much to be said for the basic idea—' a place for every man and every man in his place '—in a land where its complete removal might spell social chaos, or some worse form of State tyranny. If reasonably applied, it need not involve tyranny ; it bears, in fact, some relation to the Guild Spirit of the Middle Ages in preserving the skilled, inherited craftsman, whose work is in his very fibre ; thus tending to safeguard social standards.

We are told, in fact, by Sir George Birdwood, that during the ' mad millennium ' of anarchy, from A.D. 711 to 1707—' India's domestic, social and religious life was kept intact by the conserving and healing virtue of the Brahminical caste system '.

It is the priestly would-be monopoly of learning that stultifies the race. Even to-day, when Hindu writings have been widely printed and taught, and translated by enlightened Brahmins, the mass of Indians remain steeped in ignorance and superstition beyond the capacity of Western minds to conceive. It is this denial of common knowledge to those whom the holy ones deem ' out of caste ', that brings gratuitous tragedy into millions of harmless lives. To the stultified lot of the so-called Untouchables there exists no parallel in Europe or in the world outside Hindu India : an age-old form of slavery—body and soul—for which no justification can be claimed by men with human hearts in their bodies.

Though these hapless ones are titular Hindus, they are treated —on caste lines—as if they were less than human beings : consigned to the filthiest outskirts of any village, debarred from approaching any Hindu temple ; forbidden to draw water from public wells or to enter a public rest-house : cut off from religion, with all that it means to the Hindu, cut off from education and even the bare necessities of life. An Untouchable may be dying of thirst, but he may not drink from any village tank or pool. Even for the lowest menial service, he may not enter a Hindu household. His touch is defilement, his spirit crushed within him by that cruel knowledge. For, in their ignorance, those unhappy ones believe it is true that they and theirs are irredeemably accurst. Therein lies the essence of their tragedy.

Yet by some means they and theirs must contrive to exist—
one can hardly call it living. Their chief permitted occupation is
to carry away dead animals. On these they are graciously permitted to feed, regardless of probable disease ; and they may
also cure the skins : an occupation deemed unfit for even low-
caste Hindus. They are at the beck and call of any official who
may need them for the most degrading work, though he will not
dream of paying them for it. The only parallel to such calculated
cruelty lies in Hitler's treatment of Poles and Jews.

History proves that this blot on the caste system had no part
in its original design ; and it is to the lasting honour of Mahatma
Gandhi that he has championed the cause of these hapless pariahs
of Southern India ; has won for them the right to enter temples ;
and in many other ways has mitigated the unbelievable misery of
their lot. But, before Gandhi publicly arraigned such systematic
human degradation, their principal champion was Sir Shahu
Chhatrapati, Maharaja of Kolhapur.

Obviously education was the first necessity for these abject
items of humanity ; but England's pledge of neutrality in that
vital matter had left religious teaching completely in Brahmin
hands ; and according to their decree the Untouchables, being
outside religion, were condemned to perpetual ignorance.

Independently, much good work has been done by a Salvation
Army School and by American Missions ; but, apart from these,
the backward classes had no chance, no power to free themselves.

Imagine, then, what it must have meant for them when their
own Maharaja came down, as it were, from heaven to fight their
battles and lift them out of the dust. In the matter of education
he had to walk warily, since any village school would be con-
taminated by the mere fact of their presence. He could only
enlist the interest of leaders in each community, and leave them
to handle the delicate matter along their own lines. Not until
years later did he take the bold step of instituting free education
throughout the State.

Inevitably his first move antagonised the Brahmins, but they
were up against a strong man possessed by a commanding idea.
Openly he bestowed State posts on educated men of the backward classes : openly denounced the preserving of knowledge as
a secret possession ; asserting that the Brahmins had thus degraded
not others but themselves. A reformer so bold and resolute could
expect nothing from those high priests of monopoly but frank
hostility. Yet he continued to impress on all Hindus that the
remedy lay in their own hands ; that they alone could remove, if

they chose to do so, the slur cast on their religion and national life by such deeply-rooted and discreditable prejudices.

At that very time, it so happened that the British Government —breaking the habit of centuries—was at last moved to intervene in a matter of religion, thus paving the way for ultimate redemption of outcast millions.

The Maharaja followed suit with a frank speech that same year, in the Deccan, centre of Brahminism.

'I have', he declared, 'only one message to give you. Be not short-sighted. To dissolve the castes is a necessity. To uphold them is a sin. They hinder advance. To abolish enmity, we must abolish caste. Let us abolish it—and *be one*.'

That gage flung down to the high priests of caste-sanctity was an act of moral courage such as only those who have a profound knowledge of Hinduism can appreciate to the full. And his bold words were but the prelude to bolder actions. Extending his rôle of knight-errant far beyond the confines of Kolhapur, he dedicated himself to helping the helpless everywhere in India by a frontal attack on the whole system.

Local Brahmins retaliated by refusing to all Marathas the sacred Vedokta ceremony ; reducing them—as explained—to the peasant class. But the Maharaja had his own weapon—and the courage to use it.

He promptly suspended his ordained payments to the priesthood ; an act of boldness almost comparable to Luther's burning of the Papal Bull. His whole position was, in fact, much akin to that of the Reformation leaders.

To the priesthood he insisted, ' Let your ideal be to abolish the middle-man between God and man ; making the individual alone responsible for his acts to his Creator, instead of giving his conscience into the custody of a priest '.

The argument was identical : and, like Luther, he was threatened with excommunication by self-appointed dispensers of divine favour. But no priestly threats could turn him from a contest that virtually involved the whole warrior caste.

Endlessly the dispute raged, with increasing bitterness on the side of the Brahmins, increasing conviction on his, that the backward classes could never hope for decent human treatment while a Brahmin priesthood remained supreme. The contest and the fruits of his knight-errantry became, at length, so widely known that they reached even the heights of Simla and spurred the British Government to a far-reaching decision. The Prince himself, it was decreed, should be the final authority on all matters, religious or otherwise. The same decree annulled the Brahmins' hereditary claim to the monies that had been withdrawn : a personal triumph for the Maharaja, who promptly executed a still more drastic move.

After careful study of the whole question—including the history of the English Reformation—he dared to appoint a non-Brahmin Maratha as high priest of his household : an appointment that was to carry no caste or hereditary rights. He started a Védic School to train Maratha boys in priestly duties, to root out superstition and restore the purity of Hinduism based on the Védas. Again, it must be emphasised that no Western mind can fully grasp the kind of courage needed for such unorthodox proceedings, even by a Prince in his own right.

Alive to the risk of possible weakening in those who came after he gave special care and thought to the right education of his son, encouraging him to investigate the abuses practised by Brahmins in the name of religion.

He himself was nearly thirty before he first visited England, where he was delighted with the welcome and the honours accorded him. That visit—and all he learnt from it—emboldened him to issue his famous order, ' fifty per cent of State offices to be reserved for non-Brahmins ' : a virtual declaration of war.

But the local Brahmins were a powerful body—26,000 of them, including many anti-British extremists, who worked ceaselessly, by political means, to restore their own power. The Maharaja's life was constantly threatened. The whole Brahmin hierarchy was arrayed against him—not in Kolhapur alone. Bombay became the centre, at that time, of a revolutionary movement headed by Bāl Gangadhar Tilāk, a Brahmin leader hostile to British rule. His large following in the South made the whole movement peculiarly dangerous at a time when all political India was seething with unrest. In vain Sir Shahu warned the authorities that the disturbance needed prompt and drastic handling. Action, as usual, was delayed and grave warnings soft-pedalled ; so inherent is British distaste for facing uncomfortable facts.

It was only afterwards that the value of Sir Shahu's advice and active help were recognised, and he was accorded the personal honour of a twenty-one-gun salute—Kolhapur being only a nineteen-gun State. The enhanced prestige conferred by those two extra cannon-shots can hardly be conceived by the democratic West.

2

When the Great War convulsed Europe, Sir Shahu offered himself and his sons for active service ; but, in the event, he could not leave India. He could, however, and did, make his potent influence felt among the fighting Marathas, whether his subjects or no ; in particular by an incident that attracted widespread notice and admiration.

It was during the siege of Kut in Mesopotamia, when the garrison ran short of food, and the Maratha sepoys had scruples about eating horse-flesh. Sir Shahu, hearing of their dilemma, offered to go by air to Kut and reason with the men. Since that proved to be impossible, he sent them a strongly worded appeal that at once dispelled their scruples and helped to prolong resistance.

In 1917 the Indian situation evoked Mr. Montagu's important pronouncement, foreshadowing a definite move towards the goal of self-government. Too bold for some, not bold enough for others, it was received in India with mixed feelings, according to racial or political points of view. Sir Shahu, while welcoming the reforms in principle, feared that in practice they might tend to revive the Brahmins' waning influence. And the event justified his apprehension. The Montagu measures did undoubtedly give a marked impetus to their movement. Clearly they saw their chance for a full return to power. The Maharaja saw it also ; and to prevent that issue became increasingly the main object of his life.

More and more he extended his influence and activities beyond Kolhapur. Speaking in Madras, he boldly stated : ' I am not here as a Ruler, but as a friend and servant of millions, whose condition must excite the pity of any man carrying a human heart in his body'.

He largely financed a hostel for Untouchables, founded by American missionaries, whose work for India he admired and approved. Yet always he was hampered in his attempts to find decent occupation for those unhappy outcasts, by their utter ignorance, their pitiful acceptance of inferiority, that could only be dispelled by education and an infusion of self-respect.

As far as possible he employed them in his household and gave them swords to wear that they might publicly appear as warriors. In 1919 he freed all outcasts from the burden of degrading compulsory service in villages. He removed the ban on their use of wells, tanks and schools ; promoted them to responsible village offices, more than once displacing Brahmins in their favour. One may perhaps be permitted to query whether, in every instance, the village was likely to benefit by an exchange made purely on moral grounds : a case of the end justifying the means.

Was there ever a Prince of courage so unorthodox and unshakable in the whole hierarchy of Hindu States ?

India has known many reformers, of many types—poets, saints and scholars. But a Royal reformer, pitting himself against priestly power, and practising what he preached, she has hardly known since the distant day, centuries before Christ, when the Rajput Prince, Siddartha, left throne and wife and child to become the Buddha and found a religion that should be free from the tyranny of priest and caste : a religion that converted the Emperor Asoka—of India's Golden Age. Yet it failed ultimately in its main object—to oust Brahmin supremacy. For centuries the two rival religions contended for the souls of men ; but between the subtle persistence of the Brahmins and the ultimately sterile pessimism of Buddha's creed, Hindu priestly power came back into its own.

Now, ages after, there arose a great Maratha Prince to challenge it afresh. Everywhere and always he gave his people the supreme incentive to bold action—a personal lead. Yet he was no ascetic, no slave to one idea. A genial sportsman of the country gentleman type, he seemed—on a surface view—the last man likely to stir up a hornets' nest of outraged Brahmins by attempting the seemingly impossible. But neither threats nor open enmity could turn him from his high resolve.

Viciously criticised and vilified, he retorted : ' I am a sportsman. I am determined that all Untouchables shall have a fair chance with State professions open to them, so that they may learn to think themselves as good as other men.'

But more impressive than even his bold words and decrees was the shining light of his personal example—highest and rarest form of courage. Publicly he would ask the despised and rejected to dine with him ; would eat and drink from their hands, knowing full well that by an act so unprecedented he cut himself off from orthodox Hinduism and sacrificed, to his principles, all the hereditary privileges of his Order. Whether those for whom he so spent himself could have any conception of the price paid by their own Maharaja for their collective salvation, is a moot question ; but in no way does it detract from the value of an achievement only to be gauged by those who possess intimate knowledge of Hindu India.

Throughout, he owed much to the intelligent and devoted services of his Prime Minister, a man of notable character and charm ; while in many ways he was hampered by his own vast household, of relations, retainers and their horde of hangers-on. But the work he did has rightly been called stupendous. He lit a lamp of hope in the hearts of forty-seven million Untouchables all over India : and no other achievement entitles him to so high a place of honour.

In the matter of Mr. Montagu's promised reforms, it is worth noting that, although he believed in eventual self-government, his practical wisdom perceived the risk of making changes so vital before India had raised her all-round level of education; perceived also that the Home Rulers of that day were quite out of touch with the masses, only craving power for themselves.

'The gift of democratic government', he wrote, 'may be made or withheld by Parliament; but no such gift will cause the growth of democracy in India. Educate, educate; uproot prejudice and superstition. Only by means of social progress can political progress become a natural growth from within. If the reforms put sole power into the hands of the Brahmins, woe betide the backward classes. Heaven alone can help them.'

Inevitably, if the caste system is to continue—and it has intrinsic value—it must be made more flexible and less inhuman in its application to normal men and women. So long as there was no sign of this regeneration, Sir Shahu remained its inveterate enemy. Wide-minded and magnanimous, he was friendly always with Brahmins of liberal views. It was their arrogant system and its effects to which he was unshakably opposed. He bore no malice towards individuals. When one of his active enemies lay dying, he visited him without hesitation, talked to him and cheered him up. In all human relations his deep heart and fine character were manifest. Devoted to his one wife and son, he enjoyed an ideally happy home life that must have sustained him throughout the perpetual conflict involved in his rôle of reformer Prince.

His last public service to Government, not long before his death, was connected with Edward, Prince of Wales, and the hostile demonstrations in Bombay that led to fierce riots in which hundreds of harmless people were killed. He was also asked to unveil a statue of the Maratha hero, Shivaji, at Poona; and he arranged special celebrations to honour the event. But, before the day, his police brought warning of a plot hatched by Congress Brahmins, who were staging anti-British demonstrations, reasserting their hostility to the Prince and to the Maharaja also.

He lost no time in arranging for a counter-demonstration from surrounding Maratha villages. Thousands of his people, led by their own headmen, swarmed into Poona, overawed the astonished Brahmins and triumphantly defeated their hostile intent.

Had he lived out man's normal span of life, he might have accomplished far greater things: but he died untimely at the age of thirty-eight; having achieved more than many fine Rulers have packed into twice his span of years.

His early death was an irreparable loss, not only to Kolhapur but to India and the Empire. To the end he defied his persistent enemies, who had persistently thwarted and vilified him because he would not admit their arrogant claim to rule heaven and earth and create a hell on earth for millions of hapless fellow beings. At his own express wish his funeral rites were performed, not by the holy ones, but by students of his own Shivaji college, founded for the one supreme purpose in his purposeful life. So he passed—but his work endures ; his name lives after him. His son, during a short reign, carried on his father's progressive policy and followed his example in the matter of promoting non-Brahmins to high offices. But he lacked Sir Shahu's dynamic force of character and leadership, qualities too rarely transferred from father to son. Horses and racing interested him more actively than State affairs ; and he left no direct heir to follow him.

To the outer world Kolhapur will always signify the great Sir Shahu Chhatrapati : a Ruler who possessed the rare mingling of broad humanity with uncompromising courage—qualities that enabled him, without reservation, to act on his beliefs. As ruling Prince, he had great resources at command ; yet his high position handicapped him in many ways. In any other country he would have become the idol of all who recognised social advance as the first step to political progress. His broad views and liberal precepts would have heralded a great movement. But in caste-enthralled India, his full stature could only be measured by the few, British and Indian, who really knew the man.

His rare gift for sympathetic understanding of human nature was the basis of his charm and remarkable strength of character. It is, in fact, the basis of all supremely fine character ; nowhere more notable than in our own greatest of Prime Ministers, Mr. Winston Churchill.

Only time—that tests all human achievements—can prove whether the growth of all that the Maharaja of Kolhapur began, is to be continued, or checked—as too often—before the little leaven can take effect on the slow-moving mass that is India. In any event, it was his high privilege to kindle a torch, a light of hope, that will never be put out. Nor will his name and fame ever be forgotten among those he loved and served. Therein lies his claim to true greatness.

THE RAJA OF AUNDH

THIS cultured and original-minded chief of a lesser State in the Bombay Presidency must be accorded a brief mention, if only to prove that the smaller States also may produce remarkable Rulers and reach high standards of personal government.

The Raja of Aundh—Shrimant Bāla Sahib Pandit Prātinidhi, B.A.—is one of several well-educated and efficient Rulers in the same Presidency. Like so many of his kind, he did not directly inherit his position. It so happened that the legitimate heir, being a minor, fell out with his able Regent, and was accused of having hired a man to murder him ; a charge amply proved by a commission of enquiry into the matter. That disposed of the rightful heir ; and, happily for Aundh, the Bāla Sahib was chosen to fill his place.

By caste a Brahmin, he is a distinguished example of India's intellectual *élite* ; a great authority on Hindu law, customs and legend ; an author and artist with a profound knowledge of Indian architecture and painting. His pictorial version of the Hindu religious epic *Rāmayāna*, illustrated by himself, was produced by his own printing presses in his exceptionally well-run State. He is also distinguished as being, in theory and practice, one of the chief living exponents of physical culture, which covers a wider scope in the East than in the West. His admirable exercises *Surya Namaskar* (Sun Prayers) need concentration of mind and spirit to induce their full effect ; and the Raja himself is a living embodiment of the astonishing result wrought by regular daily practice—that major stumbling-block to Westerners, who sow, hurry and reap indigestion.

Over seventy—a greater age in the East than in the West—he looks a young and vital fifty ; supple movements, taut muscles, clear eyes and ' a mind that works like summer lightning '. For twenty-eight years he has never known illness—not so much as a common cold—which makes his tale of years more than those of the average human being, afflicted with ills that take toll of valuable life and time. His Rani, a woman of high intelligence, has never known purdah, and she plays a capable part in the management of his affairs. At forty—the mother of eight children—she is slender, supple, delicately rounded, and looks little more than twenty.

The high schools of Aundh use the same method of self-discipline as their Ruler, who himself leads the exercises that he designed for his people. He maintains that these mental and physical Sun Prayers, practised regularly in schools and homes, will create a domain from which pain, disease, worry and the frailty of old age will be gradually banished. These bold assertions are, so far, borne out by their healing and revitalising effect on himself and his family, coupled with an equanimity of mind that remains unruffled under the most trying conditions. He emphasises their ancient and traditional origin, always a virtue in Eastern eyes. They concentrate the experience of many hundred generations. He himself has only adapted and improved on them.

' In our mechanised times ', he writes, ' these natural physical movements have been lost or distorted. It restores something of the primitive vigour and one-ness of our being to revive them. The resulting lightness of body, buoyancy of mind and sense of youthfulness must be experienced to be believed.'

And he speaks from practical experience of thirty years, that led him to write and publish, at his own expense, a small book, *The Ten-point Way to Health*. Three editions went rapidly out of print; and his profits were devoted to the welfare of young people in the State. It is now published at 2s. 6d. by Dent and Sons, London.

It includes an account of his own daily programme, which has little suggestion about it of the ' Eastern potentate ' at home. Rising at 3.30 A.M., he is engaged in bathing, exercises and morning worship till 6.15. Breakfast with the family. State affairs from 7.30 to 9.30, followed by an hour devoted to painting and listening to the newspaper read aloud. Dinner 10.30 to 11.30. Reading, siesta and literary work till 3 P.M. Then three hours of official correspondence, overseeing the work of secretaries and others. Half an hour of evening worship, before the final 6.30 meal. An hour of reading ' to the Rani Sahib and children ', and to bed at 8.30, till 3.30. Sleep, which comes within five minutes, is sound and dreamless.

The advocated simplicity of life and diet will hardly commend itself to the average Westerner ; but the exercises alone, the controlled breathing in particular, can be practised regularly with surprising results.

Was ever a Raja more unlike the common conception of the word ? He follows aptly on the no less original anti-Brahmin Maharaja of Kolhapur, as a fine example of true, non-priestly, Brahmin culture and intellect, the ' wary wisdom ' that has kept religious and social Hinduism intact, through ceaseless wars and revolutions, for close on three thousand years.

According to Sir George Birdwood, a man of deep Eastern knowledge, if the Brahmin's ' conservative hold on the people is ever undermined, or Roman Catholic missionaries are not prepared to take their place, India will once again rapidly be reduced to chaos. . . .' That was written in 1914 : and India, since then, advancing with giant strides, has produced a galaxy of remarkable men in all professions and communities, as revealed in that recent, impressive book, *Great Men of India.*

In that connection, it is a point worth stressing that cultured and original men like the chiefs of Kolhapur and Aundh, and half a dozen others portrayed in this book, are nothing like so rare among the *élite* of modern India as is commonly supposed. Not many English men and women exert themselves to discover how intelligent and intuitive are Indians of all castes and creeds ; while too many books—written with a slender equipment of knowledge—have scattered broadcast wrong impressions of India and Indians as they are to-day.

Unfortunately there are few Westerners who can or will study the profound philosophy of life and religion on which the whole Hindu economic and social system is based.

My own inadequate portrayal of the greater Indian States, their Rulers and Ministers, throws a significant light on the capacity of Indians to manage their own affairs, to produce public men of character and ability as notable as any in the West. No doubt the wider opportunities open to them, under their own Princes, serve to stimulate ambition and capacity, both too often stultified when they are working under British officialdom—however just and friendly—by the fatal ' inferiority complex ' which, in Indian India, troubles them not at all.

The Raja of Aundh himself only came to England for the first time two years ago, when he spoke at the Royal Society of Arts on Indian painting : an admirable lecture written and spoken in English. His second son studied law at Oxford, where he won a place in the Brasenose College Eight, the most famous rowing college in Oxford. Thence, after studying in London, he returned equipped for legal work in the State.

Aundh is a star, if not of the first magnitude, an assurance to many lesser States that they may yet shine with a light of their own in the great constellation of Imperial India.

HYDERABAD: HIS EXALTED HIGHNESS THE NIZÂM OF HYDERABAD:
'FAITHFUL ALLY OF THE BRITISH GOVERNMENT'

HYDERABAD : SIR AKBAR HYDARI

(From *Power of India*)

TWO MOSLEM STATES

The nobility of the Moguls was based on service . . . Colourful and grandiose, they have left great memories and traditions.—GUY WINT.

HYDERABAD:
A HERITAGE FROM THE MOGULS

HERE, on the vast rolling uplands of the Deccan, we have India's premier State in every sense—in size, in wealth, in historical importance and spiritual pre-eminence; the Nizām having become the all-highest personality in orthodox Islam, since that rôle is no longer filled by the Sultan of Turkey. Geographically, the Deccan is said to be the oldest part of India, except the Himalayas; and Hyderabad State, nearly as large as France, holds a strategic position of the first importance. Flung right across the map of India, almost from sea to sea, it could, at will, isolate the mainly Hindu South from the mainly Moslem North, as it did, in effect, when the Nizām of Mutiny days decided to stand by England in her dark hour.

Both have owed much to one another; and in the whole history of British relations with India that great Principality has played a vitally significant part.

But Deccan history goes back to many centuries before the trading company from a small and distant island impinged upon its destiny and developed into a world power. It was the first great Moslem State south of the Nerbudda; and for five hundred years its Rulers have imposed a military oligarchy on a population of mixed races and religions, outnumbering them by ten to one. In the fifteenth century Bidar, the original capital—a hundred miles from the present city—was not only a fine town, with its castle and palaces and mosques, but the home of a famed university, possessing three thousand hand-written volumes and a teaching faculty recruited from all over Asia. To-day it exists only as an impressive ruin, beautified by exquisite coloured tiles that once covered the whole façade of the building.

The Deccan plateau—200,000 square miles of it—is framed on

three sides by mountains ; two of its mightiest rivers flow through Hyderabad State.   On its prairies, a century and a half ago, horses were bred for large bodies of irregular cavalry, the mainstay and pride of Moslem and Maratha armies.   Now, even here, the horse has been banished by the motor bus that needs no prairie for its maintenance ; nor can it be ill-treated, as all draft animals are apt to be in the East, not from innate cruelty, but from simple lack of imaginative feeling.

And all over that vast country remnants of vanished pride and power lend their tragic dignity to a curiously theatrical landscape : a surf, as it were, of broken hills among very blue lakes and emerald-green rice fields, diversified by fantastic masses of boulders so strangely piled and balanced on each other, as to suggest a primitive world of giants at play.   Thus they remain untouched by time, dramatic silhouettes against the blaze of sunset or dawn ; feathery heads of palm trees adding a japanesque touch to the scene.   Here and there one finds ruined temples and palaces of a Hindu kingdom destroyed by invading Moslems five or six hundred years ago ; and there are ancient forts perched precariously on crag or cliff.   Chief among these is the once formidable stronghold of Daulatabad cut out of a great isolated rock, scarped artificially to the height of nearly a thousand feet, and only accessible through its many corridors drilled in solid stone by that unsurpassed tool—the human hand.

On the utmost crag stands a colossal gun that once overawed the whole country round.   Dismantled now, it looms against the skyline, impressing only the thoughtful traveller, who marvels that any but a race of giants could have lifted it and set it there a thousand feet up.   According to legend, the marvel was achieved by an Italian engineer, afterwards put to death—in the brutal fashion of the time—lest he might betray the secret of those hidden corridors to an enemy.

More famous, and better known to the tourists who haunt Hyderabad, is the fortress of Golconda, once a flourishing city of over a million people that has curiously given its name to some of the most famous diamonds in history.   Many actually came from other parts of the dominion and were only sent to Golconda for cutting and polishing, which may possibly be the reason that those particular gems, with romantic histories, have all been written of as Golconda diamonds.

The tale of the Koh-i-Noor (Mountain of Light), first among British Crown jewels, may not be generally known.

Discovered in 1656, it was presented to the Mogul Emperor, Shah Jehan.   With the Moguls it remained, till Nadir Shah (as already told) swept down from Persia and looted Delhi, taking unto himself the Mountain of Light. Finally he was murdered —the common fate of Eastern Kings : and his murderer passed on the jewel to Ahmed Shah, founder of the Durani dynasty that ruled Afghanistan, till the fall of Amanullah, who leagued himself with Germany against the British Empire.

But the Koh-i-Noor never reached his hands. Murder and violence followed its passage from Afghan King to King, till the day of Shah Shuja, who was dethroned after the first Afghan War. From him it was cunningly tricked by his bitter enemy, Ranjit Singh, Lion of the Punjab ; and not till the Punjab itself was taken from the Sikhs did it come to rest in the regalia of Queen Victoria, ultimate Empress of India. Murder and violence followed it no more.

A lesser diamond christened Moon of the Mountains (the East has a genius for names) was also looted from Delhi by Nadir Shah to become a part of the Russian Crown jewels. And one of the finest Crown diamonds, the ' Orloff ', has its own strange tale. Originally set as the eye of a god in a temple between Madras and Mysore, it was stolen by a French soldier, caring nothing for the wrath of a Hindu deity, and sold for 10,000 dollars to a merchant of Persia. The astute Persian sold it again later, for 450,000 dollars—plus an annuity of 20,000—to the Russian Prince Orloff, at that time deeply in love with Catherine the Great. To her he gave it ; and so it passed from the eye of a god to glitter in the sceptre of Imperial Russia.

From another favourite Catherine received a second Golconda diamond, Star of the South, that passed to Napoleon the Third and was bought by a Prince of Baroda, thus returning to India after many years. Two others wandered half round the world and back again to India ; one the Akbar Shah, belonging originally to the greatest of Moguls. These by no means exhaust the astonishing list. The Crown jewels of Austria and of Saxony include—or included—a Golconda diamond.

The treasure of the Deccan seemed beyond mortal counting. It is told of a Hindu King in that region, conquered by a Moslem invader, that he presented the victor with six hundred maunds of pearls—a maund weighing about eighty pounds. There were two maunds also of diamonds, rubies and sapphires. No wonder carpets were sewn with gems in those lavish days.

And Golconda fort to-day—a name familar to every tourist— is chiefly famed for its beautiful tombs, that might well be symbols of a buried past.

Of the splendid city built by Kings of the old Deccan, little is left but the tremendous walls that now guard only quarters for troops, though the great palace-fortress, Bala Hissar, still towers in the midst of the ' city that isn't '. High up on the ruin stands a small pavilion where tourists resort to watch the sunset over a strangely wild and impressive scene. Near it stands a far more ancient Hindu temple. Long before invading Moslem Kings, it was there; and it is still there, ages after they have become shadows in a world of shadows. Ages hence it will still be there, a shrine for millions of Hindus who make up 90 per cent of Moslem-ruled Hyderabad. That is India.

These relics of the past seem more akin to the fantastic landscape than do the white modern country houses of Hyderabad nobles and landowners, who live mainly in the city, preferring its atmosphere of Moslem culture and the exciting undercurrent of intrigue that pervades the very air of Hyderabad. In every Eastern court, it pulls the strings or cuts the threads of human destinies; but here it has become a social pastime, as in our own eighteenth century; many trained and cultured brains elevating it almost to a fine art.

Some of the nobles' palaces are small towns in themselves; many of their owners Western educated, with sons sent to English schools and universities.

Far back in history, the Deccan kingdom was famed as a centre of culture and learning; and now, in modern Hyderabad, we have the one powerful Moslem Crown left since the collapse of the Moguls. Its court and aristocratic families reflect the atmosphere, if not the splendours, of Mogul Delhi. Its nobles and Ministers of State, its men of culture and big business, form a social mosaic aptly described by Sir William Barton—once a distinguished Resident and personal friend of the Nizām : ' Here you will meet Cambridge men with an Oxford accent, who will converse gracefully on philosophy or religion : men from either University, whose ethics are singularly innocent of Aristotle ; engineers who have gained highest academic distinctions in England ; lawyers, Moslem barristers, wealthy bankers who would give almost anything for an English knighthood. One of these offered £100,000 to be utilised in charity, for a baronetcy—provided the title did not descend to his eldest son, whom he hated ! '

The old school, with its Eastern culture and courtly manners, cannot much longer survive in a social element so mixed and so increasingly modernised. Hyderabad itself, the fourth city of the Empire, is more notable for its size than for any historical interest or beauty of architecture. But the well-known gateway, Charminar, has the grace and dignity of Mogul design ; and all the greater buildings blossom into the beautiful domes and minarets everywhere associated with Moslem cities.

The Mecca Musjid, largest mosque in India, contains the tomb of the Nizām's father, who died in 1911. Small and slight, with dark hair falling to his shoulders under a closely folded turban, there was nothing kingly in his aspect ; yet he ranked as the First Gentleman of India ; and those who knew the man assert that undoubtedly he filled the rôle. In the early days of motoring, he would let no car be used in Hyderabad : a grievance among his nobles, who craved the new toy that so swiftly covered great distances. But even King Canute could not check the rising tide. Nor could the completest autocrat of India check the march of progress.

Sir Walter Lawrence, in his account of the Royal Tour (1905), tells a characteristic tale of how cars came to Hyderabad.

The Prince and Princess (King George and Queen Mary) were lodged in a Palace high above the city. Sir Walter came, in his privileged car, to escort the Nizām up for an interview with Royalty. How long would it take them ? the Nizām wanted to know; and Sir Walter, remembering envious nobles, told him, ' More than half an hour in the carriage with escort ; but in my splendid car, most carefully driven, not more than eight or ten minutes.' He further dilated on the advantages of a car in so vast a State ; especially in scouring the country after big game.

The Nizām considered all that in a brief silence ; then called his Master of Horse, who heard with blank amazement that His Highness would go up to the Palace in Sir Walter's car. Pleased with the experience, he returned in the same way ; and at once wrote off an order to his agent in Bombay for eleven motor cars. His nobles, it need hardly be said, lost no time in following the Royal lead.

A Prince of hospitality, generous to a fault, he was widely liked and respected by Moslems, Hindus and British ; and the closing years of his reign concluded a brilliant epoch in the social life of Hyderabad.

Many of the great families there trace their pedigree back to pre-Mogul Moslem kingdoms ; others came in with Asaf Jah, the first Nizām, whose personality dominated all Southern India in the early eighteenth century. He has been called the most outstanding genius of his time : and undoubtedly his military prowess checked the rising tide of Maratha power that otherwise would have submerged Islam in the South, and changed the current of British history. He died in 1748 : and again, like most great men, he left none able to fill his place. As a result, his vast kingdom was weakened by wars of succession, culminating in a virtual French dictatorship, that lasted till the British ousted the French and drew up a treaty with its Ruler of the period.

From that time forward, for a hundred and seventy years, Hyderabad has been, in deed and in truth, the Faithful Ally of the British ; an alliance that proved of the utmost value during their early dazzling feats of arms. Though the foundations of Empire were laid by Clive at Plassey, the Maratha confederacy would have proved a hard nut to crack without the military backing of Hyderabad. Never have the two countries been at war : though at times—owing to a long-standing regrettable question of ceded territory—relations have been strained. It is, in fact, not too much to say that the loyalty and co-operation of Hyderabad have been one of the strongest buttresses of the British Empire in India.

During the early nineteenth century the State suffered from lax government and financial chaos. Arab mercenaries banded together and seized several forts, including Golconda. Under their own officers, they formed themselves almost into a military republic, overshadowing the rightful Ruler ; so that the State declined lamentably in power and prestige. Only a strong man could lift it from the morass into which it was sinking : and the hour—as often—provided the man.

In 1853 Sir Sālar Jung—the greatest administrator of modern India—became Prime Minister, which post he held for thirty years : a record in that line. His wise brain and strong hand on the reins brought back to life a half-paralysed government ; and in the course of those thirty years the State was virtually transformed. It was largely through his influence that Hyderabad backed the English when Mutiny flared up in the North of India and Lucknow, and an explosive atmosphere prevailed in the City. The British knew their danger. ' If the Nizām goes all is lost ' was the official conviction—not without good reason. Given a lead from the Nizām, every Moslem in India would have joined the Great Revolt. To his honour, and that of his famous Prime Minister, he gave quite another lead ; one that turned the tide of history.

There are few places now in the country where British and Indians are socially and personally on better terms : and the present Nizām, His Exalted Highness Sir Mir Osman Ali, takes a special pride in his unique title, ' Faithful Ally of the British Government '.

With a revenue of seven millions sterling, with hidden treasure of gold and gems rated at the fantastic value of thirty millions, he is reckoned to be one of the richest men in the world. But he was reared so strictly by his father that his way of life, from habit and taste, is almost Spartan in its simplicity. Unlike most Indian Princes, he cares little for any form of sport or entertainment or travel. He has never been to Europe, and he keeps horses only for his sons, who have also been strictly brought up. He himself prefers his car—an old Buick, as often as not. It is his nobles who take the air in silver-plated cars of the newest design. He likes the theatre and enjoys English plays given by touring companies for the large British garrison at Secunderabad. Literature interests him. He has written Persian lyrics ; and aims at keeping up the tradition of culture and learning associated with Islam at its best.

In himself he presents a curious blend of East and West. He works harder than most Indian Princes ; and allows himself almost too little time for recreation. His whimsical and philosophic temperament inclines him to a detached view of politics ; but he is pure Eastern in his distrust of democracy. Few Rulers more absolute have survived into the twentieth century. Short and slight, like his father, his dignity of bearing and touch of imperiousness give to his court a flavour of Mogul tradition, enhanced by the special title His Exalted Highness, bestowed on him by King George the Fifth for his services in the Great War : a title that sets him above even religion. In the great yearly fast of Ramazān that lasts a month—no eating or drinking between sunrise and sunset—His Exalted Highness only fasts on the first day, to honour the decree. After that, he eats as usual.

Sir William Barton writes that his prestige with his whole *entourage* is enormous. ' The spectacle of his nobles forming a double row in the Residency portico at a dinner party, bending double as he passes with the gesture that implies taking dust from the feet of greatness—is most impressive.'

At dinner with English guests, either in the Palace or Residency, he wears their dress surmounted by his closely folded turban— yellow, on State occasions, with a gold aigrette ; and eats as they do. There is no avoidance of wine at his table or at any other table in social Hyderabad, where, in earlier days, liqueur in a wineglass and the champagne peg were favoured by nobles of a bibulous tendency.

But his Spartan tastes are ingrained. He lives, for choice, in the house assigned to him by his father—little more than a handsome bungalow. Yet he owns two great palaces ; the original one covering more than half the city. The new one, south of the city, standing on the crest of a ridge above the river Musi, ringed with a circle of granite rocks, is an imposing pile of whitewashed stucco not comparable to the Palaces of Rajasthān, with their historical and heroic associations. It is here, behind carved and screened windows, that he houses his zenana—his one extravagance ; more than forty wives, with their attendant ladies and relations to the number of two hundred or so. Whenever he visits Delhi—an infrequent event—the whole regiment of women must be of the party ; two special trains requisitioned, and canvas screens, to protect them from the public gaze during their transfer from car to train.

In their own quarters they are strictly purdah even from English women ; though, in healthy modern fashion, they have their open courts for exercise or games. No European may visit them or even enter the city without a pass ; a precaution dating from days when the turbulent Arab was a very real danger to any outsider. Miss Tottenham, visiting Hyderabad, describes a purdah party that gave her a glimpse into that jealously guarded world of women.

' We drove across the bridge over the river Musi, through the fortress gate and by narrow streets to a towered Palace. Along the approaches stood the Amazon guards of the Nizām ; African women, dressed in blue tunics and baggy trousers, with small stiff caps on their heads. . . . An Amazon band was playing ; the bandswomen being of the same *jāt* [1] as the guards.

' The hall was one glitter of chandeliers and jewels, of satin and silk. The Palace ladies sat among fellow-Mahomedans. They wore diaphanous, delicate veils reaching to the waist, over bright-coloured satin trousers so tightly fitting that the legs must have been stitched into them. Beautiful were the jewels on ankles and wrists, hands and necks. Most ladies had their hair in two long plaits ; their oval faces and brilliant eyes giving them an unusual foreign appearance. Though they could not talk to us Englishwomen, they seemed to be gathering every detail, so closely did they observe our doings.'

One would have liked to hear their talk about it afterwards ; talk often flavoured with a wisdom culled from life, not from books. For there is much intelligence and shrewd interest behind the purdah—so-called—in these changing days ; too little knowledge ' outside ' of India's secluded women and their ways.

It may surprise some Westerners to learn that, in the social and moral code of the Koran, the Moslem woman is given higher legal rights than any others of her kind, except in a matriarchate like Travancore. In law, her footing should be equal with man.

[1] Breed.

In marriage—a civil and social, not a religious act—the husband has no power over her property or over the sum he settles on her. Of her son she is sole guardian up to the age of seven or nine ; of her daughter till she marries. She can deal with her own property ; and neither father nor husband have legal authority over her after she comes of age.

The Prophet, in fact, assigned to Moslem women a better all-round position than even her Western sisters, until very recent days.

But custom can produce puzzling anomalies between sacred decrees and common practice : anomalies mainly caused by purdah in its old, bad, orthodox form that mentally and physically stultified the lives of women ; a state of life certainly not enjoined by the Koran. The idea could be based on one text only, telling women to hide their beauty from men ; an injunction that might logically apply to the body rather than to the face. The fact remains that Mahomed's daughter led an army into battle, and his first wife was no *purdah nashin*, but one of the most remarkable women in Arab history.

As it is, complete purdah for the middle classes and aristocracy has profoundly affected the whole social and religious atmosphere of India, both among Moslems and Hindus, who adopted the custom in order to protect their women from the covetous Moslem invader. With all its obvious drawbacks, there are those, even now, who still uphold purdah in its healthiest form, that gives secluded women a select social life of their own : bridge and games and free intercourse with male relations on both sides. Here is the view of one who has intimately known and admired the *purdah nashin* of India : ' These women are thoroughly women, beyond all else. . . . Here are the clear brow and smiling faces of those who know ; those to whom sex is a necessary part of life, mother-hood a pride and duty. Their very aloofness and seclusion gives them half their charm ; and they know it ; know that it is for women, veiled and separate, that men crave : captives of passion at a first quick-taken glance. A wife who is not the familiar companion of every walk and game—with what delight the husband seeks her at last in the inner apartments, where she awaits him with smiles and flowers.'

And again here is purdah, seen from the different angle of an American woman, who lived for some years with Indians as one of themselves. ' It may be a question of temperament, but one can grow to like the idea that purdah represents. There is more sympathy, more freemasonry among women in the East than in the West. Men of the West have their clubs and circles where women don't go ; and one felt a distinct lift in status finding places in the East, where women could be at ease among themselves and men were not allowed. It seemed to me that both sexes deserved that occasional freedom from each other. One noticed that Indian ladies who made a point of breaking every restriction, going to dances and so forth, seemed to lose something of their distinctive charm and attraction. One found them less wise, less tender, less graceful.'

The last sentences, like most generalised opinions, are too sweeping. The Indian woman's peculiar quality is inbred from centuries of specialised living. The bloom is not rubbed off by even a decade of living otherwise : but again it is a question of individual character. All purdah women are not angels in *saris* and the less admirable will more swiftly succumb to very mixed influences of the ' outside '.

But the Moslem woman, purdah or no, has never become so completely subject to man as her Hindu sister. In her family she wields great power and influence ; and many Moslem husbands are, to some degree, henpecked. Social conditions also make it possible that—as in Turkey—the women of Islam will have a better chance than the Brahmin-ridden devotees of Vishnu and Shiva, to gain complete inner and outer freedom of spiritual life. Many Moslem women in Hyderabad have left seclusion and are doing valuable social service work.

As to the decree permitting many wives, four is the given limit in the Koran, on the condition that all ' must be treated with equal favour and cherishing ' : a counsel of perfection so nearly impossible that it almost cancels the permission. One of the Mogul Rulers—more human than holy—suggested a choice of four wives to meet different needs : a Persian for talking to ; a Kermani for housework ; a Hindu woman for nursing the children—pre-eminently the mother; and a Turki to whip, by way of deterrent example, to keep the other three in order.

Shades of the Prophet who wrote, ' Paradise is under the feet of the Mothers '.

In most cases economy, like the Prophet, advocates one wife. Few men can afford more in these times ; unless it be the richest man in the world, lifted by his wealth above economic hindrances and by his title above religious decrees.

But in spite of rigid purdah for the Palace ladies, the Nizām's unmarried daughters appear free from its restrictions and are seen at dinner parties, garden parties and the many race meetings that are a feature of social Hyderabad. His two sons, men of wider ranging interests, have visited England and travelled in Europe.

The elder, the Prince of Berar, married the beautiful daughter of Turkey's last Sultan : and the younger married his niece. Both are women of Western culture and Eastern charm. Both have done good work for the advancing women of India ; and through them the Nizām is linked by marriage with the spiritual head of orthodox Islam. Perhaps for this reason—lacking the Caliphate in Turkey—India's ninety million Moslems show signs of transferring their spiritual and cultural allegiance to His Exalted Highness of Hyderabad. The Shiah sect of Mussulmans have, as their spiritual head, the Aga Khan, a world-known personality, who, however, owns no territory in India.

As for Congress politicians and Hindu extremists, the Deccan merely offers them a wide field for subversive propaganda, which can do little damage to a State founded on a basis of rule at once so firm and so liberal that it has been called a species of constitutional autocracy, if the two are not a contradiction in terms.

British India, outside official circles, appears to know little of Hyderabad, except as a racing centre and a paradise for tourists on account of Golconda tombs and the vast sculptured caves of Ajanta and Ellora.

Mention of these brings us to the chief artistic and architectural glory of the Deccan : an impressive assemblage of cave monasteries and cathedrals, sculptured from a wall of perpendicular rock some two hundred and fifty feet high sweeping round in a hollow semicircle, over the Waghara river.

These astounding caves contain twenty-four monasteries, with countless monastic cells, and five cathedrals ; all originally inspired by Buddhism—India's third great religion—when it penetrated the Deccan. The frescoes that adorn many of the caves depict the imagined experiences of Buddha in his many incarnations ; and they date, all told, from the second century B.C. to the eighth century A.D.

The caves and rock-cut temples at Ellora were built at intervals from the fifth to the ninth centuries by Buddhists, Jains and Hindus, ages before the industrial machine made a fetish of time to the detriment of craftsmanship, that aimed simply at perfection. Here three great religions have engraved their spirit, side by side, into the rock : and, among many wonders, the most wonderful is the Kailās temple built for Shiva. A massive monolith, richly hewn and carved, it stands in the centre of a vast court supported by four rows of pilasters with colossal elephants and other animals among them giving that mighty temple an effect of being suspended in mid-air.

For more than a thousand years—in these recesses of rock and cave—they lay forgotten or unknown till 1819, when an explorative company of British soldiers happened to stumble on them with amazement ; thus, by an apparent accident, bringing them back to human ken.

Yet it was not until 1843 that the Royal Asiatic Society persuaded the East India Company to take an active interest in preserving the Ajanta frescoes that are the more marvellous because they were not conceived and executed by one inspired man, or even by some great artist and his pupils. They were simply carried on by many generations of unknown artists and craftsmen ; yet, all told, they astonishingly reveal a consistent unity of conception, detail and design. It is written of them that ' in the delicate colours, in boldness and subtlety of execution, in vitality of conception, the Ajanta paintings are unrivalled '.

It is also told how, sixty years after that awakening to their beauty and value, a zealous Moslem official had the frescoes—their chief glory—whitewashed all over, ' to improve the look of things ' in honour of a visit from Lord Curzon, the one Viceroy for whom the preservation of India's art and architecture amounted almost to a passion.

Needless to add that the whitewash was removed without damage to the paintings, that are, to-day, in a state of preservation largely due to the zealous interest of Hyderabad's most able Prime Minister, Sir Akbar Hydari, backed by generous aid from the Nizām ; an achievement that puts in their debt all the world's genuine lovers of Eastern architecture and art.

Of Sir Akbar Hydari himself it may be said that he stands out—with the impressive figure of Sir Salar Jung—as perhaps the greatest Prime Minister in all princely India ; one who looks beyond the good of his own State to the good of India as a whole —an ultimately united India in which he profoundly believes. By his practical acumen as Finance Minister, his breadth of mind and vision as Prime Minister, he served Hyderabad with tireless energy and zeal for more than forty years. A product of India's fine old merchant families, he is descended neither from Moslem conquerors nor from converted Hindus ; so there is no fanatical strain in his blood ; and his faith in Islam does not blind him to the value of other creeds for other men. Like the sagacious Maharaja of Baroda, he has striven always to minimise discord in all matters of religion, custom and tradition : an asset of practical value in a Moslem State numbering 90 per cent of Hindus.

Educated by Jesuits at their Bombay College, he probably owes to them, in part, his mingling of tolerance with subtlety in diplomatic affairs. He began his career in British service, but was afterwards lent to Hyderabad, where he remained for the greater part of his working life.

In appearance he is short and stout, white-haired and bearded, with a fine breadth of brow and keen eyes twinkling behind his glasses. In his court dress, with knee-breeches and cut-away gold-laced coat and sword at his side, he has almost an eighteenth-century air ; no turban, no distinctive mark of the East. In daily life, caring nothing for appearances, he looks very much otherwise. A patch on the seat of his oldest trousers may horrify his wife, but it will please him mightily as a triumph of economy. To that very wife, who died in 1940, he owed an appreciable measure of his success. A woman of strong character and shrewd judgment, she shared his cultured tastes, and made possible, through real partnership, his strenuous way of life.

And in his method of work there is little of the traditional, leisurely East. Seven days a week and eighteen hours a day hardly suffice for his whirl of mental and official activity ; endless committees, endless business interviews : letters dictated and telephone-calls even at meal-times : and, at the end of his arduous day, he remains, as ever, a fresh and stimulating companion, interested in all that happens outside his complex corner of the world.

Two hobbies absorb his few free hours : art and philanthropy. Of the last he says no word, preferring not to let his left hand know what his right hand offers to those in need. Both in politics and education Hyderabad has gained by his breadth of mind and vision—that rarest of qualities, the power to see ahead and see true.

The idea behind the famed Osmania College is an experiment in education that may yet have far-reaching effects on the mental outlook of all India. It provides higher education in Urdu, not in English ; an idea that has been adversely criticised—the fate of most bold experiments. But, when all is said, it inculcates self-respect and reverence for traditions of culture essential to a United India. It also releases the student from methods that stifled originality and from the strain of coping with a foreign tongue at the expense of the subject in hand. Witness the pathetic futility of Indian students mangling lines from English poets in their genuine attempt to wrest some meaning from unfamiliar words and ideas.

Take, as an instance, Keats' beautiful lines,

> Thou wast not born for death, Immortal bird,
> No hungry generations tread thee down,

solemnly rendered by a promising Indian pupil : ' He say the nightingale is not the game bird for the dinner table, therefore the hungry sportsman spare to tread on it '. The paraphrase may be a gem of humour ; but its educational value is precisely nil.

Again, higher education in Urdu rather than English must enable the students to teach others in their own tongue, and thus narrow the gulf that yawns between literate and illiterate : a consideration that may well confound the critics. No human design can be without a flaw ; and it is always easier to criticise than to create. The fact remains that Sir Akbar, in the Osmania College, has sown the seed of a practical idea that may bring forth good fruit in due season.

Along political lines also his broad views and forward-looking mind have been of service to more than Hyderabad. At the Round Table Conferences, representing the Nizām, he impressed all who came in contact with him as ' the equal of both Eastern and Western statesmen '. A mixture of realist and idealist, he foresees a united India, while recognising that the changes involved must be gradual ; that the position of all Indian States must be modified and even certain privileges surrendered, if they are to play a real part in achieving the desired end. But the realist in him insists that Congress cannot be expected to take all and give nothing : a programme congenial to extremist mentality, if less nakedly expressed. Hence opposition to the normal safeguards demanded by the States, to ensure their present stability and future integrity.

They take their stand on Dominion rank for India within that brotherhood of nations, the British Empire. But the unity aimed at has yet to be achieved—not by the waving of a wand, but by men of goodwill and experience working for the goal of All-India first, last and all the time ; men with wide and tolerant minds that alone can envisage the best traditions of the old blended with the most fruitful ideas of the new.

Of such, undoubtedly, is Sir Akbar Hydari, who in 1941 was called from his high office to a wider sphere of action and responsibility, in the Viceroy's Enlarged Executive Council ; a council in which Moslem and Hindu were given the chance to work in unison against the forces of evil that threatened India no less than the rest of the civilised world.

And when the time comes for detailed settlement of India's ' New Order ', Hyderabad, in which Sir Akbar played so great a part, will be found to afford a fine working example of what Indians can achieve in the way of self-government. Working under Englishmen, they are apt to shrink from initiative ; for which reason it is mainly the Indian States that have produced men of notable talent, real thinkers along sane lines, like Sir Akbar and others of his quality. Thus we find in Hyderabad, both political and social, ' the future is being moulded on the solid basis of what is enduring in the past '.

*   *   *

Since this chapter was written, the news of Nawab Sir Akbar Hydari's death has deprived India, at this critical juncture, of a statesman second to none in vision, courage and grasp of world affairs ; one whose breadth of mind, in all matters religious and political, was the true solvent of communal hatreds that are rightly deemed to spring more from hatred of labels than of actual men and women.

His personal and political sagacity and prescience were of a very high order. It was Mr. Churchill who called him ' the ornament of the Round Table Conference ' ; and, after his death, Sir Philip Hartog justly wrote, ' If there were more Hydaris among the leaders in India, the political situation would clear up as if by magic '.

Is it too much to hope that his mantle may fall on a younger pair of shoulders ?

BHOPĀL:
KING OF THE EARTH

FOR the second important Moslem State, Bhopāl, we fare north-ward again to the wilds of Central India. Here we reach the stronghold of purdah upheld by veiled Queens unknown else-where in the East.

To have been ruled for over a hundred years by four remark-able Begums in succession, all maintaining the strictest purdah, is the singular distinction of Bhopāl. The last one, mother of the present Nawab, Hamidullah Khan Bahadur—was perhaps the most distinguished of the four. A woman of education, a traveller, a lively talker, she ranked as one of the most outstanding personalities among modern Indian Rulers—all men.

The strength of mind and character shown by that singular sequence of Queens may have been partly due to the Afghan descent. For Bhopāl, as now known, was founded two centuries ago, by an Afghan General who distinguished himself in the service of Aurungzeb. Fifty years he spent in a violent struggle to form a stable kingdom from some disconnected fragments of the doomed Mogul Empire : a kingdom that dates from 1723.

But the original Bhopāl, like Hyderabad, goes back into legend-haunted mists of Hindu India. Its very name springs from a union of two Sanskrit words : *Bho*, the earth ; and *Pāl*, a king. The kingly city of those far-off times was built upon the shores of a veritable inland sea. Lake, it was called : but the word gave no idea of its dimensions. Here were islands bearing whole villages ; the shelving mainland thronged with palaces, temples and more temples. From these there rose, morning and evening, the music of daily worship : Buddhist chants sung by saintly men and women. For Buddha endowed women with freedom to join holy orders and devote their lives to good works.

His story—immortalised for English readers in Sir Edwin Arnold's *Light of Asia*—tells how he put behind him his three chief treasures, throne and wife and child, in order to lead the first open revolt against Hindu priestly power and restrictions. Boldly he demolished caste divisions that increased Brahminical hold over the masses, especially the women, whom he set free to seek unhindered the knowledge so long withheld from them. He gave them the right to stand everywhere—in sacred or secular

BHOPÁL : HIS HIGHNESS NAWAB MOHAMMED HAMIDULLAH KHAN
BAHADUR OF BHOPÁL

BHOPĀL : THE NAWAB OF BHOPĀL : A GENIUS OF THE POLO FIELD

life—free and equal with man ; his own wife and aunt openly becoming his first disciples. His bold action challenged the age-old rivalry between priest and woman for lordship over the body and soul of man, with results that were eventually dramatic and overwhelming.

Perhaps too suddenly the prison doors were flung open. Changes too abrupt, even for the best, are apt to bring more harm than good. Thousands of nuns thronged the monasteries, eager to escape from perpetual widowhood, from lives of isolation, or the heartbreak of losing children.

The wholesale movement, in fact, threatened to withdraw from their normal functions the life-bearing, home-tending half of the race. Women freed, mentally and socially, from the shackles of ignorance, would obviously have been far more valuable as wives and mothers than they could ever be as nuns, seeking spiritual freedom through the ascetic life. Buddha himself is said to have recognised the danger—too late.

That cardinal error, and the pervading pessimism of his creed, gave intellectual Brahminism its chance to regain dominion over the majority of Hindus. Slowly, resistlessly, Buddhism was thrust east and north, to Burma and Tibet, where it may have been more in keeping with the mentality of the people.

But in those early days, when its votaries thronged the islands and shores of ancient Bhopāl, the new creed was making headway everywhere. In Bhopāl it flourished till Moslem invaders came sweeping down from the north under the green banner of the Prophet : conquerors and fanatical destroyers of all idols made with hands. Monks and nuns, by the thousand, were killed or scared away, in fear of their lives. Temples and shrines were ruthlessly demolished by those Eastern Calvinists whose religion was the Sword. They made of beautiful Bhopāl and its sacred buildings ' an heap of stones '. They drained away its vast lake till a ' pool ', hardly two miles long, was all that remained of those shining waters. The rest, becoming an unhealthy swamp, bred an epidemic that killed off the hapless people and plagued Bhopāl with many diseases for close on thirty years. Eventually, trans-formed into fertile land, it produced a succession of wheat fields, rice fields and pasture for a happier generation : and the ravages of malaria troubled them no more.

Centuries later, Moslem Bhopāl arose from the devastated shrines of Buddhism. The dwindled lake was enlarged ; with the result that we now have modern Bhopāl, one of India's most attractive cities ; its gleaming palaces and mosques mirrored in

M

six miles of shining water : an oasis of beauty and fertility in an arid land.

Its original founder, the Afghan General Sirdar Dōst Mahomed Khan, boldly refused to become an ally of Asaf Jah, first Nizām of Hyderabad ; a powerful Ruler who owned, or held in fief, the greater part of South and South-east India, including most of Madras. The Sirdar's independent Afghan spirit nearly cost him his country—but not quite. Reluctantly he was compelled to give up his son as hostage ; and at his death, that son—Yar Mahomed —was installed as a willing ally of Hyderabad.

Not until the middle of the eighteenth century did Bhopāl's first Begum, widow of Yar Mahomed, appear on the scene. Pure Afghan in her shrewd judgment and strength of character, she took complete command of State affairs, when her son, the Nawab, gave up his throne to become an ascetic—as only Easterns ever do. Through fifty years of that turbulent era, she guided Bhopāl with a masculine vigour allied to a feminine capacity for winning the hearts of her people.

She it was who, in 1779, laid the foundation of Bhopāl's long friendship with Britain, through an episode that occurred during one of the four Maratha wars of which so much has been told. Warren Hastings, India's brilliant Governor-General, anxious to counter Maratha moves in Bombay, hazardously flung a small force, under General Goddard, from Bengal right across India, through regions unmapped and mainly hostile : the kind of thing that only an Englishman could attempt and achieve. Everywhere Goddard encountered and overcame local opposition, till he entered the State of Bhopāl, where he found a spirit of friendliness as unlooked for as it was welcome.

Orders, it seemed, had been issued that the English force be welcomed, and given every possible help : orders that were carried out with zeal, often at great risk to the people themselves. And they paid a high price for their show of good feeling. No sooner had the English passed on, to complete their wonderful march, than the Marathas descended in force on Bhopāl to exact vengeance for help given to the hated enemy.

After that gallant episode, it is distressing to record a sequel that sprang from reactionary political influences, when the recall of Lord Wellesley—a later Governor-General—cancelled his policy of extending British protection to Native States as a buttress against war. With the end of his brilliant era, his policy of subordinate alliances lapsed for a time.

So it came to pass that, when a later Nawab of Bhopāl pressed for alliance with the British, as a protection from Maratha onslaughts, the request was refused : a seemingly ungenerous response that doomed that plucky little State to years of strife. For the Marathas gave Bhopāl no respite. In 1813 they besieged the capital with a strong mixed force, against which the Afghans held out obstinately for more than nine months ; finally dispersing their invaders without British help. But the most persistent raiders in history returned again and again ; and not until the little kingdom was on the verge of collapse did the East India Company at last intervene with armed assistance that, if given earlier, might have saved Bhopāl from prolonged and devastating conflict.

That was in 1817, nearly thirty-eight years after Goddard's death ; and even then, the desired treaty was, as usual, too long delayed.

In 1844 the failure of a male heir gave Bhopāl the first of its four successive Begums, making it the only woman-ruled Moslem State on record—well and wisely ruled, from all verdicts available.

It is a curious fact, attested by history, that women, as Queens, have a remarkable record of distinction. England's three Queens have each given their name to an era ; though Queen Anne lacked the dominant personality of the other two. Catherine of Russia also stands out—a conspicuous figure ; not admirable, but in-dubitably great. And in Central India the Marathas have pro-duced a famous Queen : the great Ahalya Bai of Indore, who began as Queen-Regent in 1765, and, on her son's death, became virtual Ruler of the State. She saved her country from invaders, raised her capital from a mere village to a flourishing city, which she ruled capably for thirty years, showing sympathy and con-sideration to all classes of her subjects. Her neighbour, the first Maharaja of Gwalior, so admired her fortitude and capacity that he actively helped her to maintain her unusual position. She takes a high place among India's heroines ; and the Age of Ahalya Bai is still regarded as the Golden Age of Indore.

Four Bhopāl Queens add their distinguished reigns to the record ; especially the first and last of the four.

And more recently we come to the Queen-Regent of Mysore, mother of the saintly Maharaja, who died in 1940, and great-aunt of the present Prince. For seven years, while her son was a minor, she practically ruled from behind the purdah ; a seclusion so strict that even the doctor must look at her tongue, or the dentist pull out her teeth, through a slit in the curtain that shut off the inner apartments ; and her ladies must follow suit. Like the Begums of Bhopāl, she triumphed over all imposed limitations ; but unlike them she could not easily move about, because of

purdah restrictions. They, being Moslems, could envelop face
and figure in the tent-like drapery known as a *burkha*—folds of
fine white material gathered into a close-fitting cap, with a mesh
across the eye-holes, that blurs all objects and confuses perspective,
but admits a curious form of semi-detached intercourse with their
kind.

It was the second of the Bhopāl Queens, Sikander Begum,
who appointed as her Commander-in-Chief a certain Sebastian
Bourbon ; a strange non-Indian name that sprang from a family
history stranger still. For the Bourbons of Bhopāl are descended
from the Bourbons of Navarre ; and the story of their founder,
who fled from Brittany and made his adventurous way to the
court of Akbar, is a tale as romantic and dramatic as even India
has produced : a tale that throws an interesting light on the
centuries-old link between these descendants of a French aristocrat
and the Moslem State of Bhopāl.

It was in 1560 that Jean Philippe de Bourbon de Navarre, kin
to the renowned Henri IV, had the ill luck to kill another high-
born Gascon in a duel. Fleeing from Brittany, he made his way
to Portugal, thence to Goa in a Portuguese vessel, with two
friends and a family priest. The friends died on the voyage, and
the other two adventurers made their way to Southern India,
where the priest remained to shepherd a small community of
Indian Christians. Jean Philippe, alone, sailed round the coast
to the north of the Hoogli. Thence he travelled by boat, mooring
every night, up the rivers Ganges and Jumna to Delhi, where
Akbar was at the height of his imperial power. Letters of intro-
duction obtained him an audience with the greatest of Moguls,
on whom he made an immediate favourable impression. Tall
and of gallant bearing, he coloured the tale of his own achievements and high family connection, in true Gascon style : and so
impressed the Emperor that he was given a grant of land with
the title of Nawab. Nor did his good fortune end there.

Shortly before his arrival, two lovely Portuguese sisters had
also reached Delhi in the adventurous fashion of the time. Shipped
from Lisbon with other young girls of good family, they were
destined for Portuguese India—then at its zenith—to become
wives of Royal officials and soldiers out there. But too often it
happened that pirates got wind of these attractive cargoes ; and
in this case a boatload of noble orphans was waylaid by a Dutch
privateer. The crew carried off their prizes to Surat for sale to
the highest bidder, a harsh fate for sheltered girls of breeding and
education. But to some of them Fate was merciful. One young
lady found herself throned Queen of the Maldives ; while the two

beautiful sisters, Maria and Juliana Mascarenhas, were bought by one of Akbar's agents, deputed to find fresh inmates for his imperial harem. That these young women were Christians did not disqualify them as wives for the most tolerant and catholic of Mussulmans. Their beauty sufficed. Delighted with his purchase, the young and ardent Akbar's choice fell on Marie, and he made her his Christian wife. How she fared among Moslems and Hindu princesses has not been told : but it was she who adorned a wall in Fatehpur Sikri—Akbar's rose-red city —with a painting of the Annunciation ; and her tomb, outside Agra, is still cared for by the British Government.

My tale of the Bhopāl Bourbons hangs mainly on the fate of Juliana, who was given the post of doctor (qualified or no) in charge of the imperial zenana—a very colony of women numbering five thousand all told. But no woman of that period could be left husbandless : and what bridegroom could be more suitable for a Christian beauty than the splendid young foreigner, Bourbon de Navarre ? Could his own account be believed, he must be, next to Akbar himself, the finest warrior alive. Nor did he quarrel with the Emperor's gift of a wife. As Juliana's husband, he was appointed governor of that vast seraglio ; she receiving the title of ' Imperial Sister '. Before she died, she built the first Catholic church in Agra, and was buried in it. Her son and grandson both carried on the office created for Jean Philippe ; but by that time India's greatest Empire was breaking up. Many of the Bourbon family were murdered by a small Raja who coveted their land. The rest escaped to Gwalior under Salvador de Bourbon and were found inside that mighty fortress by the English when they captured it in 1780 ; a brilliant feat of arms. Captain Popham, who escaladed the fortress, gave the stray adventurers an estate in Sindhia's dominions ; a form of generosity that Sindhia did not relish at all. He proceeded to make himself so unpleasant that Salvador and his cousin Pedro betook themselves to Bhopāl. That friendly State welcomed them and gave them land for their maintenance : a hospitable act that was repaid over and over in the years that followed.

Salvador himself proved so gallant and capable that he was given command to lead an army against the perpetually hostile Marathas, whom he dealt with successfully in a manner all his own.

Instead of fighting them, he sent a flag of truce to Sindhia's General, who happened also to be a Frenchman, Jean Baptiste Filose. Salvador, after greetings, proceeded to argue that as both were Christians—a Bourbon and a Filose—they ought not to fight one another. The sane argument proved so effective that instead of exchanging blows the enemy Generals exchanged hats. Jean Baptiste withdrew his astonished army ; and it is not told how Salvador accounted for his bloodless victory at headquarters.

He certainly lost no prestige ; for his son, Balthazar, found favour with the next Nawab of Bhopāl and also helped the English against bandit Marathas, thereby at last procuring the long-desired treaty of alliance between the East India Company and Bhopāl. Thus—by the devious route of this romantic family history—we revert to Sikander Begum and Sebastian, son of Balthazar, who held the office of Prime Minister in the dark and critical year of 1857. Through his great influence over the Begum, he kept her staunch to her treaty of alliance with Britain ; though her own mother—who had long since abdicated—was pressing her to join the mutineers. And her adherence was more than passive. She sheltered and rescued numbers of white men and women who fled to Bhopāl, through dangers and terrors indescribable, and found themselves amazedly among friends.

That remarkable family still remains intact, with here and there an Indian wife ; still remains Christian in faith and outlook.

No member of it played a special part during the rule of Sikander's daughter Shah Jahān, who is chiefly remembered for her building of the first State railways and the making of many roads ; hampered though she was, in private and public life, by the vicissitudes of her romantic but ill-advised second marriage.

' A wandering minstrel ' he, with little to commend him beyond good looks and a gift for writing Persian lyrics. With or without design, he captured the heart of a veiled Begum, who could succumb to his charm without herself being seen. Any idea of marriage seemed unthinkable ; but when a Queen loves, there are ways and means to the desired end. A small post at court kept her in touch with him ; and step by step she assisted him till he became one of her officials. In that position, marriage, however inadvisable, seemed a practical proposition : and the minstrel-into-officer had no quarrel with the proposed change of status. As minstrel, he may have had some merit. As Nawab-consort he proved a lamentable failure. Many years younger than his infatuated Queen, he proceeded to make the most of a position that would end with her death. Unscrupulously he filled his pockets ; robbing and torturing those who were not persuadable ; and so complete was his ascendancy over the Begum that he alienated her from her eldest daughter, Sultan Jahān. For years she and her husband were almost prisoners in their own palace.

Finally he became virtual leader of Bhopāl, though it was laid

down that no Nawab-consort should have any say in State affairs.
The reversed position amounted to a scandal.

The British Resident could do no other than advise that the
adventurer be deposed. The A.G.G. (Agent to the Governor-
General) backed up the suggestion ; and the Government of
India proceeded to consider the matter.

While that leisurely process was still in hand, the Viceroy of
the day, Lord Lytton, held a reception at Simla for Central Indian
Chiefs ; and among them came the discredited Nawab, representing his purdah wife.

Lord Lytton, himself a poet, became enthusiastic over a
lyrical Indian Prince, who was no Prince. Either not realising
or ignoring his discreditable record, he greeted the stranger with
fervour as ' my brother poet ' and impulsively embraced him in
Eastern fashion, to the disgust of high English officials, who were
present at the scene.

If the Nawab felt elated, his elation was short-lived ; and the
Viceroy found himself, not long after, in the awkward predicament
of having to sanction the deposition of his ' brother poet '.

The delicate affair was carried out by a deputation from Simla :
a surprise visit on the ill-matched pair ; a summons to attend a
ceremonial durbar, with all officers of the State. There a further
surprise was administered in the form of a viceregal decree
depriving the Nawab-consort of his titles and salute ; forbidding
him to have any further concern with the Bhopāl affairs.

The shock to both hit the devoted Begum hard. Stoutly she
upheld her worthless lord and did all in her power to have him
reinstated. But the decree was never annulled : and the Nawab
—wrecked in health by every kind of excess—conveniently settled
matters by dying years before his time.

His ill deeds, unluckily, did not perish with him. He left the
Begum and her daughter Sultan Jahān still estranged : a tragedy
for both, acutely felt by the daughter, who writes of it with sorrow
in a translated account of her own and earlier times in Bhopāl.

At the ripe age of forty-three she herself was installed as fourth
successive Begum ; and almost at once a cruel sorrow darkened
her life. Her own Nawab husband, to whom she was devoted,
died suddenly in his sleep only a few months after her accession.
His help had been invaluable ; her hostile and extravagant step-
father having left the State almost bankrupt. Now, bereft and
heartbroken, she must needs carry on alone with a Minister too
jealous of his own prerogative to afford her any real support ;
while all her old enemies were busy sowing seeds of discontent
and suspicion.

In her sorrow and many difficulties, she had the very real comfort of three young sons, who seemed likely to break the curious feminine sequence of more than a century. Undaunted by grief and loneliness, sustained by her heritage of statecraft, ability and courage, she consecrated her life to one purpose—the redemption of half-ruined Bhopāl. To her lasting credit she did succeed in launching the State on a new era of prosperity. Strictly maintaining her veiled apartness, she chose good men to work for the great end in view.

Again, soon after her accession, she was deeply and sincerely grieved, by the death of Queen Victoria—that far, unseen woman-ruler who had acquired such an abiding hold on the imagination of India. From the highest ranks to the simplest villagers, she had become in their eyes—through her long reign—almost an immortal. Many simple folk, even to-day, believe that she still rules in London ; that through her alone they enjoy the security of tending their cattle and sowing their crops in peace.

Sultan Jahān herself wrote, in sorrow and admiration, ' The grief that shook India, as the distressing news fled from district to district, from village to village, is not for words to express. Nor is it for my humble pen to recount the virtues of one whom the world has acknowledged as a peerless woman, a peerless Queen. The story of her life and its example will be an heritage to mankind for all time.'

Queen Victoria herself might have appreciated so generous a tribute from an Indian Queen hardly less revered in her degree.

From first to last education was her watchword, more especially for women. Girls, in Bhopāl, were to be educated as thoroughly as boys ; though her woman wisdom insisted on more than book learning for the mothers of the race. They must possess knowledge of household management, so that their feminine duties might be carried out with intelligence and skill. Yet at the same time she insisted on their remaining *purdah nashin*. She went so far as to open a school for well-born girls on those broad lines ; and among conventional-minded mothers disapproval was rife ; obstructions multiplied. But they were dealing with a woman who knew what was best for her people and intended that they should have it. So by degrees the scheme was accepted, partly because of its Royal origin. Forty girls, under nine, attended in the first year ; closed carriages being provided for the daily outing —itself an event in their restricted lives.

More serious was the difficulty of finding women teachers equally versed in English and Urdu ; but even that problem was eventually solved by the ever-resourceful Sultan Jahān.

Though immersed in State activities, she found time to undertake the care and training of her own children ; so strongly she deprecated the custom of leaving them constantly with paid ayahs. The teaching of her youngest son Hamidullah—her destined successor—she began precisely when he was four years, four months and four days old, proof that even her vigorous brain was still under the spell of numbers, prevalent everywhere in the East. Clearly she recognised that India could not be fruitfully served either by mission or Government schools, however well intentioned. She would have her own system for training the young ; a system that should be free from priestly domination, especially among Hindus.

A popular Brahmin saying gives the measure of their repressive influence : ' Educate a woman and you put a knife into the hands of a monkey '. That knife, they had good reason to know, would be used to cut the cords that had bound Hindu women, spiritually and mentally, for centuries. In fact ' the monkey '—writes Freda Hauswirth—' seems now to be getting in an effective retort to its male tormentor ; and when the monkey behind the knife begins to talk—woe to the Brahmins ! '

The importance of woman as a social factor has percolated very slowly into the male Indian brain ; but the pace has quickened in the last decade. There remains a quiet reserve of strength, still untapped, in millions of Indian women, that bears within itself untold promise for the days and years to come.

In Moslem Bhopāl there was no priestly opposition to the Begum's bold education schemes ; no hindrance except her own insistence on the purdah rule of life, for her subjects as for herself. Honestly she admitted that purdah did not form an active part of Moslem religious ordinance. It was mainly a matter of local considerations. To her mind, its chief motive in India was to prevent undesirable intercourse between men and women—not foreigners, but men of their own race, whose conception of women and of woman must be readjusted—a change already in progress—before free mixed intercourse can become as natural as it is in the West. The significant fact remains that not all Eastern women desire that form of freedom by any means ; nor do those who have closely associated with the cultured *purdah nashin*, and have come to recognise the profound influence of the zenana, the honour in which the veiled woman is held and the peculiar, disciplined charm of Indian family life. Its formalities can be overdone and become irksome to lively temperaments. But it does confer on the emerging, educated Indian woman a spirit of dignity and responsibility that are not least among her assets in a world of shaken standards and lost footholds.

History proves that many Eastern women have lived fruitful and influential lives behind the veil : nowhere more so than in the purdah Palace of Bhopāl.

Her Highness Sultan Jahān spoke her mind on the subject at a woman's conference. ' If the system were readjusted ', she said, ' and placed on a more reasonable footing, most of its evil effects on female education would vanish ; while, at the same time, we should be spared from the kind of situation that is causing anxiety in the West.'

That last expresses the view of a good many Indian women, who do not invariably envy or approve of the Western woman and her works.

So the latest Begum, for all her mental energy and breadth of vision, retained her self-imposed apartness : and in later years became known as ' the sanctuary of purdah '. Yet she travelled widely and attended many ceremonial occasions ; her short, stocky figure shrouded in a *burkha* or *yashmak*—of lilac and silver embroidery almost to the knees ; or, at high functions—like the Coronation Durbar—she would be draped in gold from head to foot. Over this shimmering formless garment, she wore ropes of pearls and her glittering order the G.C.S.I. ; the gathered folds fantastically surmounted by a jewelled crown, mainly of diamonds. And beneath it all—a curious anomaly—she would often be wearing a Western dress. From her draperies there would emerge a small, shapely hand, for greeting ; and the eyes behind her meshed eye-holes, observed more than those of many average women who, having eyes, see not. Her soft yet deep-toned voice —the face invisible—had a curiously detached quality ; and from the small shrouded figure there emanated an impression of dignity, not only Royal, but racial ; the innate dignity of India, based on a patience and endurance that the West can never fully understand ; even as it can never fully share India's frankly expressed interest in things of the mind and spirit.

In her talk with English friends the Begum was lively and witty, shrewd and knowledgeable ; preferring her own language where it was understood ; and often removing the *yashmak* with those whom she came to know well. Her wide range of interests, that made her a delightful companion, included a taste for water-colour painting rare among Indian women ; though few changes to-day are of better augury than the revival of all the arts among them. Music, singing and dancing, too long associated with the courtesan or the professional performer, are at last taking their rightful place among cultured women of to-day—and to-morrow : the first devotees of art since ancient days.

The Begum's staunch adherence to the Empire and recognition of India's debt to British rule were well expressed soon after her installation : ' Since the year 1857, the States and peoples of India have enjoyed a period of peace and progress without parallel in the history of that country. Under the British Government they possess freedom and security such as the rule of no other world power could give them. The only drawback arises from the fact that, after a time, too much prosperity led the people to indolence and pleasure-seeking, which unfitted them for work in their State. As a result, too many important posts, especially in the Army, had to be filled by outsiders ; and the only road out of that impasse— as out of most others—is the highway of better education.'

In pursuit of it she never flagged: and later she drew from the A.G.G. of Central India a tribute as sincere as it was richly deserved.

' It is my experience,' he said, on a public occasion, ' as of many others, that to know her Highness better is to respect her more. And for this reason : not only is she a lady richly endowed with the virtues of her sex ; but, as Ruler, she can vie in ability and energy with any Chief in India.'

High praise indeed : but not one whit too high, as most of her fellow Chiefs would admit.

In 1904 she made the sacred pilgrimage to Mecca ; a journey of many difficulties and hardships, yet the crowning ambition of every Moslem woman. There is a quiet nobility and courage in the figure of an old, untravelled woman, shrouded in her *burkha*, reared within the shelter of purdah, self-schooled to face the crowded port, the steamer, the unknown Arabs of the desert. Thither went the Begum Sultan Jahān, simply as a pilgrim woman among scores of humble worshippers. And in 1911 she crossed ' the black water ' to England for the coronation of King George Fifth, afterwards attending the Great Delhi Durbar of that year.

Then came 1914 with its call to arms ; and her response was more than equal to that of any princely ally among them all.

Nearing seventy—a great age in the East—she at once offered personal service ; and would fain have led her own troops into action. Though that could not be, her example and her zeal for the British cause ' served as a torch throughout the realms of Islam '. Like the Nizām of Hyderabad, she issued a manifesto, not only to her subjects but to all Indian Moslems, urging them to defend the Empire and maintain its rights, an injunction loyally obeyed. Countless were the good services she rendered during those critical four years of war. But thereafter age began to tell upon her, weighed down as she was, in heart and spirit, by the loss of her two elder sons. Wisely, after twenty-two years of beneficent rule, she abdicated in favour of the one that remained —Nawabzada Hamidullah Khan.

Four years longer she lived, more or less in seclusion, loved and honoured to the last, proud of the distinction, accorded to her by King George, of a personal seventeen-gun salute, as if she were still a Queen.

So she passed, leaving Bhopāl the richer in every way for her memorable reign ; leaving to it also the first ruling Nawab since 1844.

Her son, a man of fine and resolute character, is proving in every way a true successor of his remarkable mother—and that is saying a great deal. From early manhood he has given much time and thought to politics and the perplexing problems of an All-India Federation. He has played a distinguished part in the Chamber of Princes, as the one Moslem Chief in an assembly that is mainly Hindu ; and has already become a leading figure among the younger statesmen of India. At the Round Table Conference he was in accord with the group of his fellow Princes known as the ' Big Eight '. And, in addition to his ruling qualities, he is famed everywhere as a polo player of genius, an all-round sportsman and a brilliant shot. He shoots tigers with a ·270. He will walk straight up to a wounded one, and finish him off with the same weapon.

He rules Bhopāl on liberal lines, while maintaining his Oriental point of view. His revenue is administered by a British civilian ; his military portfolio is held by a British Colonel. Here, as in Hyderabad, the two races are on a very friendly footing. There is an affinity of outlook and attitude to life between the English-man and the Moslem that makes for cordial working in unison. There is affinity also, of another kind, with the princely Rajputs, through their aristocratic and soldierly traditions—links of mind and character that have been of inestimable value in the past ; and in the future, with the advent of changing relations, may prove more valuable than ever.

The Nawab himself has a strong personal leaning towards English tastes and English ways, as his Palace life bears witness. A man of courage and common sense, he speaks his mind vigor-ously, but without rhetoric, on all important subjects ; and his considered opinion carries weight, as it deserves to do. Frankly he recognises that, in the A B C of progress, A stands for educa-tion, B for social and C for political advance ; frankly indicts an irresponsible democracy as ' the greatest danger to any country '.

He would far rather improve upon the existing edifice than scrap it in favour of theories not indigenous to the land.

His enchanting capital, dominated by the Palace, is reflected in the Lake already described ; and even its more modern buildings are in keeping with the best of India's tradition. His forest jungle—inhabited by one of the most primitive tribes extant—gives him and his guests fine scope for sport, big, game and small. His people expect, and receive, good government, which for them implies a continual personal interest in their affairs. These may be seemingly trivial ; but the right kind of trifles make life worth living. And, for the peasants—backbone of every kingdom—the liveableness of life hangs on their work, their huts and the scraps of land that are their all. ' It is better to be too little governed than too much ' is the wise verdict of India, beginning already to foresee that too much government will be her portion if ever Congress gains its political ends.

By some curious persistence of fate the woman-rule sequence, broken by the Nawab Hamidullah Khan, will be repeated at his death. Again there is no son to follow on ; but there is a notable daughter who seems to have inherited the mind and spirit of her famous grandmother, in ultra-modern guise ; and she has now been recognised as her father's heir. Already she is reported to be an active force in the State ; and she is probably the most original figure in India to-day. Small and short, with olive skin and cropped hair, she rides and shoots and plays polo, drives her own car and flies a fast 'plane. Yet, with all her taste for sport, with the muscles and daring of a man, she has the soul of a musician. To see her at the piano is to see her transformed. Her brief marriage proved a failure ; and restrictions of purdah are not for her. No Begum in a *burkha* will ever again rule Bhopāl. The lead she has already given to the woman move-ment will gain ground when she comes into her kingdom.

Her mother, the Begum, is a very charming woman who runs the attractive Bhopāl Palace much like an English country house, plays tennis with her daughters, joins them in their Girl Guide activities and other social work of modernised India. They are lively, intelligent young women delighting in any up-to-date, impromptu form of sport. A favourite diversion is to dash out after dark, with their cars, into the forest and shoot stags by spot-light, an exciting test of marksmanship : one girl holding out a powerful torch, the other, with rifle poised, awaiting a rustle or a shadowy form to give her a chance of catching her stag. Wary and swift, the nervous creatures are no easy target ; and a cloud of dust from the car may abet their chances of escape from these all-round, competent girls of very modern India.

The sharp contrast between their lives, their characters and those of the gentle-mannered, secluded women of two generations ago, is in its way more revealing than any political upheaval ; witness to the living force of ' change unchanging ' at work in every phase of Indian life. Even now in many regions, as in Udaipur, the old order lingers ; women are still hampered by the dead hand of the past. But more and more, as in Bhopāl, they are freely and actively of the present ; and on the whole in very promising guise. For the teaching of India's philosophy is reflected in the practical wisdom of her people : and her modern women, though forsaking the ordained way of abnegation, may yet find fresh ways to realise the age-old ideal of ' Sita—perfect wife and mother '.

SOUTHERN INDIA:
LAND OF TEMPLES, LAKES AND PALMS

The symbol of Rajputana is the rising sun. This is the country of the horned moon . . . an India of paddy fields, palm trees and thick jungles, where elephants move silently from sunlight to shadow, and tigers slink through the long grass . . . this is the South, where old, old magic survives.—MICHAEL PYM.

MYSORE:
THE RULER-SAINT

I

THE Ruler-Saint—Sir Krishnaraja Wádiyar Bahadur—was a man of rare personality; one that must dominate any account of modern Mysore, though he died regrettably in August 1940 at the early age of fifty-six.

Like Sir Shahu of Kolhapur, his death was a grave loss to India, no less than to Mysore.

He combined in himself the arresting contrast of a Ruler steeped in advanced ideas, in education, politics and industry, while he yet remained an orthodox Hindu in faith and life. More than any other Prince, it was said, he symbolised the ancient Hindu ideal of a King. Below middle height, but slim and very erect, he carried himself with a Royal air and dignity that added a cubit to his stature; and his manner had the innate reserve of Royalty without a hint of its pomp. There was little of the typical East in his finely-cut features, in the small mouth and beautiful eyes, with their hint of sadness. And his outward charm was matched by the beauty of a mind that found its deepest satisfaction in religion and music and a more than filial devotion to his wonderful mother, from whom he derived much of his saintly personality.

During his minority—for he came young to the throne—she had ruled Mysore capably from behind the purdah: and thereafter she still remained a vital force, dominating her family by sheer intellect and character. Few decisions in State affairs were made till the Maharaja had submitted them to his mother. Her clever, ascetic face and brilliant dark eyes were remarkable even among many distinguished Indian women. Like her son a devout Hindu, she yet shared his progressive views and schemes that lifted Mysore to pre-eminence among the many model States of Royal India.

The Prince himself, inherently a saint, combined culture and breeding with skill in all forms of sport. In his young days a fine polo-player and horseman, he enjoyed riding to hounds over the rolling uplands of Ootacamund, his summer home. At fifty he still played a first-rate game of tennis, racquets and squash. But his interests centred chiefly in things of the mind and spirit. An exquisite critic of the fine arts, he was also a skilled player on the piano, the violin and 'cello, taking most delight in severely classical trios and quartets of the masters. So there was much music in the Palace, the best of both kinds, Eastern and Western ; organ recitals and a string band for classics. His English guests were always treated to concerts in the noble music-room, colonnaded with pillars of blue and gold, its doors inlaid with ivory ; one end devoted to the Maharaja's private collection of musical instruments. Two archways, hung with cloth of gold, screened an inner room where the Mysore purdah ladies and their friends were assembled to hear the concerts and look through crescent slits at all that passed in the world outside their own.

As the Maharaja grew older, State affairs and the demands of duty too often prevented him from giving all the time and attention he would fain have given to the art he loved. There is no record of any other Indian Prince so musical in taste and in accomplishment as His Highness the late Maharaja of Mysore : and in spiritual quality it would be hard to find his match, almost ascetic as he was in his simplicity of personal tastes and way of life. It is worth quoting a sincere tribute paid to him, in early years, by Sir Stuart Fraser, K.C.S.I., originally his tutor and afterwards, for five years, Resident in Mysore.

' The Maharaja's quiet strength of character, his sense of duty to his people and high conception of all it involved, marked him out, even during minority, as one destined to make a name among the greater Princes of India. His people, it is true, have a rough idea of his devotion to duty and to their welfare ; but only those in close touch with him can appreciate what it really entails in constant thought and high aspiration, constant activity in a hundred ways.'

And few worked in closer touch with him than His Moslem Dewān—or Prime Minister—Sir Mirza Ismail, who has been described as a Dewān after His Highness' own heart. A Mussulman of Persian descent, he was chosen, in boyhood, to work as a student with the Maharaja. Later he graduated from Bangalore Central College, and at once he entered the Mysore Civil Service. Only three years after that he was taken on to the Maharaja's personal staff : and so valuable was his help in every way, so genuine his devotion to the State and to the Prince, his closest friend, that eventually he was advanced to the more intimate post of Private Secretary—a step towards the highest honour of all.

As Dewān he had full scope to prove his quality and capacity for handling State affairs ; Prince and Dewān worked together in complete accord, rare enough in any case, and the more significant where one was an orthodox Hindu and the other a Mussulman— wide-minded, singularly free from communal bias.

Later still, at the Round Table Conference in London—representing Mysore and Southern India—he proved himself a man who would never sacrifice great issues to lesser loyalties, a man whose democratic outlook was balanced and tempered by inherited aristocratic tradition.

The Maharaja himself, though a religious devotee, took a broad view of life and politics, spending one-fifth of his revenue on education, and insisting on equal opportunities for all his subjects, even for the backward classes. At one time an ' Untouchable ' student was top scholar in Mysore College.

More potent even than a spirit of benevolence is the spirit of personal sympathy to win and hold the heart of a people ; as witness an episode quoted by Sir William Barton.

He and his wife, driving across country to a tiger shoot, in a bullock tonga with the Maharaja, passed through a small village, where they were greeted by an eager little crowd, clapping vigorously, as Indians do, where an English crowd would cheer.

The leading man advanced towards the cart holding up a portrait of His Highness garlanded with flowers. Those behind him salaamed profoundly and again clapping rattled through the crowd.

His Highness checked the cart and explained, with apologies, to Sir William that the villagers were giving thanks to him on account of a school he had provided for them out of his private purse, when their request for one had been turned down by the education department because the village was considered too insignificant to be favoured with means of learning. That their own Maharaja had thought otherwise and had himself given them the coveted school was a simple act of kindness that would endear him to them for ever.

It was but one of many, typical of the spirit that pervaded the

N

whole Palace family ; a family so ancient that its origin is shrouded
in legend ; but the traditional romance that links it with two young
fourteenth-century Rajputs is so generally believed that it may
fairly be accepted as history.

It is said that a feudal chief of that time, holding the small
principality of Mysore, wandered off into the forest, in a characteristically Indian fit of mental aberration, leaving his wife and
young daughter without protection. A hereditary enemy, seeing
his chance, demanded the daughter as bride, and threatened to
invade Mysore and carry her off if the request were refused.

The two helpless and reluctant women were at his mercy ; or
so it seemed, till two young Rajputs came riding out of the landscape, in fairy-tale fashion, seeking adventure. What more congenial to youth and Rajput chivalry than the chance to rescue a
distressed damsel from a dreaded suitor ? Promptly the two
brothers proclaimed themselves as her champions, rallied the
State's forces and invaded the would-be invader. Him they slew
and annexed his land. Then did the elder brother marry the
grateful daughter of Mysore and through her he raised up a new
dynasty for the State that grew eventually into a kingdom two-
thirds the size of England.

The name Mysore, like the family, has an ancient and legendary
origin in accord with the ultra-Hindu background of this ultra-
progressive and well-governed State. It derives from *makesh*, a
buffalo, and *assurna*, a demon ; the two words telescoped, to
signify the slaying of the buffalo demon by Mysore's patron
goddess Chamundi—a manifestation of the terrible goddess Kali,
who still demands the blood of sacrifice on her altar stones. In
these days it is mainly the blood of goats, the abomination of
human sacrifices having been long since abolished.

But Chamundi radiates a potent influence from her temple
set upon the hill that bears her name : an isolated granitoid mass
three thousand feet high, its last thousand feet rising abruptly
above the model city at its base ; legendary past struck sharp on
progressive present, the twin elements of Mysore.

No forests mantle the rocky hillsides ; only the grey-green of
jungle and scrub, patterned with spiral roads that lead to houses,
temples and palaces commanding views over the plain where lesser
hills rise like ant-heaps here and there. Its crowning temple is
reached by a thousand stone steps worn slippery by the feet of
many thousand pilgrims : a form of ascent favoured only by
devotees. The undevout visitor prefers a carrying chair.

Up and up, past Shiva's sacred bull, an impressive monster,
sixteen feet high, hewn out of solid rock nearly three hundred

years ago. Here the patient bearers take a brief rest. Then up again to the towered temple gateway, carved with a procession of figures, human and vital, symbolising the creative profusion of Nature. Into the actual shrine none but Hindus may enter. Only a glimpse of it can be seen beyond the square-sided silver pillars : a glimpse of the seated goddess, jewelled and garlanded, weirdly lit by the flare of torches ; her attendant priests moving to the sound of strange music in their daily ritual of worship.

Beyond the temple, in a lofty shed, stands the lion car, twenty-five feet high ; the lion rampant, breathing flame ; on his back a seat for the goddess, who will be placed on it under a gold-fringed umbrella for the October procession, the great religious festival of the year.

Mysore State has been described as ' one of earth's magic regions ', a land of superlatives : mighty peaks, primeval forests, waterfalls of unequalled height, temples adorned with unrivalled carving, birthplace of the fabulous King Chandragupta, a contemporary of Alexander.

Mysore contains the only gold-mine worth mentioning in India. Its coffee and silks are known throughout the world. The silk industry, in fact, ranks only second to the gold-mining. Great mulberry trees, home of the silkworm, cover 55,000 acres ; an area that increases every year.

The country itself is full of varied charm. Its rolling uplands form a high plateau roughly two thousand feet above the sea, flanked by outlying buttresses of the Ghauts rising, southward, to the Nilgiri Hills. Outbreaks of rock in ridges recall the Deccan features of Hyderabad. Magnificent forests, west and south, provide big game shooting of the best—bison, elephant, tiger : a form of sport more congenial to the Prince's guests than to their host. So genuine was his love of all animals that he could take little pleasure in killing them ; though tigers—prolific as cats—must be kept within limits if they were not to ravage the land and become a terror to isolated villages. The upland climate enjoys two short rainy seasons and a temperate warmth in summer, followed by a winter of endless sunshine, with a welcome nip in the air early and late. Mysore's capital—a model city *in excelsis*—lacks the glamour, the romance and heroic associations of Rajput cities : but, comparisons apart, the impression varies with the eye of the beholder.

Here is the view of an enthusiast on the subject : ' Roads a hundred feet wide are bordered with shade-giving trees and pavements. Western ways are only adopted in part. No trams or buses or overhead wires deface those noble thoroughfares

Though much of the city is modern, it is not garish. Many fine old houses remain with their massive carved doorways and windows. " Hygiene enthroned, beauty deposed " is not everywhere the case. Picturesque parks and gardens are thronged with citizens hardly less picturesque. Too many Eastern men have discarded their national costume ; but the women, more wisely, retain the gracious curves and delicate colours of the *sari*, a form of dress unsurpassed in the world. People constantly exclaim, " The most beautiful city ever seen ! " But this is fairyland.'

And here, for contrast, is the impression made on eyes and mind more deeply imbued with Indian India, an American woman who had lived some years with Indians as one of themselves.

' Mysore ', she writes, ' is the show State of India, " the place you simply must see ". But it seems hardly a living place. The city itself has been aptly described as " fairyland, deserted by the fairies ". It is perfectly beautiful as a setting for the wonderful pageants that are staged by the Maharaja, for State festivals and processions, attended by thousands of visitors ; but it is all too clean, too ordered to seem perfectly true ' : an impression confirmed by other writers and travellers.

To capture Mysore's true Eastern flavour and historic interest, one must look beyond the city to Chamundi's Hill ; and again beyond that to the great carved monolith of Nanjāngud, and the ancient temple at Vijāya Narayāna : a remnant of far-off days when Mysore was part of a vast Hindu Empire in the South. An immense rock-statue of the Jain apostle Gomāta, fifty feet high, has towered over the countryside for a thousand years, that in the sight of Hindu India are but as yesterday.

For a thousand years Melkote, the High Fortress, has crowned the holy hill of Yadugiri beyond Seringapatām. The upward road climbs to the colossal Gopāl Raya gateway, passing two clear small lakes, the Twin Sisters, fern-fringed and hung with blossoming trees. Thence it drops again to the walled Fort and its famous fountain. But even here one cannot escape the incongruous clash of present and past.

Hard by the ancient temple car, a Boy Scout may be tinkering at his motor cycle. Huts of old Mysore, holes in the roof for light and air, cower beside a brand-new weaver's house, complete with loom, pet dog and parrot, and a very new baby in charge of a guardian great-grandmother. Larger buildings, bearing the modern legend ' Bus Office ', ' Municipal Office ', ' Co-operative Bank ', form an incongruous background to a stately Brahmin woman in the silken *sari* of the centuries, a small Scout beside her exulting in shoes and stockings, shorts and shirt, badge and whistle : a fragment of future India.

On the granite throne of the hill-top stands the Narasinha temple ; three hundred and sixty carved steps, tiers and tiers of grotesque prancing figures. From its massive gateway one looks out over miles and miles of rice fields and gleaming lakes, homesteads of Melkote, tiled and mellowed ; here and there a splash of red where some new house has been built. The temple lakes reflect its many shrines. Butterflies of every tint and tone quiver in the level sun rays. Clear along the sky-line a wash of softened blues and mauves indicates the hills of Coorg.

The sun dips and disappears. Through the evening mist comes the clang of a temple bell, blare of music and patter of feet. Lights flicker here and there till they outline the temples, lakes and dwellings. Night falls, swift and sudden ; but the fairy lights keep up their dance, ' like a last flight of elfin wings '.

It is time to descend from the High Fortress, from shrines and lakes and the dream of ' a day that is dead '.

2

Between that dream-day of ancient empire and this immediate Model State lies the inevitable period of Mogul conquest and dominion that has set its own imperishable seal on Mysore as elsewhere.

Whoever has a taste for the perspective of history, a haunting sense of the past, must drive out to Seringapatām with its Moslem architecture that so finely expresses, in concept and design, the simplicity and strength of that virile creed. It expresses also—in forts, *musjids*,[1] tombs—the emphasis of Islam on battle, worship, death, in contrast with the Hindu emphasis on life and creation, symbolised by the overcrowded frieze or fresco, often to the detriment of proportion and beauty. Impressive, alike to the eye and imagination, is the noble domed mausoleum built over the tomb of the famous (or infamous) Tippu Sultan, son of the great Hyder Ali, the Mussolini of his day : two redoubtable leaders who for nearly half the eighteenth century defied British arms and dominated Mysore.

No colour here, no riot of carving, but the stark simplicity of black and white marble interpatterned with exquisite effect ; doors and pillars of black marble inlaid with ivory : a wonder work of beauty and craftsmanship.

The American writer, who failed to appreciate Mysore city,

[1] Mosques.

found in that stately mausoleum an inspiration of ineffable peace ' like a clear light about the silent building ' . . . strange aftermath of a man who can have known little peace in his tempestuous life, and who was killed while fighting against the hated English.

Yet another mausoleum, in the garden of Tippu's summer Palace, was built by him over his father and mother. The Palace itself, Sarya Daulat (Wealth of the Sea), is a building of rare and remarkable beauty, its walls adorned in richly coloured arabesques that rival the Palace of Ispahan. There is no other work of the same kind and quality in India. With its gardens and the two mausoleums, it breathes an air of tragedy and splendour quite other than that of ancient Hindu Mysore.

Alone, outside the Fort, there stands a very different shrine of tragic memories : a commonplace bungalow, empty and deserted since the distant day—a hundred and fifty years ago— when it was the home of a certain Colonel Scott, with his wife and two daughters.

One day, it is said, he returned after a brief absence to find all three of them dead from cholera. Stunned by the shock and shattered with grief, he walked blindly away from that house of death—and was never seen again. Nor has anyone since lived in that sorrowful bungalow.

Empty and desolate, there it stands, in complete preservation, not having even attained the dignity of a ruin. Nor do even the ghosts of that sad family wander through its once homely rooms and verandahs. There stands the old-fashioned Indian furniture, watching the years go by. The rooms are high and cool. Steps leading down to the river are framed on either side with small stone pavilions. More empty it seems, that shrine of home life and sudden death, than Tippu's tomb and the mausoleum he built for his father. They shelter at least the dust of greatness.

It was about the middle of the eighteenth century that Hyder Ali, an adventurer of genius, emerged from the ranks of the Mysore army, made violent history and became virtual dictator over the Raja and his people for more than thirty years. So strangely and so often do great men seem to arise, as it were, from nothing, the source of their innate genius hidden from human ken.

As a soldier he proved himself absolutely fearless : and his courage, allied to skill in battle, led to rapid promotion, with results that may have astonished him no less than his fellows. By sheer brains and daring and a natural gift for leadership— the insignia of greatness—he raised himself from a mere soldier to the highest position in Mysore. He restored its finances. He built up its army and made it in every way greater than it had ever been before. As *de facto* head of the State, he maintained the old Hindu dynasty in name and form, even as the King of Italy has been maintained by the Fascist leader. There was still a Raja of Mysore ; but, like his modern counterpart, he was eclipsed by the virtual ruler and greater man.

In organising the army, Hyder Ali owed much to the French and their officers, whom he greatly liked ; a fact that brought him up against their rivals, the English. When war broke out between them, he was pledged to a friendly neutrality at least ; but his warning to Madras that he would defend the French ports was ignored by a Government for whom its own countrymen had no good word to utter ; a Government that brought discredit on the whole East India Company. Its moral atmosphere at the time was briefly stigmatised as ' pestilential ' ; an adjective approved by the historian as ' felicitously exact '.

Hyder Ali himself supplied a scathing analysis of the Company's political record ; adding the terse comment, ' I leave you to judge on whose part engagements and promises have been broken '.

Thereafter, inevitably, ' incidents ' multiplied, till in 1780 he launched into open war, flooding the province with his armies that surged up to the very walls of Madras. Edmund Burke, in his vivid fashion, described the scene of woe and desolation those armies left in their wake : ' All the horrors of war before known or heard of were as nothing to that new havoc, which blasted every field, consumed every house, destroyed every temple ' : a foretaste of ' total war ' as waged in the civilised twentieth century.

A small British force, launched against Hyder Ali under Colonel Baillie, was unbelievably deserted by an officer of repute sent to relieve him—an event seldom recorded in the annals of Great Britain. The unfortunate Colonel Baillie was, in consequence, overpowered and his troops massacred ; few only were reserved for an imprisonment whose horrors were to become notorious. That tragic fiasco left Hyder Ali complete master of the Carnatic ; a serious threat to British power in India.

At so critical a juncture, England was fortunate in being represented by a daring and brilliant Governor-General, Warren Hastings. With equal courage and wisdom, he took the war into his own hands ; placed Sir Eyre Coote, India's most competent soldier, in command of the Madras army, and himself made overtures to the inimical Dutch. These failed, and war with Holland was added to his many perplexities. Sir Eyre Coote, in Madras, defeated immense Mysore armies : but Tippu Sultan—also in the field—destroyed a force of two thousand, while the French navy, under a distinguished seaman, appeared off the coast.

Followed a conflict of many vicissitudes, of desperate fighting by land and sea. The English in their astonishing fashion survived several indecisive sea fights ; a second force, despatched by Hastings, backed up Sir Eyre Coote ; and, as matters began to improve, the unexpected happened.

The formidable Hyder Ali suddenly fell ill and died, which brought the whole affair to a standstill—for a time.

Though that born leader left a son to inherit his war and his hatred of the English, the younger man was not comparable to a father whose greatness was undeniable. Hyder Ali, faults and all, possessed the vision and the tolerance of an Akbar. Even of the hostile English he wrote that he had ' committed a great error ' in making them his enemies, on account of dissatisfactions that by no means justified four years of war.

' The defeat of many Baillies and Braithwaites ', he sagely admitted, ' will not destroy them. I could ruin their resources by land but I can never dry up the sea.' That has been the crux of all English enemies, even to this day of air fleets that seem to have rendered her no longer an island.

From Hyder Ali, Tippu Sultan inherited an inconclusive war and an implacable hatred of the English, who made peace, of a sort, with him two years later, on a basis of restored territory and prisoners. But to both sides it was clear that there could be neither true peace nor safety till one or other power had been destroyed.

The British had ' lost face ' through the ill-repute and actual misdeeds of their Madras Government : and Tippu, though by no means the equal of his father, was a man of character, energy and ability. Unlike his father, he was bigoted and fanatically hostile to the British, whom he treated, as prisoners, with abominable cruelty. Again unlike his father, he completely shelved the Raja and his family ; kept them in durance and proclaimed himself Sultan of Mysore. As a Ruler he did great things for the State ; but he could not remain at peace with the British. Shorn of half his dominions by defeat, he cherished against them an inveteracy of hatred that would end only with his life.

' Mysore ', writes the historian, ' had shown itself by far the most formidable foe the Company had met : no subsequent wars, not even the Mutiny, were to bring them so close to ruin as Hyder's had done.' And now there remained the tremendous task of placating or making an end of his successor. Hyderabad, dissatisfied with the French, had accepted, *faute de mieux*, an alliance with the British : an alliance recognised by Warren Hastings as the keystone of the political arch in the Deccan. Remained Mysore and the Marathas, bent on Empire : a tug of war that could but be a matter of time.

Tippu must be dealt with first ; no light affair. An attempt at making terms with him failed—not surprisingly. The terms were too harsh : the ceding of his whole Malabar sea coast ; and the dismissal of all his French element, with the admission of a British Resident by way of last straw.

Tippu, the Tiger of Mysore, would kneel to none nor could he steel himself to any further sacrifice. Sooner would he face a life-and-death encounter. But, as the onrush of his doom sounded nearer, his mind settled into a fatalistic despair. . . . In the vivid narrative of Wilks the form of Tippu stands out against a sombre lurid background ; a fate-laden atmosphere suggesting Greek tragedy.

Sir Arthur Wellesley, glorying in ' the finest army that ever took the field in India ', was using half of it to net ' the Beast of the Jungle ' at Periapatām ; the other half pushing on to Seringapatām ; a swift movement, straight to the heart.

For Tippu, the certainty of destruction loomed threateningly nearer ; and the tale of his council of war—when that certainty could not be hidden from himself or others—was deeply moving, were he ' Beast of the Jungle ' or no. Again it is Wilks who portrays that scene. ' The dark obstinacy of the Sultan's mind grew clouded with omens and conflicting superstitions. . . . Crazed with humiliation, he declared he would sooner die like a soldier than live dependent on the infidels. And a week later, like a soldier he died—desperately wounded and killed by a British private, who coveted the gold buckle of his sword belt. Even into death he carried such a vivacity of hatred that Arthur Wellesley, standing over him in the flickering torch-light, could not believe him dead till he had felt the heart and the pulse.'

His death ended the war and glutted the victor's passion for vengeance that had been intensified by a report of British prisoners strangled on Tippu's order. He was given honourable burial and his sons received kindly treatment from the Governor-General. Seringapatām itself was sacked and plundered, the troops, drunk with victory, being called to order only by the severest measures that Wellesley could inflict.

The Summer Palace, where he rested after the battle, still stands in its quiet garden, a sanctuary of peace, its inner rooms panelled in dark woods, lightened with paint and gold ; a sanctuary favoured, in his gentler moods, by the man whom they called the Tiger of Mysore. The Tiger's life—for all its dark blots of bigotry and brutality—had its glorious aspect for himself and for the State, to which he and his father left legacies that remain to this day.

With the passing of Tippu Sultan, the Moslem sway passed from Hindu Mysore for ever. Curiously enough, that bigoted Mussulman left behind him a Hindu Prime Minister who carried on ably when a reduced Mysore—two-thirds the size of England —emerged from the drastic process of dividing the spoils. The storming of Seringapatām, a brilliant feat of arms, was a success equal to Clive's victory over the French at Plassey. That success had established the Company as a power in the land. The conquest of Mysore raised England to the position of the Power Paramount, from that day forward.

Wisely and rightly the State was not annexed. The old Hindu dynasty was restored in the person of a five-year-old boy, rescued from the ruins of Seringapatām; and for twelve years—till the boy Raja turned seventeen—it remained a vassal State in charge of Tippu's very able Prime Minister. Finally it was handed over, with a handsome cash balance, to an inexperienced Prince, with little idea of finance and a large capacity for spending. The goodly sum transferred to him soon slipped through his fingers, and an attempt to mend matters by taxes and exactions merely goaded his people into open rebellion. British troops were called in to quiet the turmoil, and eventually to restore a good working government.

A carefully chosen Commission was appointed to run the State with Sir Arthur Wellesley as Commandant. Only officers were chosen and members of old Anglo-Indian [1] families; a band of right-minded, like-minded men who, in character, capacity and achievement, almost equalled the brilliant band of young men— also mainly soldiers—who settled the Punjab, fifty years later, under Sir Henry Lawrence.

India, in those days, was attracting the best that England could give. More than ever, now, it is essential that she should attract the best again. Indians have an unerring eye for character and breeding. They detected at once a falling-off in quality after the last war. ' When are the *real* Sahibs coming back to India ? ' was the question that troubled the Indian army, where ' the real Sahib ' is an asset beyond price.

Forty years of British rule set a high standard for Mysore, when at last it was handed over to a Maharaja of the Wádiyar dynasty—this time with such complete success that the State was

[1] Using the word in its true historic sense.

freed, once for all, from restrictions laid on it at the time of transfer.

Colonel His Highness Chamrajendra Wádiyar Bahadur, father of the late Maharaja, was not only a sound Ruler,. but a man of great personal charm and goodness like his son. No name was more loved and honoured throughout the land. His Ministers were well chosen: and under them the State leaped towards its present pre-eminence ; a standard maintained and surpassed by the enlightened administration of his successor, the greatest Maharaja of Mysore.

3

At the age of eleven, Sir Krishnaraja Wádiyar was installed, with his remarkable mother as Regent. He was fortunate also in his tutor, Mr. Stuart Fraser, I.C.S., a man of culture, character and experience, having already distinguished himself as tutor to the Maharajas of Kolhapur and Bhaunagar. At eighteen the young Ruler was fully installed by Lord Curzon ; his tutor exchanged for a British Private Secretary, a post initiated by the Viceroy because a succession of strong and able Dewāns had usurped an undue share of power in State affairs ; and he was rightly resolved that a Prince who promised so well should be master in his own house and State. A Private Secretary of Civil Service experience could relieve His Highness of drudgery and exercise his influence in keeping the balance of power.

Again the choice was a happy one ; and Mr. Evan Maconochie soon found himself, like Mr. Fraser, deeply interested in the attractive personality of his chief, who carried a head of singular maturity on his young shoulders. In choosing his English friends, he showed rare powers of discrimination, never making a mistake in the quality of the men and women whom he admitted to that privilege, and in handling State affairs he would take stock of his officials ' with an intuition amazing in one of his years '. But with all his unusual ripeness of judgment he was very much a boy at heart, delighting in games and sports, devoted to animals, especially to horses and dogs. A beloved terrier was his constant companion ; and his two hundred polo ponies received much personal care and attention. He had a great liking for the English, being fully aware of all that his country owed to those fifty years of British rule ; and there soon sprang up between him and his Private Secretary a genuine friendship, quickened by a shared taste for music.

Both being violinists, they keenly enjoyed their many evenings of chamber music, His Highness playing first violin. Love and understanding of music, especially the same instrument, begets a closer understanding all round, since any art loved and practised permeates the whole mind and character ; a fact still too scantily recognised in the curriculum of education.

For His Highness that close contact with the older man must have been an asset of value during the first years of his rule, that were not all smooth going by any means.

Through these early difficulties the wise young Prince pursued his purposeful deliberate way, undeterred by criticisms of the prejudiced or dissatisfied. His decisions, once made, were unalterable. His patience was inexhaustible. ' He was never the young man in a hurry ', writes Maconochie, who served with him for seven years, ' but one scheme after another of his own planning was realised with a completeness that was impressive and an entire absence of fuss or disturbance that was not less remarkable.'

Of those seven years the same writer adds that his task throughout was of absorbing interest ; and his association with a man of singular depth and strength of character was a labour of love.

It was during the Maharaja's minority that his Palace had been partly destroyed by a disastrous fire ; and the new one took more than seven years to complete. Built of massive stone, granite, porphyry and marble, all from local quarries, its details and design brought skilled craftsmen together from many parts of India : yet the whole resulting effect was impressive rather than beautiful.

Designed by an Englishman, on Hindu lines, it has not quite escaped traces of British influence that fail to harmonise with the Indian conception. Too consciously elaborate for true artistic beauty, its details of curves and carvings are admirable. Its marble architraves, with floral arabesques in softest colours, are inlaid with shavings of semi-precious stones and exquisite seashells from Madras. Decoration, everywhere decoration ; not an inch of bare space to repose the eye and mind.

Through a vast archway one enters the inner courtyard guarded by eight bronze lions flanking four flights of steps. On the first floor, between open arches, silken draperies screen off the women's ' Inside '. Above that again we reach the great Durbar Hall, beautified by a long series of arches, their pillars designed in jade green and gold ; walls and ceilings one blaze of colour. A centre door of silver and side doors in rosewood strike notes of simpler beauty ; but again the critical eye is jarred by the incongruity of an appalling Western carpet, as described by Miss Fitzroy ; ' green with a chaste design of pink roses giving too few glimpses of an inlaid marble floor ; and above it a painful roof of stained glass.

The carpet and the roof, in such a Durbar Hall, are crimes ! '
One passes with relief from the almost garish new to the oldest
treasure in the building—the Lion Throne ; a mellow harmony
of detail and design in figwood and ivory, gold and silver. What
Edward the Confessor's Chair is to the English, that throne is to
the people of Mysore. His Highness, as an individual, offers
worship to it before he ascends to his seat in full Durbar. Seated
on it, as enthroned Maharaj, he becomes to his people a very
symbol of God.

In the music-room alone one finds the simplicity and dignity
essential to undisturbed delight in ' the concourse of sweet
sounds ' : sweetest of all perhaps, a favourite duet played by
light finger-tips on two glass bowls half filled with water, the
tone varying with the amount of water, the music so liquid, the
notes so clear and true. Everywhere there is encouragement of
Indian music and the Mysore anthem became a part of the people's
lives : daily sung by thousands of school children, heralding
always the arriving and departing of their Maharaj, whose nature
was in essence kingly, not by any display of wealth and power,
but by purity of life ; by the atmosphere of dignity and restraint
in which he lived and moved ; by his self-dedication to the higher
interests of his people.

The creating of model villages for them ranked among his
favourite pursuits ; and perhaps next to music he loved mountain
scenery ; two influences that are apt to meet in one character.

Especially he loved his highland home in the Nilgiri Hills at
Ootacamund—familiarly known as ' Ooty '—the chief hill station
of South and Central India. Lacking the grandeur of the Himalayan background, it has the advantage of beautiful lakes, only
shared by Kashmir and Naini Tāl. Its wide rolling uplands
admit of carriages and cars. For hunting and golf enthusiasts
it is a station unequalled in all India. Its social atmosphere
includes Generals, Members of Council and the Government of
Madras. Here also two of India's chief Princes, Baroda and
Mysore, have their English-looking summer homes. With the
Baroda house, Woodstock, we are already familiar.

The Mysore house, Fernhill, was as English in appearance as
its name, but strictly Hindu in its way of life and the complete
purdah of its ladies. The moon-faced young Maharani had given
her Prince no son. There was no direct heir to that fine heritage :
a fatality strangely common to many of India's ruling houses. But
the Maharaja took no other wife ; so his brother—also without a
son at that time—was Yuvaraj, heir to the throne. Some years
later a son was born to him and educated as Prince by his Royal

uncle to become eventually the present Ruler of Mysore.

At ' Ooty ' the Maharaja enjoyed racing and hunting and liberal entertaining of the large English colony. Dinners and dances were admirably planned by his English Military Secretary ; but he himself could never dine with his guests, nor could his purdah ladies appear at balls or garden parties. They could only look on with interest through curtain-slits or trellised windows.

Always, at ' Ooty ', there was much to-and-fro visiting between the Mysore and Baroda families. The brilliant and travelled Baroda Maharani enjoyed lively conversations with the untravelled but actively intelligent Queen-Mother of Mysore ; the two exalted ladies talking English together as their only language in common. Like all women of South India, the Mysore ladies wore their saris with a difference ; not drawn over the head, but round the neck, in folds on the breast, and caught with a brooch on the left shoulder. These purdah Princesses delighted in attending races ; seeing, unseen, from a private retreat of their own at the back of the grand-stand ; and as eager to bet on the horses as any Western woman. Miss Tottenham would get tips for them, lay their money, and return with (or without) the result.

Those yearly informal meetings went far to deepen the close friendship, already recorded, between the two distinguished Princes, so far apart in age, so unlike in temperament ; alike only in devoting all their energies to the welfare of State and people, with signal success. Both laid special emphasis on the need for education, first, last and all the time, if industry and social advance were to be developed along the right lines.

But there remains the regrettable fact that it is possible to force the pace unduly even with so great a good as education. It is Mysore's proud boast that ' We spend one-fifth of our revenue on Education '. And herein precisely lies one of the few real difficulties encountered by this favoured State, as by the smaller yet equally over-educated State of Travancore. In both States industry and the land are important factors, more especially in Mysore, whose industries, during the last thirty years, have flourished exceedingly. Intelligent young men are as urgently needed in the lower grades as in the higher grades of every working concern. But ambitious, college-bred students demand responsible posts with good money ; and there are not enough of these to go round. Hence discontent and middle-class unemployment. Idle hands and active brains breed a tendency to political ferment ; and thus create promising material for Congress agents—local or seeping in from British India—exploiting dis-content with facile promises of a new heaven and earth if the disgruntled will persistently harass those in authority.

Mysore is not free from such ' political excrescences ' as Councils of Action and Congress Dictators—self-styled—counting largely for support on those very disgruntled unemployed ; since the people themselves—content, well-governed and devoted to the Ruling House—are either indifferent or opposed to political agitation ; though probably few of them ever realised how much they owed to their Ruler's personality.

The Baroda Maharaja had also his own share in these growing-pains of Indian India ; and in all State problems the two devoted Rulers had much in common. The older man's experience, the younger man's admiration, drew them into a close personal intimacy, valuable to both ; and between the two States intermittent visits were arranged.

One of these, from Baroda to Mysore, centred in an event worth recording, since it is peculiar to Royal India.

In certain States, every five years or so, increasing herds of wild elephants must be thinned out, lest they multiply dangerously and destroy vast areas of coffee, crops and sugar-cane. For no field or plantation can be fenced off against them. The elephant, in fact, can only be dealt with at all because his curiously tractable nature makes him seemingly unaware of his superhuman strength. Man, little and cunning, turns that strength to his own advantage in a dozen ways other than tiger shooting and State processions.

In forestry, the tamed elephant is invaluable for the hauling of planks and felled trees : in building, for his power of lifting weights, his untiring capacity for work. If he has a drawback it is that his appetite matches his size. The wild elephant eats without ceasing for the whole twenty-four hours on end, with snatches of sleep at intervals ; and the State elephant of a Maharaja will content himself with a modest daily ration of thirty *chupattis* [1] (made of 50 lb. of flour), 150 lb. of hay, 200 lb. of grass or grain, all washed down with 150 gallons of water. It takes a Maharaja to satisfy a stableful of thirty elephants more or less on that scale : and there are gourmets among them who will unerringly choose a *chupatti* made by a woman rather than one made by a man. Your civilised elephant will pose consciously for his photograph, sluice himself, fan himself, and offer to fan you. The machine may oust him yet : meantime he retains unchallenged his place of use and honour—the one remaining giant in a pigmy world.

When the jungles are over-stocked, and the crops, especially sugar-cane, are receiving unwelcome attentions, the time is ripe for a *kheddah* [2] drive. The date is fixed : invitations are issued

---

[1] Unleavened cakes.   [2] Stockade.

for English and Indian guests, always eager to witness a form of capture only justified by necessity and the fact that, in six months' time, 90 per cent of the great beasts will have become useful, even contented servants of the State they would otherwise ruin.

Months beforehand a wild herd is located ; and elaborate preparations are made by practised *shikarris* to enclose that part of the jungle. Slowly, cautiously, day by day, the herd is propelled in the desired direction. By showing flares of fire and light, the elephants are drawn towards the river-bed at a sharp bend, with low banks on the near side and high cliffs opposite.

That done, they are manœuvred through a prepared passage into a triangle formed by the river ; their retreat cut off by an army of beaters, who ' raise hell ' with guns, horns, drums and bamboo clappers. Up the river and down, escape is barred by lines of tame elephants, who assist in the capture of their fellows with cynical unconcern. There remains only one way out for the terrified herd ; up a ramp leading to the large stockade, often as much as a mile wide.

When all are in, the pressing of an electric button closes the gates—and the imprisoned beasts are left to settle down. The first phase is over.

Before the Baroda visit all had been arranged to secure a herd that, for some years, had been devouring crops, smashing huts and endangering the lives of hill men. Nearer home a small army was engaged to prepare for the distinguished visitors a forest camp such as only India can achieve at comparatively short notice.

A low hill cleared of jungle was encircled by a red road and twenty-four brand-new tents : the hill itself crowned by a forest bungalow transformed within and without ; a small impromptu garden, with a fountain playing in honour of the royal pair. Tents close by were to house the purdah Mysore ladies ; and the Maharaja had planned a bamboo ' look-out ' to give his favoured guests a far view of forest and ravine and the Nilgiri Hills. Under the look-out was a shelter for the band to play. Electric light had been everywhere installed, and a heliograph station for signalling news. The main tent was furnished with armchairs, books and papers, even the latest novels ; evidence, in every form, of the kindly personal thought that counts for more than the most lavish expenditure.

Many guests had arrived from Bombay and Bangalore ; and just before sunset an escort of Mysore Lancers heralded the royal cars of Baroda and Mysore. Flags were run up to announce their coming. Dinner awaited them—no jungle dinner by any means. And the second phase was complete.

MYSORE : SIR KRISHNARAJA WÁDIYAR BAHADUR,
LATE MAHARAJA OF MYSORE

TRAVANCORE : SIR CHITRA THIRUNAL, MAHARAJA OF TRAVANCORE

The last phase performed by elephants, willing and unwilling, by daring and skilful *mahouts*,[1] was staged in the smaller stockade, where the roping of the captured completed the painful process of subjection.

The smaller *kheddah* was enclosed by immensely strong palisades twelve feet high, its uprights and sloping supports bound with strong hide rope to the nearest trees. Around and above it rose a spectators' gallery, ten feet high, unlikely to be noticed by the elephants, who—perhaps because of their great height—seldom look up. A light roof, added in case of rain, converted the ramshackle affair into a kind of forest theatre, complete with steps and seats, commanding a view of the larger jungle stockade and the manœuvring of the captives into the smaller one for the final roping process.

That last is often a ticklish business, demanding skill and courage from the *mahouts*, seated on the necks of trained tamed elephants, armed with an iron-tipped *ankus*,[2] their knees tucked behind the huge ears, their scanty clothing, brownish grey, hardly distinguishable from elephant's hide. The fury of the great tuskers on finding themselves trapped had in part subsided. So also had their first terror of man : and at this final indignity they might begin to give trouble.

At eight o'clock of a brilliant December morning, the air pleasantly cool, all spectators, except Their Highnesses, had climbed into that impromptu theatre with the lesser enclosure directly under them. The stirring note of a horn announced royal arrivals. Trumpeting and squealing from the arena suggested an orchestra tuning up.

Away down the river a pair of gentle, but skilled *kumkis*[3] came splashing through the water ready for their task of barring the wild ones from attempting to escape, or hustling them into the *kheddah*.

Out of the dark jungle moved a huge lone tusker, flapping immense ears. Stepping into the water, he casually squirted trunkfuls of it over his back : a stranger, it seemed, to the rest of the herd, some fifty strong, who now came plunging into view, swimming straight for the mouth of the *kheddah* : mighty tuskers, cows lifting babies in their trunks—unaware of impending fate.

Suddenly one of them scented danger. Wildly trumpeting, the whole herd turned in mid-stream, trying to break back ; charging the *kumkis* who stood firm, prodded and encouraged by their *mahouts*. Curiously enough the wild elephant either fails to see the little brown man seated aloft, or fails to recognise him

[1] Elephant drivers.   [2] Goad.   [3] Tamed elephants.

as the real enemy, whom he could sweep off his perch at a blow and trample to death.

Baulked of their bid for freedom, the doomed beasts came on again, making for the funnel-shaped entrance to the final stockade, disguised in a camouflage of bamboo and jungle leafage, so as not to awaken suspicion. For the wild elephant, acutely intelligent, is alive to the least hint of man's presence. He will even shy away from chopped wood ; by what instinct who can tell ?

Puzzled and curious, they were almost venturing in, shepherded from behind, when they scented the presence of onlookers : and once again they broke back in a state of squealing, trumpeting excitement, plunging into the stream.

Dismay in the forest theatre. It looked as if the drive had failed. Not so. Men who handle wild elephants must be masters of resource ; swift, skilful, never losing their heads at critical moments, when sheer brute strength seems fated to prevail.

Once again clappers, beaters and coolies raised pandemonium. Once again the thirty elephants, male and female, poured into the river. Thence, through the funnel-shaped opening, they passed to their doom.

When as many as possible had been forced into the stockade, including the lonely tusker, word was given—and the drawbridge gate crashed down behind them, shutting in a dozen *kumkis* and their *mahouts* to deal with the captured victims, not yet resigned to their fate by any means.

Roping operations are sometimes painful to witness. Those lords of the jungle in their fight for freedom seem nobler than the pigmies who have trapped them and must occasionally wound their bodies to break their spirits. Until the beasts are trapped, it is a fair fight between instinct and skill ; but the final subduing process is inevitably nothing short of brutal. Creatures of the wild, monsters of their kind, cannot be tackled in kid gloves. Dauntless leaders have, in some cases, been unable to survive the shock of capture and defeat.

On that occasion the first desperate struggle was short ; but some of the biggest tuskers turned savagely on their tame oppressors. Silently they contended for mastery ; the huge foreheads pressed hard against each other ; *mahouts* goading the wild ones with spears ; jabbing at their heads with the *ankus*, unmoved by the sight of their faces streaked with blood and tears.

Meantime the outer bower of bamboos had become a scene of rage and fear : the wild things trampling and storming ; tame

ones thrusting their great bodies into the middle of the stockade ;
mahouts and foresters yelling to one another—' *Maro, maro !
Dānt do !* ' (Strike, strike ! Give him the spike !), with here and
there a yell of triumph, ' *Arre—arre—hai-yai !* ' : onlookers,
fascinated yet fearful, intent on the daring ' ropers ', who must
hobble the hind legs of the tuskers, if they are to be secured and
gentled in kindly fashion, with voice and touch.

The tame elephants, their allies, worked in pairs, one on
either side of the jungle lord, leaning against him with all their
weight, while he trumpeted and struggled. The ropers, slipping like lightning down the hindquarters of their *kumkis*, must
contrive to fling a noose of oiled hide round the hind legs of the
captured, evading—as by a miracle—the obvious fate of being
trampled to death in that fury of thundering feet, each one as
powerful as a steam hammer.

The audience, half incredulous, watched those wisps of men
plying their dangerous trade ; sheltering under their *kumkis*,
dodging in and out as the creatures moved ; hobbling the huge
hind legs of the captive, and swarming like monkeys up the tails
of their own all-enduring beasts, back to safety, breathless but
triumphant.

But those who grappled with the huge lone tusker were not
allowed to rest on their daring achievement. Finding himself
shackled, his fury flamed up again. With one powerful kick he
snapped his fore-leg ropes as if they were thread ; swung round
with startling speed, became aware of spectators and headed for
that precariously perched theatre-gallery full of men and women.

Uncontrollable now, with tusks and trunk he began purpose-
fully breaking up the supports. In that moment of frozen fear,
it looked as if all must crash to a hideous, inevitable death.

Then fear unfroze into a wild stampede ; a rush for ladders
and gateways ; the most agile boldly essaying the ten-foot jump
to earth out at the back, sooner than face those terrible tusks ;
the crowd beyond the stockade scurrying in all directions like
ants from a broken ant-heap.

In that confused and critical juncture, the Maharaja's brother
—then Yuvaraj—showed a remarkable coolness and courage that
probably warded off wholesale destruction. Rallying his foresters,
he spurred them to a concerted attack on that formidable monster.
Resolutely they drove him back into the stockade with shouts and
blows and pricks from long spears in tender places. The ever-
ready *kumkis*, intelligently playing their part, closed round him
when he tried to break back ; till, at last, by some means, his
hind legs were crossed so that he lost his balance and crashed

sideways to the ground. Fortunately, no live thing was within the area of that monstrous falling body.

While he lay helpless for the moment, brown men swarmed all over him, once more securely roping his feet and his neck. That done, they left him for the night to his confused sensations, foresters taking turns to keep an eye on him. Even prostrate, he could still make things unpleasant for his captors.

Next morning he must be removed to the kraal, where many others were tethered, to be handled by the boldest *shikarris*, most practised in the art of taming wild things by hand and voice.

But his spirit was not yet broken. Once they had him on his feet, much forceful persuasion was needed to get him safely out of the stockade. Roped head and tail, three *kumkis* in front and three behind, it seemed that he must at last accept his fate. But, as the drawbridge gate was raised, he dug in his huge fore feet and refused to move an inch.

Vainly the three front *kumkis* strained at their ropes, while the others prodded him unfeelingly behind.

Suddenly a thrill of horror ran through the venturesome ones, who had returned to the gallery to see the end of him at any risk. Unmistakably the loosened head ropes were slipping off. One more tug and he would turn upon them all, smash through the gateway and regain his freedom.

Warning cries rang out as the *mahouts* backed their tame animals into the stockade, fastened the slipping ropes and told the tusker in unmistakable terms they could master him, do what he would.

Trumpeting vain protests, he was pulled and pushed and prodded at last into the avenue, across the stream—where he drank thirstily—and on into captivity.

There his hind legs were tethered to a huge tree, giving him six feet of rope to allow movement. Neck ropes and fore legs were fastened to another tree, while tame elephants stood round gently talking to him, prodding him when he restlessly swayed to and fro.

By next day twenty-one of the wild herd had been dealt with —exhausting work and dangerous ; for the captives who remained ceased not from straining to escape their doom of lifelong servitude to man—they, lords of the jungle ; a match even for their rivals, the tiger.

That was a memorable *kheddah* drive for all concerned ; made more so by an after-exploit in which the Maharani of Baroda distinguished herself as a sportswoman of skill and daring.

The great drive ended, she and her Maharaj went off into the hills after big game : she, in her *sari*, turned forty-five, as eager for a taste of skikar as any modern young woman of them all.

On the second day they had hugely enjoyed chasing wild elephants ; and, on their way back, they were told that the road was unsafe ; all camp visitors warned to keep within bounds. They had not yet, it seemed, finished with the elephant-people.

During the night a big lone tusker, known as a ' rover ', had come in from the forest to try and visit his friends in the herd. The Barodas—eager for more sport—discussed the possibilities with Theobald, the white hunter, learned in elephant lore.

Decidedly, he said, the rover might prove a danger to the camp. If he could not be captured, he must be killed. But it would need a marksman to hit, unerringly, the one fatal spot behind the beast's ear. That fired the ambitious Maharani. With directions from Theobald, she would make a sporting attempt to rid the camp area of its unwelcome visitor.

The hunter, willing enough, placed her between two *kumkis* on the roadside near the kraal of picketed captives : and there, facing them, stood the unsuspecting rover, a hundred yards away.

Keeping very still, they must wait till he turned sideways. Then Theobald moved his hand. The Maharani fired with perfect precision ; hit the vulnerable spot, and held her breath as the huge beast staggered and fell over sideways—killed outright.

It was a trophy fit for a Queen. The rover measured close on nine feet from heel to shoulder. Thirty-five, the hunter reckoned his age : killed by a woman, in the fullness of his strength and vigour, when he was probably biding his time to tackle the other tusker who would never again know freedom or the joy of combat with his kind.

And so an end of the elephant episode ; the five-yearly defeat of jungle herds at the hands of man.

After the *kheddah*, by way of contrast, visitors must be driven out to the western district of Mysore : first to visit the most famous temple of the Jain religion in South India ; then on to an incomparable masterpiece of Nature—four cascades that rank among the greatest waterfalls in the world.

The approach to that sublime spectacle, over sixty miles of high tableland bordered by noble forest, had once an appropriate dignity of its own. But, even in these wilds of India, motor traffic has worked its fatal will, changing the noble approach into a commonplace highway ploughed by buses, lorries, carts and cars, taxing all the resources of the district to keep the road in decent repair.

Yet, even now, the forests on either hand make amends with their unspoiled splendour, monkey-haunted, clothed in orchids and rambling creepers. Here long stretches of bamboo, most graceful among forest trees, there great *goni* trees larger than a giant oak ; their dense canopy of outflung boughs often measuring as much as four hundred and twenty feet round. Massed areca nut palms shoot aloft to the height of sixty feet and more, crowned with spreading leaves and bunches of fruit. Lithe semi-naked gatherers, who swarm up the stems, fling themselves like monkeys, from tree-top to tree-top, never descending till their day's work is done. From afar off comes the organ thunder of those mighty cascades—*forte*, *crescendo*, *fortissimo*—as a sudden turn in the road reveals the beauty and majesty of the Arrow-born river in a stupendous leap over a precipice of eight hundred and thirty feet ; its four separate cascades bridged, as it were, by a vast rainbow. Low down in the chasm that rainbow, formed by sun and spray, begins in a complete circle, gradually broken, as day draws on, till it forms a bow above the welter of foam. The whole wonderful scene is enhanced by the wild beauty of the immediate country round ; by many-hued rocks, by thousands of pigeons and swallows, that nest in cliff crevices, and ' flash like drifting leaves through the spray '.

And for nine months of the year the whole place is alive with butterflies innumerable, their brilliant colours and wide wings flickering in strong sunlight, huge black-and-white ones striking a note of contrast.

In December, when the sun rises behind the falls, they remain for half the day in deep shadow. Broken rainbows flash and fade ; and at noon the whole scene is filled with a blaze of dancing light : every pebble and pool, every tree, rock and fern making arabesques of light and shade. Dusk brings a ghostly radiance of silvery veils and columns of wind-tossed spray. And in the unearthly light of a full moon, the elusive gleam of lunar rainbows, the eerie beauty of it all must be seen to be believed.

The king of the four, aptly named Raja, excels Niagara in height ; his terrific leap being five times as great, though Niagara is made more impressive by its volume of water half a mile wide.

The Roarer dashes into the Raja half-way down, while the Rocket descends in a series of playful jets. Last of the four, a little apart, the Rani, a very Undine, glides over the cliff in a dazzle of lace-like foam.

Each fall, isolated, would be a world-wonder. The four of

them, with their mighty orchestration of falling water, unforgettably impress the mind and imagination. Exquisite effects are produced by searchlights playing all over the falls and gorge, and by rockets of golden rain ; but nothing can excel the natural magic wrought by sun, moon and stars ; the fourfold leap into the gorge, with its pool, eight hundred and thirty feet below.

The supreme event of the year in Mysore is its great religious festival—the Dussara : an elaborate sequence of ceremonies ten days long, such as the soul of India loves.

It is an autumn festival of very ancient origin, falling in September or October according to their changeable calendar. Kept with pomp and circumstance all over Hindu India, it is nowhere more reverently or more magnificently carried out than in Mysore.

Under its outer garb of processions and ceremonial, it is an eminently religious feast, celebrating the central episode of India's great epic, the *Rāmayāna*. Sita, beloved wife and Queen of Rāma the hero-king, was, through trickery, left unprotected in their forest home ; and in Rāma's absence she was carried off by Ravān, the ogre-king of Lānka, the old name for Ceylon. The epic tells how she was traced by Hanuman, general of the small and cunning monkey-people ; her innocence proved by a ring-token sent to her lord, who came with a great army, defeated Ravān and released his Queen.

But the feast of Dussara is concerned with a deeper significance : the light—a stainless Queen—shining in darkness, and the defeat of darkness by light. Every part of it symbolises, in some way, the conflict of right and wrong, the subduing of passions and the spirit of worship.

The chief objects of worship, during those ten days, are six : Chamundi, Mysore's patron goddess ; Ganesh, the friendly elephant god ; the nine planets ; the State sword and ivory throne ; and finally, above all, the Maharaj himself. For that brief time he puts off the mantle of mere royalty and becomes very god in the eyes of his people, who believe him to be surrounded by an invisible aura of divinity. The passing spell of god-head is conferred on him by Chamundi herself, his divine ancestress and hundreds of times great-grandmother. He opens the Dussara by a visit to her shrine on the hill above the city. There she endows him with the honours and drawbacks of divinity ; for, during the days of his twofold majesty, he must not be touched by human hand. As a god, none can logically wash or shave him,

As Maharaj, he may not wash or shave himself : a dire dilemma that can no doubt be partially circumvented, as he remains throughout secluded in his Palace.

Not least among many ceremonies laid on him was the blessing and salutation of the sacred horse and elephant, people of importance in every State procession. The State horse, a cream-coloured Arab, would have his tail stained in rainbow tints ; his body, bearing the twelve essential marks and curls, would be veiled in a golden mesh and harnessed with jewels, with knee-caps and anklets of gold-worked velvet. Six attendants restrained his prancing and capering. A guard of honour went before and the State elephant followed after, also clad in gold and many colours from tusk to tail.

Twice daily that brilliant cortège must repair to a pavilion by the lake, where the favoured creatures would be garlanded and worshipped ; submitting with bored resignation to the waving of incense-burners and showers of blossoms. Returning, sanctified, they would approach and salute His Highness : the elephant trumpeting with lifted trunk ; the horse on his knees, head bowed to the ground.

Not until the ninth day was the Maharaja released from the honour and burden of his sanctity. In the privacy of his State tent he could now be washed, shaved and clothed, as befits a Prince about to review his army : a process that may take many hours.

First, installed at the Elephant Gate of the Palace, he himself must bless all his sacred creatures—horses, elephants, cows and the like—an ancient ceremony brilliant and dignified. The whole courtyard would be thronged with troops and bands, carriages and decorated animals, all waiting to pass His Highness ; and everywhere, beyond them and beyond, masses of people, orderly and joyous, a surging blaze of colour.

Not until sunset could he be ready to head the final procession on caparisoned elephants—the whole court and royal family gorgeously arrayed—to a vast open space crowded with his loyal subjects and his entire State army.

A climax of splendour was the march back by torchlight from the Field of Assembly to the Palace accompanied by happy crowds, who had regained their human Maharaja until the yearly return of this Great Feast.

That joyous day culminated in a ceremony of quite another kind peculiar to Mysore : the European Durbar, at which he received in State the official English colony of Mysore. No Indians would be present at the function except himself and the royal family with their attendants. The Resident and the Prince, in cloth of gold, wearing magnificent jewels, entered the Durbar Hall to a fanfare of trumpets, the whirling of silken banners and the calling of the Maharaja's many long-winded titles. Before ascending the gold and ivory throne, he must offer it formal worship ; the Resident being assigned to a gilded chair on his right hand. On his left sat the Yuvaraj, and beyond him all members of the ruling family, all officers of State.

Beyond the Resident sat the English guests in full evening array ; the whole effect heightened by decorations of the Hall itself and thousands of electric lights. Two among them—each of two thousand candle-power—played directly on His Highness, the brilliant centre of brilliance, a scintillation of jewels, arms, neck, ears, chest and fingers encrusted with them ; his Yuvaraj, beside him, only a shade less regally arrayed.

Many among them were jewels of astonishing size and splendour, worn only on high occasions, and that in no mere spirit of display. Always, in India, seek the symbol behind her bewildering extremes of ceremonial, asceticism and lavish adornment. The Hindu endows jewels with magical powers. An Indian Prince— it is decreed—must wear his jewels so that their virtues, passing through his body, may spread prosperity, security and glory throughout his dominions. Thus, at this great feast, as always, the welfare of the people is symbolised in the glory of their King.

Like most other Indian festivals, Dussara is arranged to co-incide with the approach of full moon ; her mysterious influence on all things terrestrial being more instinctively apprehended in the East than in the West. So this most significant religious feast reaches its climax on the night of full moon in a vast assembly of the people on a certain hill-top round the ' Lake of a Thousand Lights '—the name itself an inspiration.

No more than a tiny mere, framed in wooded shores, hardly noticeable in daylight, this lonely, sanctified spot enjoys its appointed hour of glory.

Here all Mysore assembles long before sundown, to await the launching of a sacred raft bearing their Maharaja in his silver pavilion. The wooded banks are packed with people—often as many as three thousand—seated among flowering bushes, or perched on branches of trees—tamarisk and wild olive ; each family with its own bunch of coloured lights and cheap fireworks. Around and across the lake hang lines of coloured bulbs that will, at dusk, become coloured lights.

In a semicircle reserved for women, jewels and bright silken *saris* enliven the scene. Palace peons, in strange costumes, stroll here and there carrying lily-shaped standards. The hours of waiting, however long drawn-out, are part of the thrill to those simple Eastern folk for whom time is of no account.

As sunset fades and dissolves into the violet-grey of India's brief transit from dusk to dark, family fireworks crackle and flare, leaving a trail of smoke that softly blurs rocks and boulders, outlines of trees and the massed crowd, waiting patiently for moonrise—a moon just past the full.

Suddenly a silver-gold rim among black boughs printed on the sky heralds the coming of their King in his silver pavilion on the sacred raft.

In the gloom, lit only by the rising moon, with a few lamps and fireworks reflected in the still water, that fairy-like structure seems almost to be resting on the lake itself.

Then—the climax ; he appears in person. Simultaneously, a thousand lights, controlled by a main switch, spangle the dim scene and the dark shore. They reveal the decorated raft resting on the backs of four huge white swans with gilded beaks and ruby eyes, their long necks garlanded with flowers and chains of gems. At the corners, four priests stand erect.

Now and then a rocket rises : a breathless moment of admiration ; a sigh from invisible thousands as it falls in golden rain. Lights on the raft and ashore are switched on and off with magical effect as the great birds, moved by inner machinery, sail slowly round the lake ; the sense of magic deepened by the utter stillness of that enraptured, invisible throng.

The raft vanishes ; the lights flick out. Moon-radiance washes the darkened scene, as the silent thousands melt away like ghosts, leaving the lake once more a tiny mere hardly noticeable by daylight.

' The high song is over ' ; but its hour of glory will return. Will the four swans bring again, to his waiting people, that same beloved and worshipped Maharaj ?

4

Sir Krishnaraja Wádiyar Bahádur IV celebrated his last Dussara in October 1939. In August 1940, at the early age of fifty-six, death took him from his genuinely adoring people, from the State that was his pride and first concern in life, from all those —his inner circle of family and friends—who loved him as a man. His passing was an irreparable loss, not only to Mysore but to the whole of India. Those few words are easily written or said ; but what they convey to those who suffered that loss—above all to those nearest him in life and love—no phrase ever coined could express. As Ruler, he commanded unqualified admiration : as man, he won all hearts. Universal lamentation accompanied him on his last journey to the place of burning. An unceasing stream of telegrams and tributes flowed in from all over the world to the bereaved city at the foot of Chamundi Hill.

The farewell procession of his mourning people might almost have been a finale to his last Dussara celebration. For there went his caparisoned cream-coloured horse and elephant. But none now sat on the throne where the horse he loved would kneel for a salute from the royal hand. No slender, dignified figure sat on the elephant to receive a people's salutation. Instead there he lay on a simple bier under the open Royal Umbrella, receiving the tribute of men's tears ; the beautiful familiar face, under its turban, serene as if in peaceful sleep.

When the bier paused before his Palace, a military band struck up the muffled beat of Chopin's funeral march, with its ' immortal lament for human mortality ' ; and through it, like the cry of sea-birds, came the wailing of women who watched his passing from the upper windows. After the cortège came a surging throng of old men, young men and boys from all the streets and alleys of his capital, moved by one irresistible impulse of homage and grief.

' Kings might come and kings might go ; but for them, it was as if their father had died.'

That pervading sense of a personal relation touches the inner mystery of Indian kingship. Through all theory and practice of life runs the instinctive need of a personality who commands not only respect, but allegiance of the heart : and the Maharaja, in his life and character, commanded both in a remarkable degree.

' All the world was his kin ', wrote Dr. James Cousins, the poet, ' but his State-people were in truth his family. When he went, their father died.'

He lived the life he believed in : a harmony that was the essence of his greatness. A devout Hindu, he was surrounded by the followers of all faiths. He chose a Moslem Prime Minister as ' the ideal Dewān ', and he numbered many Christians among his closest friends. There are scores in England who will cherish his memory ; not least the members of our own Royal Family. It was Lord Lothian who wrote of him, ' It will be long before one meets with such a very perfect gentleman again '. A wreath sent by *The Times* from London was coupled with a tribute to the Maharaja, ' who had set a standard for the whole of India '. World tributes were unending, from Washington, Melbourne,

Canada, from every corner of the Empire, from all his fellow Princes, from men of culture East and West.

Perhaps none more perfectly portrayed him as Ruler-Saint than Paul Brunton, mystic and writer, who came to know in a measure the secret mainsprings of his character.

' The Maharaja, as I knew him, was both mystic and philosopher. He had scaled the heights of religious aspiration and plumbed the depths of philosophic thought. His clear mind never lost itself in a sea of vague dreamings. It has been the fate of India's *rishis* [1] to be much misunderstood; so that people came to revere the lethargic hermit or self-centred monk, as long as either donned the white ash and yellow robe of sanctity. . . . Contrary to common opinion, research has shown that the deepest solitudes do not produce the divinest men. The Maharaja, for one, practised spirituality amid activity, not apathy. . . . Both in public and personal life, he mingled artistry with austerity and did not oppose them as incompatibles. He was artist to the finger-tips and saint to the inmost core of his being.'

In the words of Sir Stuart Fraser—his tutor, his Resident and lifelong friend,—' A man whom it seemed almost impossible to overpraise '. Of such an one it may truthfully be said, his name liveth for evermore.

[1] Wise men.

TRAVANCORE:
LAND'S END OF INDIA

THIS small but prosperous and very individual State brings us to the utmost South. Walled in by the Great Western Ghats, it seems a world apart, a region of the blest, where rice fields gleam and lagoons reflect their fringe of palm-fronds, and boat-traffic saunters along charmed waterways : a world more than two thousand years old. Yet singularly advanced, on Western lines, in politics, welfare work and education.

Shaped like a conch—as if symbolising its link with the sea —that favoured land, a hundred and seventy-four miles long, lies entirely between hills and the sea, Nature's most sublime elements : hills clothed in primaeval forests, with all they provide of beauty, rainfall and rivers that save Travancore from being scorched into a barren sandy sea-board. By the mercy of these forests, it is cool and green at all seasons ; a paradise for Nature lovers, so brilliant and varied are its jungle flowers, butterflies and birds ; a fruitful land of rice fields and tea plantations, acres of tapioca plants—and palms, everywhere palms, cocoanut, sago, areca : their graceful stems and crown of leaves adding enchantment to the backwater lagoons, only found here in all India. And her natural ramparts, with their sixteen mountain passes and impenetrable jungle, have protected Travancore from invasion.

Widest at the northern end, the land narrows as it ranges southward to the stark edge of all things, Cape Comorin—Land's End of India.

There three oceans meet, the Arabian Sea, the Indian Ocean and Bay of Bengal. There, among rocks and more rocks, one stands as it were in mid-ocean. Sea to the right ; sea to the left ; sea before and beyond to the utmost horizon : in rough weather, foam and thunder of breakers ; soft lapping of blue-green waves when the air is still.

Here only, in all India, one may see the sun rise on one hand, traverse the heavens and set in the same waters, though they are called by different names. More : on a night of full moon—the crowning marvel—one may experience the strange beauty of sunset and moonrise at almost the same hour, again over the same ocean. Here the bewildering variety of India is resolved into the majestic simplicity of Nature's three most sublime elements, hills and sea and sky.

Inevitably Cape Comorin ranks as one of the seven most sacred pilgrim-haunted places of India ; only saved from complete erosion by a natural breakwater of the Western Ghats, coming right down to Land's End. Almost at the very water's edge stands the local temple ; shrine of the virgin goddess Kannya Kumari, who has christened the Cape, her second name corrupted by the English into Comorin. Virgin she remains—a plight unknown in the Hindu hierarchy—having missed her chance of marriage with the Lord Shiva, husband of Kali the. Terrible.

According to the legend, all things had been arranged for her wedding at the Cape ; but the bridegroom delayed his coming. Kumari, feeling anxious, set out in search of him under cover of night. A long way she went, all to no purpose ; and fearful of being caught in daylight seeking her bridegroom, she fled back to her temple on the rocks.

The delayed Shiva could only reach Suchindrām—many miles from the Cape—by daylight. So there he must seek refuge in a small temple, where he lives to this day ; the disappointed goddess also living on alone, unwed.   All the food prepared for the marriage feast was turned into sand ; and the credulous are shown pebbles like grains of rice scattered abundantly along that coast among sands of many colours.

The eastern gate of her temple is opened only twice a year for certain festivals, when the goddess looks directly out to sea : and a story is current of long-ago mariners attracted by flashes of light from the jewels in her head. Believing they beheld a miracle, they mistook their course and crashed to death among the rocks : a legend that recalls the German *Lorelei*.

The wild and sacred character of the Cape is not enhanced by intrusions of a Royal Palace, a Residency, a Cape Hotel over-looking the ocean, and a first-class travellers' bungalow. But man must be served, as the goddess herself is served by the inescapable Hindu worshipper. Pilgrims swarm—not only at the Cape. Travancore is thronged with temples. Legends abound ; and Brahmin priests profit exceedingly by the unlimited credulity of ignorance ; though of late years their power and influence have notably dwindled in a land where Christians are more numerous than in any other part of India.

The advent of Brahmins from the north—bringing Aryan culture and caste divisions—may be reckoned a comparatively recent event in the immense backward vista of Travancore, with its curious contrast between isolation from India on the east and its western maritime contact with many lands. The shipping and world-wide trade of its harbours—Alleppey and Quilon—date from the earliest dawn of merchant-adventurers, the Phoenicians, in search of ivory, sandalwood and spices. A thousand years before Christ, King Solomon sent his ships to Tarshish and Ophir —said to be a little coast village still extant, south of Trivandrum : and it has been definitely proved that Greece and Rome and also China traded largely with the coast of Travancore. Ships from Persia and Arabia were familiar ; and in 1497 came Vasco da Gama bearing letters from the King of Portugal. In 1588 the first English traveller, Master Ralph Fitch, appeared in Malabar —the geographical name of western Travancore ; but there was no trade, till 1608, with the East India Company, who found themselves forestalled by the Dutch, with a backing from their strong home government. Finally Holland captured Cochin from the Portuguese and ordered English settlers to leave ; an act that antagonised the English and eventually led to war.

But wars between other States and other nations have never actively disturbed Travancore ; nor was it appreciably troubled by India's turmoil of anarchy and bloodshed in the last half of the eighteenth century. The Moguls never came so far south ; and even the predatory Marathas were daunted by the Western Ghats. Hence the unbroken line of Hindu Kings that have ruled Travancore for two thousand years.

In its present form, about the size of Wales, it was created by its warrior King, Raja Martanda Varma, who subdued all neighbouring chiefs, dedicated himself to the patron god of his line, and thus raised his status from mere Ruler to vice-regent of deity. He it was who formed an alliance with the East India Company ; and his successors fought under the British in the Mysore wars. For those good services the higher title of Maharaja (Great King) was bestowed, in perpetuity, on the Rulers of Travancore.

The first British Resident, Colonel Macaulay, was appointed in 1800 and remained there for ten years. That gave a man full chance to become closely acquainted with the people and the country, and to leave his mark on both. Colonel Munro, who followed him, urged—wisely or unwisely—the sending of missionaries to temple-haunted Travancore. The first came in 1816 : men of limited knowledge and imagination with no conception of the deep philosophy underlying the mass of Hindu ritual and superstition. No doubt assailed them as to their own rather superficial method of light-bringing, or as to possible after-results.

Even the activities of St. Francis Xavier, a genuine saint, leave a question mark in the non-missionary mind as to the lasting value of his hurried mass conversions. Fervently he writes of explaining to unlettered peasants ' the elements of Christian doctrine, three persons in one God ' (himself unenlightened as to the complex Hindu Trinity), of ' persuading them to make the sign of the Cross three times and repeat the Paternoster '; of sending them, after baptism, to demolish their temples and break their idols. ' I cannot describe ', he adds, ' the joy this spectacle affords me. . . . In the space of one month I have baptized over ten thousand.'

So unbounded was his energy and zeal that one can hardly believe he spent only three months in Travancore. Did he ever have time or opportunity to return and discover the effect of his whirlwind conversions on those he left behind ? With equal zeal he devoted his energies to the practical relief of suffering among the fisher villages ; and, in the case of an actual minor invasion, he allied himself with the Raja of Travancore, whose hastily gathered army was in danger of defeat by a stronger foe.

St. Francis, lifting his crucifix, walked alone towards the enemy, crying in a loud voice, ' In the Name of God, the Terrible, I command you to halt ! '

They halted. Others behind them pressed forward, but they could not advance. ' A giant, they said, was barring the way : dressed in black, his face so resplendent that it blinded them. High officers ran up to see what had happened ; but the army, seized with indescribable terror, fled in disorder.'

True or no, the tale is not past belief. So invincible is the conjunction of unswerving faith and courage.

The Salvation Army, in its own fashion, has done remarkable work in Travancore as elsewhere. Caring for the bodies as well as for the souls of men, it has many hospitals to its credit, a leper colony and 175 village schools.

Education takes high rank in Travancore. The State prides itself on standing third, as to literacy, in all India ; with Burma first and Cochin second ; whereas in the rest of India only 15 per cent of the men and 3 per cent of the women can read and write. In English literacy Travancore ranks fourth, after Cochin, Bengal and Bombay. In fact half her men and one-sixth of her women are literate : a school to every two square miles ; a hundred and twenty English newspapers and periodicals. As in Mysore, one-fifth of the revenue is spent on education ; and eight colleges are affiliated to the Madras University.

These details, neither romantic nor sensational, are matters for legitimate pride, the more so that they have been carried through without excessive taxation.

TRAVANCORE: FIRST PRINCESS OF TRAVANCORE. AS ELDER SISTER
OF SIR CHITRA, HER SON WILL REIGN AFTER HIM

THE PUNJAB-PATIĀLA : THE LATE MAHARAJA OF PATIĀLA IN A FEW
OF THE STATE JEWELS

But here, as in Mysore, the advantages of education bring their own peculiar drawbacks. Congress emissaries and advocates, who can make little headway with illiterate India, find fruitful soil in educated Baroda, Mysore and Travancore. For here, again, the towns are over-stocked with ex-students, who far prefer the pen to the plough ; having lost, through the benefits of education, both their mental and physical heritage. Travancore needs trained men on the land, needs foresters and planters : but asks for them in vain. This is a serious problem for the State, and a handicap for young men who find themselves too well equipped, on the wrong lines, for the kind of work that urgently needs doing. It pushes them towards politics and journalism, and makes for discontent : a conjunction too often favourable to anti-British, anti-Princely congress outlook and aims.

Nor is it only young men who find themselves educated on wrong lines. That advanced State—small though it is—contains more college-bred young women to the square mile than any other in Royal India. Side by side with countless temples and distorted *sadhus*,[1] with putrescent holy tanks for bathing and drinking, one finds colleges for women on ultra-modern lines, where ' flower-like girls talk English among themselves because they find it easier than their native tongue, and elegant young women in the loveliest of draperies make laboratory experiments with light '.

Women everywhere are prominent in public life, largely owing to the curious system of matriarchal heritage, that obtains nowhere else in the world. It is not a case of being woman-ruled, as in Bhopāl. The actual Ruler in Travancore is, and has always been, a man. But although he may reign in his own right, he cannot transmit that right to his son. Inheritance goes through the woman. The heir to the present delightful, intelligent young Maharaja is the three-year-old son of his eldest sister, known as the First Princess—a beautiful woman of brains, character and charm.

The Maharaja's wife—in this odd, sideways fashion of inheriting—has no more status than a commoner. It is his young-looking mother who bears the title of Maharani ; and together they rule the State : a fine blend of the riper mind with the experimental enthusiasm of youth.

Far-seeing both, and full of enterprise, they are alive to the fact that Travancore depends mainly on fruits of the soil ; that intensive industry and mass production were not its true highways to prosperity. Wisely they aim at rural reconstruction that should tend to make agriculture more attractive, as a calling, to the college-bred unemployed.

[1] Holy men.

P

Their capital city of Trivandrum is set like an island in a sea of tropical verdure : Residency, Training College, schools, University and College of Science ; High Courts of Justice, hospitals and museum—all on the latest lines. Yet Travancore, tolerant of all faiths and modern points of view, has never merely imitated the West. More than any other Indian State it has compassed a mental attitude frankly modern without becoming pseudo-European. The Palace in itself, more like a vast white house, stands on high ground sloping to a lake, looking out over dense groves of cocoanut palms, that surge over the whole coastal landscape : their long, curved fronds drifting like light green smoke to the rim of the horizon.

Life in the Palace, with mother, brother and sister, is very simple and pleasant, on English family lines. Sir Chitra Thirunal —who owns seven names and a string of fifteen titles—never dines with non-Hindus ; though he is less rigidly orthodox than the last Maharaja, who had to take a purifying bath if ever he shook hands with a white man.

Sir Chitra, reared on English lines and trained for administration in Mysore, was only nineteen when he went to England, where he made a special study of economic questions. An invitation to British Broadcasting House pleased him the more because their programme was altered so that he might speak through the microphone direct to his own people six thousand miles away.

As in all States, the Prince's birthday is an occasion for great rejoicing ; and here, as in Mysore, the Ruler's family has genuinely won the heart of its people. His Highness goes in procession to worship at various temples, superbly clad, carried in a green-and-silver litter, escorted by State elephants, Bodyguard, Brigade and State officials.

His twenty-fifth birthday (November 1936) was distinguished by a proclamation of which Travancore felt rightly proud. It is known as the ' Temple Entry Proclamation ', giving to Untouchables the freedom of all Hindu temples in the State. The poor, the needy and backward, Travancore may still have ; but never, hereafter, an ' Untouchable '. Worship in the temples is denied to no Hindu. In his own words, ' There shall henceforth be no restriction placed on any Hindu, by birth or religion, entering or worshipping at the temples controlled by Us and Our Government '.

The magnitude and after-effects of that freedom only the years can reveal. It does honour to the young Prince, whose name will be blessed by millions for ever.

He employs British officers freely in the army, education,

police and other public services. Even his Dewān was for some time an Englishman, who could deal impartially with quarrelling sects, Christian and Hindu.

In appearance the Maharaja is not tall, but very slender, with features ' like an ivory miniature ' ; the unfailing courtesy of his manner as attractive as it is rare in any modern young man. Like His Highness of Mysore, he is so fond of animals that he can find little ' sport ' in destroying them. Instead, one of his primaeval forests has been converted into a sanctuary, where elephants and tigers, bison, elks and panthers have nothing to fear from the arch-enemy, man.

The Palace, woman-ruled, is furnished mainly in English fashion, with unusual good taste and sense of colour. The drawing-room, with walls, curtains and furniture of palest blue, harmonises exquisitely with the silken draperies and dark un-covered heads of the women. Travancore having never endured invasion or conquest, her Hindu women have never known the *sari* or the veil. Through their system of matriarchal heritage, they exercise a widespread influence and authority that makes them feel actively responsible for the welfare of their country. In all walks of life they abound. Women teach and lecture at men's colleges. Women practise as doctors and lawyers ; and only a few years ago the first woman judge presided in their law courts. Yet, throughout, they keep their intrinsic charm, their essentially natural poise of body and mind. In the home they are inevitably supreme. For a matriarchal family may consist of all who can trace their ancestry on the female side to one woman : a mother and her children, her daughter's children, her brothers and sisters and her sister's children.

Not only the throne, but inheritance among the noble families, carries on through the woman. Chief among these, the great landholders, are the Nairs of the Malabar Coast : a community of high-caste Hindus found nowhere else in India. They are said to be the original people of this coast, having evolved their own civilisation and way of life long before the Brahmins brought Aryan culture from the North.

They have always been mainly nobles, never demeaning them-selves to touch commerce or handcrafts. Warriors all, noted for their courage, their prowess in the art of war and, not least, for the astonishing beauty of their women. Down the ages, from earliest French tourists to those of to-day, the lovely Malabar woman has been praised by travellers, by writers and poets of their own land. It is told how even an English official, attracted by their grave and simple charm, was moved to protest by a comment in the census report, ' Excess of females in the Nair population '.

' Excess ! ' he cried in mock wrath. ' The most beautiful women of India, however numerous, could never be excessive ! '

It was partly on account of their women that the Nairs are said to have been singled out by early Brahmin priests as people of the highest human type : and from those holy ones, who favoured their lovely daughters, came a large infusion of Aryan blood ; adding to their beauty the distinction of fair skins and regular features that visibly lifts them above the dark Dravidian masses of the South.

Seldom in any country has its womanhood received so universal a chorus of praise. A tribute from one writer of knowledge must suffice : ' Very clean and well-dressed, they hold it a great honour that they know how to please men. For them the bath is more an article of faith than a daily ablution. . . . Beside each house is placed a large private tank with steps leading into it ; and there will be women bathing and laughing in it at almost any hour of the day. No dress, however slightly soiled, will be worn again. A sense of almost hieratic purity breathes from them like an emanation.'

And their houses produce the same impression ; each aloof and dignified in its own quiet grounds, with its bathing tank and luxuriant garden ; the rough stems of jack-fruit trees, the slender grace of palms and the large-leaved banana plants. In flowering time, enormous lilies—orange, yellow and tawny red—make bold splashes of colour in the prevailing green.

The homestead itself houses their mixed families, all related in the female line. On the ground-floor a large kitchen and store-rooms open on to a courtyard. Two staircases ascend to the upper storey ; one used only by the men, one only by the women ; their rooms above kept completely apart. The women predominate and rule. Sisters, cousins and aunts, all growing up together, necessitate a large measure of order and discipline that is an integral part of Hindu home-life ; a self-effacing restraint and deference to the wishes of elders that can, under a martinet mother or grandmother, be carried too far. All that is impulsive and self-assertive must be smoothed away, as stones, shaken together, are smoothed into pebbles. The result is seen in the manners of young women ; a shade too serious and self-contained, though sweetened by much human feeling and lightened by touches of worldly irony.

Their extremely simple dress—if dress it can be called—is no more than a length of soft white material swathed round the figure from waist to knee. All the upper part of the body remains bare, but for a necklace round the throat, and occasionally a gold belt, or gold bosses in the ears. Simply and modestly, innocent of the veil and its lure, the Nair woman goes everywhere thus, uncovered and unashamed. It is the law of the community ; and habit governs the mental attitude of man and woman to all questions of dress, or undress. When travelling the Nair women may sometimes wear a shawl round her shoulders and breast, for warmth or conformity with others. In such a case the unnatural covering will make her feel more shy and immodest than the normal woman would feel in discarding her accustomed bodice.

Her amusements are as simple as her dress : singing, dancing and swinging, especially at yearly festivals. The children delight in making flower carpets, weaving patterns with blossoms or petals, and building over their lovely handiwork a booth festooned with flowers. Then neighbours are invited to come in and admire. But the gravely sweet Nair women, with their intrinsic charm, are the loveliest flowers of all.

And marriage ? It is not surprising to find, in a woman-planned community, that wives are usually on the happiest terms with their husbands. Not seeing too much of one another, their mutual pleasure and affection are not blunted by over-familiarity, or dulled by tiresome minutiae of daily living. It is a curious but undoubted fact that, with the woman mainly in control, there is apt to be less friction between man and wife. If the two prove incompatible or tend to quarrel, they separate simply and naturally, without sense of wrong or unkindness, to seek more suitable mates. The ideal simplicity of such an arrangement takes no count of the inevitable crux of all easy divorce : both may not wish to part. The children, in such a community, would no doubt remain with the woman and swell the composite family of the homestead.

These isolated *tarawads*, or communal homesteads, are more characteristic of Travancore than the village community that is the human unit of India.

For the origin of these and the Nair family system, one must look back to ancient days of isolation, every man's hand against his neighbour, or against the countless beasts of prey who came out of the jungle seeking their meat from God. In those days the men of the family were mainly hunters, living a nomadic life in the foothill forests of the coast. When they, later, settled down in semi-fortified homesteads, they became also warriors, and surrounded their compounds with thick stone walls. Their main entrance was a small door cut in a huge gateway ; over the gateway a watch-tower room, with slits for firing on attackers or doubtful intruders.

With the men constantly absent from these family hives, the chief care and upkeep of their property devolved on the women, who evidently proved so efficient and created a family life so favourable to all concerned, that the arrangement became a system lasting well into the twentieth century.

Only now, in this day of many changes, the Nair homesteads show a tendency to break up. New professions, new activities are drawing the young men and women away from their home duties and their work on the family estate. Many old communal properties have now been divided ; and the matriarchal system, while retaining its hold on the ruling family, is being gradually superseded : whether for better or worse remains to be proved.

The Nairs are essentially of the ' county family ' order, having little taste for the cramped life of towns ; and their pleasant home-steads are found mainly among the beautiful backwaters that are yet another unique feature of Travancore.

These 'captive seas ', as they are picturesquely called, are the outcome of a perpetual conflict between flooded streams and mon-soon waves. At one time all must have been actual sea ; but India's heaviest rainfalls and the loose soil of Malabar rivers have combined to push the sea back, as it were, by imperceptible degrees, while the rivers have gradually silted up new shores to mark their advance into the unresting ocean.

It is these becalmed shallow lagoons that are called the back-waters of Travancore, a beautiful feature of its coastal scene ; the largest fifty-two miles long by ten miles broad. Limpid and still, they dazzle under the sun or shimmer under moon and stars. So clear the reflections that spaces of night-sky seem fallen to earth, fringed by the inevitable palm groves and diversified by palm-decked islands large and small. The beautiful eight-pronged lake, just outside the port of Quilon, has been called the Loch Lomond of Travancore. But most British travellers—their eyes surfeited with tropical luxuriance—would give the palm to the Queen of Northern Lakes, reflecting the brittle glory of its November woods.

Yet these tropic lagoons have their lotus-eating charm, never more lovely than on clear nights of moon and stars. Linked by rivers and canals, they create the famous waterways of Travancore —the State's peculiar blessing, never yet, nor ever likely to be, quite superseded by road or rail. From the borders of Cochin, to within easy distance of Trivandrum, they cover some hundred and fifty miles : a water journey more restful and attractive than any that the land has to offer in this region, especially if timed to coincide with a waxing moon. The night effects are magical. Moon and stars above ; moon and stars below ; and between them a dark mysterious mass of palm trees, their fronds printed sharply on a grey-violet sky.

Drifting slowly, with hardly a sense of movement, one has the restful illusion of journeying from nowhere to nowhere ; time obliterated for that brief interlude ; the traveller feelingly persuaded that there are more things in heaven and earth than the wearying urgency of haste and speed. In these dream surroundings, it is ' the fever and the fret ' of modern life that seem almost as unreal as life on another planet.

At the little village of Varkāla, rich in folklore and in future possibilities, the land breaks off abruptly in dizzy cliffs. Here is a temple, with three springs of peculiar sanctity and purity. To these, centuries ago, weary travellers came in search of peace. Now the practical modern mind—intent on profitable development —foresees a flourishing sanatorium : sea-bathing, outdoor life and springs of remarkable purity to ease the ailments common to those who drink hard water.

Varkāla is also the birthplace of the only teacher and religious movement native to Travancore. The holy one—Prophet of Peace—was born there more than eighty years ago. Like most of his kind, he early recognised the evil elements in rigid caste divisions, the tragedy they involved for those underlings of humanity, the Untouchables. Being a practical philosopher, he preached that the chains of servility are forged mainly by oneself ; and his basic principles were condensed into the simple motto that flies, figuratively, over every church he consecrated, ' One Caste, One God, One Religion '.

His reforms were far-reaching, his consecrated temples open to all Hindus, even Untouchables, decades before they were championed by the great Maharaja of Kolhapur. He abolished idols ; and in their place he set mirrors, to remind those who worshipped that ' as we are, so our gods are too '. There spoke a holy man with brains and a knowledge of human nature that went far to account for his widespread, lasting influence towards truer, cleaner living. He founded no sect. When his disciples wished to exalt him as leader, he forbade it, as Krishnamurthi has done in this later day. But his devotees, who are trained at Varkāla, go forth to serve their kind in whatever way they are needed to do. The memory of such a man deserves to live and will live. ' By their fruits ye shall know them.'

The magical water journey ceases at Trivandrum, the palm-engulfed capital. Beyond the town another fifty miles of busy Grand Trunk Road brings us back to Cape Comorin, the hills and the sea, having traversed the entire coastal length of lovely varied and prosperous Travancore.

The mountain region offers grandeurs of primaeval forest, lake and rushing rivers that many may find more to their taste than palm trees and dreaming lagoons. But all that is most unusual in that strip of a State—including the unusual beauty of its women —is to be found along the coast of Malabar. Happy is the nation that has least history : an aphorism that seems applicable to Travancore. Compare it—in that sense—with beautiful and tragic Udaipur, the splendour and terror of Tod's Rajasthān. Yet tragedy has its heroic compensations. Who would not be a Rajput and pay the price for that high privilege ?

Let us leave it at that. Comparisons are invidious. The world has need of all types ; the desert-bred, the soldier, the man of peace and progress. Among the constellations that make up Royal India there is equal room for the fiery effulgence of Rajasthān and the placid gleam of tropical Travancore.

SIKH STATES OF THE PUNJAB :

Everything passes : Emperors, Kings, adventurers, generals, saints and beautiful women. Cities rise in splendour, and decay forgotten among the wheatfields or the sands of the desert. The peasant has seen it all—and goes on. To-day, to-morrow, yesterday : it is really the peasant who holds the Punjab.—MICHAEL PYM.

THE SIKHS

' THE Punjab ! But of course I am prejudiced about the Punjab ' : words written by an American woman who fell in love with India and things Indian ; words that might with truth have been written by myself. My father's long service there, my own connection with the Lawrences of the Punjab have, from early days, given the whole Province a special claim to my interest and affection. Yet, as a land, it has neither charm nor splendour. Like a strong, unbeautiful face, it is more satisfying, as an index of character, than any languorous loveliness that charms the senses, but makes no stern demands on those it may captivate.

The Punjab, from end to end, possesses a unity of character, of atmosphere, curiously compelling to all who have come under its potent spell. That same American writer, who calls herself Michael Pym, conjures up in a few sentences the essence of the Punjab scene on an evening of spring, that is no prelude to summer, as England understands the word, but a whispered threat of the furnace seven times heated in May and June, before Indra, God of thunderbolts and storms, ushers in the Great Monsoon.

Here is her impression of an evening hour in April when out in the jungle the scarlet *dāk* tree flowers and all the different kinds of jasmin, yellow and white, fill the air with intoxicating smells ; air that quivers with heat. ' Dust devils rise and whirl into nothingness. Everywhere the sound that is India : wood doves kuroo-cooing languorously in the trees ; and far off the thudding of a *tabla*—a small drum beaten with the palm of the hand and the tips of the fingers ; a voice rising and falling on long-drawn Indian notes that finish in the air as if the singer went beyond ordinary hearing. From somewhere near by comes a long slow creaking, as a Persian wheel turns and turns ; bringing up water and emptying it, bringing up water and emptying it. Far and far stretch the wide fields with their low hedges of cactus. From a clump of trees two graceful minarets spring upwards. About half-way towards the horizon some peasants, with a team of buffaloes, are ploughing. How slowly they move like people in a dream. Three or four women, in the deep reds and yellows of India, walk in single file, their full skirts swinging rhythmically. . . .

' Sunset and long lines of cattle coming home in a golden haze : the smell of wood smoke, the quick harsh chatter of monkeys fighting as they go to bed ; and again far off, the throb of a *tabla* and a boy's voice singing. . . . The whole thing composed into an *adagio* movement hypnotic, dreaming, timeless : those wide fields, those far-off trees, minarets like white flowers, the buffaloes moving slowly, slowly . . .'

Timelessness : that is the note of the Punjab : and the village is its authentic human unit. Here we are two thousand miles removed from Cape Comorin : scene and climate and people the very antithesis of Travancore. No lotus-eating atmosphere in this Land of the Five Rivers, as its name signifies. Here we have a land of extremes : fierce heat and fierce cold, fierce antagonism and fierce loyalties ; mile-wide, slow-moving rivers : and everywhere dust—unlimited dust; the long silent fight of the peasant against drought and delayed monsoon and the Indian desert. Crops gleam in the river regions and in the Canal Colonies, marvels of irrigation ; but the general aspect becomes ever more barren as the train runs northward to the Salt Range beyond the Jhelum ; and beyond again towards the jagged hills of the North-West Frontier : a dun-coloured, sun-smitten landscape, fearsome in its lack of vitality, its aspect of an embodied Fate. Only in the utmost north, faint silver peaks of the far Himalayas lift their supremacy of strength and beauty high above the Punjab, above Kashmir.

Essentially the Punjab breeds peasants and fighters ; tall, sturdy men with the blend of many martial races in their veins, descendants of Aryan invaders, of Scythians, Greeks, Afghans. Every invader of India has passed through the Punjab, leaving his trail blazed by fire and sword, leaving also a legacy of racial qualities finely blended in the Punjabis of to-day. Among these are many Jāts of Rajput stock, more noted for courage, honesty and industry than for intelligence ; Punjabi-Mussulmans—mainly Rajputs of the North converted to Islam ; and the small but potent brotherhood of Sikhs—a far-famed religious and military community belonging to the Punjab and only to the Punjab. As founders of a sect and makers of history they rank high among India's manifold peoples. Indeed, the rise of the Sikhs from an obscure and persecuted fraternity to a great and formidable empire is one of the most dramatic records of Indian history. They have no legendary beginnings like the Rajputs though their present ruling families trace their origin back to a Rajput chief of Jaisulmir.

The actual founder of their brotherhood, Baba Nānak, was born in 1459 in an insignificant village near Lahore : an event of no greater moment than the fall of an acorn to the ground ; yet, like an acorn, the seed of great things to come.

The son of a village accountant, with no money sense and a taste for unprofitable meditation, he must have seemed to his family and fellows an unsatisfactory human specimen, hardly fitted to make a livelihood, by no means fitted to make anything else of importance to himself or others. Sent as a storekeeper to the small town of Sultanpur, he married and fathered two sons ; but more and more his inner self became detached from practical or worldly affairs. After his uncongenial day's work he would slip away into the forest, where he spent the night in fervent prayer and the singing of hymns to his Creator.

On one occasion, lost in meditation, he failed to return for three nights and days—a curiously common number in mystical experiences ; and those who loved him for his kindly deeds feared he must have been drowned in the river. But on the third day he returned, not realising the lapse of time ; and was greeted as one risen from the dead.

Questioned anxiously as to what had befallen him, he only said like a man dazed, ' There is no Hindu and no Mahomedan '.

Those seemingly senseless words expressed the core of his future creed : the basic truth proclaimed by all seers and dedicated men : ' God is one : whether we worship him as Allah or Rāma. The Hindu god dwells in Benares, the god of the Moslems at Mecca. But He who made the world lives not in any city made with hands.'

So spake Kabir, the inspired weaver-poet. And Baba Nānak, born twenty years later, was in the true succession of seers who believe in the *life lived* and frankly denounce the ascetic injunction to ' flee from a world pervaded by love, joy, beauty—the proper theatre of man's quest '.

In one of Kabir's Hundred Poems, translated by Rabindranath Tagore, he eloquently expressed that same belief :

Know whilst you live, understand whilst you live ; for in life
deliverance abides.
If your bonds be not broken whilst living, what hope of deliverance
in death ?
It is the Spirit of the Quest that helps. I am the Slave of the
Spirit of the Quest.

A slave of that spirit was Baba Nānak, who spent the latter
days of his life wandering from country to country, from city to
city, making disciples and disputing with holy men of every caste
and creed ; preaching always a purer morality between man and
man ; not how to escape the world but how best to live worthily
in it ; not how evil may be avoided, but how it is to be met and
overcome. Neither in Moslem nor in Hindu scriptures could he
find God : and throughout his life he was for ever seeking some
common bond between these two irreconcilables ; seeking to con-
vince them that ' there is but one God whose name is true—the
Creator, infinite and invisible '.

His wanderings took him southward to Ceylon, northward to
Kashmir, and there was no transport in those days but river,
horseback or country carts. It is said that he even adventured
to Mecca and Medina. A legend characteristic, if not verified,
tells how an Arab, finding him asleep on a hillside, woke him
and reproached him for sleeping with his feet towards the House
of God (Mecca).

And Nānak answered aptly, ' Show me where the House of
God is *not* '.

Questioned by a thoughtful Moslem Governor as to the
principles of his religion, his answer was simple yet impressive :
' Make Love thy mosque ; Sincerity thy prayer-carpet ; Justice
thy Koran ; Courtesy thy *Kaaba* ; Charity thy creed ; and the
Will of God thy rosary '.

He preached no new religion, and claimed no divine or special
powers. He desired only to restore Hinduism in its ancient
purity. He forbade *sati*, the killing of girl children, and the
element of sacrifice in worship. He required only a spirit of truth
and simplicity ; neither ritual, incense nor burnt-offering. Everywhere he preached without ceasing ; in mosques, in Jain temples,
in all places of pilgrimage where crowds assemble : and he drew
countless men after him. These followers he named Sikhs, or
disciples, from the word *sikhna*, to learn. Him they called their
' Guru '—teacher : the head of a succession of Gurus, who
established the Sikh brotherhood on purely peaceful religious lines.
Later, through force of circumstances, their creed took on a
political and military character. In those turbulent days, only

the fighter could hope to survive : and the Sikh has proved himself a fighter of the first quality.

But Guru Nānak remained a man of peace all his days.

Beset by illness, he felt that his end was near ; and lying with closed eyes he heard his sorrowful disciples arguing over the manner of his burial ; the Hindus insisting on a funeral pyre, the Moslems on earth burial.

Since neither would give way, the saint opened his eyes and quietly settled the matter.

At his death, let fresh flowers be heaped on his right hand by Hindus, on his left hand by Moslems : and in the morning those whose flowers remained freshest might claim his body.

There he lay all night, after death, flowers heaped on either hand : and in the morning all still remained fresh. The puzzled mourners, who had received no answer, lifted the winding sheet —and behold, the body had vanished.

But, in those who came after, his spirit survived and accomplished great things.

Nānak preached peace and ensued it ; but there was no peace for the Sikhs, or any Hindu cult, in the day of the great Moguls. Under the benign rule of the three first Emperors—Bābar, Humayun and Akbar—they flourished unmolested. It was Akbar himself who gave to the fourth Guru a tract of land where the holy one dug the now famous tank, Amritsar—the Pool of Immortality. Here eventually his followers built the Golden Temple as a shrine for their bible, the *Adi Granth* (First Book). It opens with a complete exposition of the Sikh faith, which every orthodox Sikh must learn by heart and repeat every morning. In the Temple it is daily read aloud ; and a copy of the Granth Sahib is carried at the head of every Sikh regiment.

The famous shrine owes its beauty chiefly to a coating of beaten copper covered with thin plates of gold. Set upon a platform in the middle of the tank, it shines resplendent, and is mirrored with dazzling effect in the green water framed by a marble pavement five hundred feet wide. Here Sikh men and women sit under the wild plum trees, reading or discussing their scriptures, while others bathe in the sacred pool. From the Gate of Adoration, with its doors of silver and ivory, a marble causeway leads to the centre platform and the shrine ; its doors of chased silver always open to the four winds. Worshippers entering by the western door bow reverently, drop their simple offerings on a sheet laid down for them, and pass out by the north door.

The scene within had been aptly described : ' The semidarkness, the rich colouring, the wailing voices and tinkling strings, scents of marigold and jasmin, the sheet strewn with poor offerings ; the mixture of reverence and indifference, the splendour and the squalor : an epitome of India '.

Trouble began for the Sikhs with the advent of Emperor Jehāngir, when the swift development and growing influence of the Sikhs in the Punjab led to false accusations and persecution of the fifth Guru. Cast into prison, he died under torture, leaving to his son and successor an injunction to defend the brotherhood by force of arms and forsake the futility of preaching peace where there was no peace. Thus it came about that Har Govind, sixth Guru, more soldier than saint, fired his followers with military ardour and soon had an effective force at his command. Even in those early days the Sikhs gave such clear proof of their great fighting qualities that Jehāngir became alarmed, seized and imprisoned their leader, who managed to escape, but died soon after.

For thirty years Mogul persecution raged unabated ; but it is a commonplace of history that oppression and cruelty invariably defeat their own ends. It was, in fact, the ruthless ferocity of Aurungzeb, last of the Moguls, that welded the Sikhs into a great warrior clan implacably hostile to Moslem power.

The ninth Guru, Tegh Bahadur, taken and imprisoned, refused to change his faith whatever torments of the flesh he might be called upon to endure. Accused of gazing, from the roof of his jail, towards the royal harem, he answered, in strangely prophetic words, ' Emperor, I am not gazing at thy royal apartments. I am looking across the sea towards the men, fair-skinned and wearing helmets, who shall come from the west to avenge my death, to tear down thy purdahs and destroy thy Empire.'

His prophecy was so firmly believed by the Sikhs that they used it as a battle-cry in the Mutiny, when fighting for the English, outside Delhi, against the last shadow Emperor of the Moguls.

After Tegh Bahadur came the tenth and last Guru, destined to raise the Sikhs from a fighting sect to a military nation. Only fifteen when his father was cruelly executed, he fled to the hills, fearing a like fate. There, for twenty years, he brooded on his people's wrongs ; and emerged from retirement a dedicated man, resolved on nothing less than the overthrow of the Moguls and the setting up of his own Sikhs as an independent power.

Thousands flocked to join him ; and at a great assembly he announced his mission, binding them more closely by a baptismal ceremony at adolescence, by the title Singh (Lion), hitherto reserved for Rajputs, and by five distinctive items of dress, known as the five *Kakas* ; all, in the vernacular, beginning with the letter K : *Kirpān*, the Knife, readiness for battle ; *Kara*, the iron bangle for fidelity ; *Khanga*, the comb ; and *Kes*, the uncut hair on which it is used ; *Karchh*, the shorts to the knee, possibly for a sign of manhood, since their women wear trousers. The Sikh fellowship was known henceforth as Khalsa—the Elect or Pure.

Govind Singh, like Nānak, insisted on purity of life, loyalty, honesty, chastity, justice. But on a level with these he placed brave deeds and readiness to die fighting in defence of the faith. A Sikh, for some reason, must never cut his hair. His beard, untrimmed, must be rolled round an oiled string and fastened under the chin, his long hair twisted into a knot under the high and handsome Sikh turban. The Khalsa has always been largely recruited from that hard-working race of husbandmen, the Jāts : men of splendid physique, tall, spare and muscular. Neither intellectual nor cultured, they make up in courage, honesty and thrift what they lack in brain power. Law-abiding in times of peace, in war, they are fighters of the first quality.

With the death of Govind Singh—murdered by a Pathan in 1708—the line of Gurus came to an end. He left no successor ; telling his disciples that their mission was ended. Their spirits henceforth would dwell in the *Granth Sahib*, their bible, and would pervade the Khalsa.

' I have entrusted you ', he said, ' to the immortal God . . . wherever there are five Sikhs assembled, know that I am in the midst of them. Henceforth the Guru shall be in Khalsa and the Khalsa in the Guru. I have infused my mental and bodily spirit into the *Granth Sahib* and the Khalsa.'

In the eighteenth century, throughout the great Anarchy—of which I have told—the Punjab, like most of India, was in ceaseless turmoil. Afghans from the north, Marathas from the south reduced it almost to a no-man's-land. Eight times it was invaded by the Afghan Chief Ahmed Shah : and for twenty years the Punjab reeled under his repeated, relentless visitations. He captured Lahore, and plundered Agra, leaving his son Timur to strike at the heart of the Khalsa by a surprise attack on Amritsar. That also was captured, the Golden Temple demolished—the sacred tank filled up with rubbish.

But, like many ruthless conquerors, he miscalculated the effect of that supposedly mortal blow. Destruction and pollution of their holy city fired the inexorable Sikhs to a white heat of fury. Uniting under the leadership of a carpenter, Jassa Singh, they ravaged the whole Province, routed the victor and drove him back into his father's domains. They seized Lahore and proclaimed the Khalsa an independent State.

But if the Sikhs were inexorable, the Afghans were insatiable : and many fierce struggles, a ding-dong of defeat and victory, intervened before Lahore became at last undisputed capital of the Sikhs ; and a certain chieftain of Patiāla, Raja Àla Singh, became Chief of a Province, thus founding the present ruling family of Patiāla.

When Timur succeeded the terrible Ahmed Shah, he left the Sikhs unmolested. They had given him too sharp a taste of their quality. But, like the Irish, they must be fighting someone. Failing a common enemy to unite them, their Sirdars, each with his own force, split up into twelve clans and began fighting one another.

At that time the Sikh character lost many of the fine qualities instilled by their Gurus. Mutual jealousies hindered the fulfilment of Govind Singh's prophecy—ultimate defeat of the Moguls. Their only law became the law of the sword. They still awaited a master hand that should weld them into a nation.

Then was born their Man of Destiny, Ranjit Singh (Lion of Victory), he who was to become the redoubtable one-eyed Lion of the Punjab.

At ten years old he witnessed his first battle, from the back of his father's war elephant, in a fight between rival clans, and was nearly killed by a man who climbed the elephant, only to be cut down before he could harm the boy. At the age of twelve he succeeded his father ; and endured, impatiently enough, a period of petticoat dominion, under his mother and mother-in-law. The two fierce and warlike ladies led their own armies in person ; and completely neglected the boy Ranjit, not even teaching him to read and write. But native genius has never been baulked of achievement by lack of education.

When his mother died, his wife's mother—ambitious and unscrupulous—dreamed of dominating the whole Punjab. But Ranjit Singh at sixteen had his own high ambitions in view. For all his lack of education he was an enlightened young man, with a bold, enquiring mind and an insatiable lust for power ; and the would-be Queen, intent on using him as a stepping-stone to power, found herself cast for that rôle by her uncrushable son-in-law.

After some show of resistance, she was captured and sent to ' honourable confinement ' in a distant fortress : leaving young Ranjit at length master in his own house : a step towards mastery of the Punjab and lands beyond the Punjab, as the event proved.

Before very long he gained possession of Lahore, still nominally under Afghan rule. He had the good fortune to be there in person when the Amir—making one of his intermittent raids—was recalled in haste and obliged to leave behind him twelve precious guns that could not cross the river Jhelum in flood. Artillery, of all arms, was the most precious in those days : and the shrewd young Sikh saw his chance. He undertook to salve the guns and convey them to Peshawar, if the Amir would recognise him as Ruler of Lahore. The Amir granted the request and kept his word, though the grant actually meant no more than permission to take Lahore—and to keep it, if he could : a doubt that would not be likely to trouble Ranjit Singh.

He proceeded to defeat lesser Sirdars, envious of his power ; and, in July 1799, he triumphantly marched into Lahore.

Three years after that he annexed Amritsar and demanded the surrender of the famous Zamzamma gun that had been captured by Ahmed Shah thirty-seven years earlier. It was regarded as ' The Luck ' of the Sikhs, and was mounted on the fortress of Multan. When that fort fell to the British in 1849, ' The Luck ' passed into their hands ; and it now stands outside the Lahore Museum. It is said to have been cast from copper water-pots collected, as a kind of poll tax, by Moslems from Hindus.

The capture of that famous gun must have pleased Ranjit Singh almost as much as his capture of the city. His two master passions were horses and guns. Never did he lose a chance to capture a gun. Let him hear of one in a fort, and he would not rest till the fort was taken or the gun surrendered to save the fort.

With the capture of Amritsar, Ranjit became leading Chief of the Punjab ; took to himself the title of Maharaja and a good deal else before many years were out. It was he who built up the formidable Army of the Khalsa that proved its fighting strength and skill nearly forty years later against the British in two Sikh wars. Meantime it was his unshakable resolve to become master of the Punjab.

His tactics were astute as they were effective. News of any quarrel or disturbance would give him the chance first to act as mediator, then to start operations and further depredations on his own account. Successfully he annexed the strip of wild hill country now known as the North-West Frontier Province, and eventually the delectable Vale of Kashmir that was still an outlying tract of Afghanistan.

He assumed few outward signs of Royalty ; but none who were

Q

admitted to his presence could fail to be impressed by his extraordinary qualities, his intelligence and acuteness that almost dispelled the effect of his unprepossessing aspect. ' The penetrating look of his one restless fiery eye, which seemed to dive into the thoughts of those he talked with, the rapidity of his laconic but searching questions, denoted the activity of his mind and his insatiable curiosity.'

A born conqueror, he still had his difficulties nearer home in dealing with his most powerful Sikh confederacy : a group of Chiefs, east of the river Sutlej, known as Phulkián. These seven brothers became ancestors of several Sikh ruling families, their leader being the Patiāla Chief Āla Singh, great-grandfather of the present Maharaja. He and his fellows, wishing to hold their own against the ever aggressive Ranjit Singh, appealed to the British for protection. This was finally granted, and Ranjit forced to recognise the Sutlej river as the boundary of his kingdom. Within that boundary, on the word of the British Government, he need fear no aggression ; and his political sagacity told him also that the English were safe friends, but very dangerous enemies. So a treaty was signed in 1809 ; and for twenty years he remained a firm friend of the Paramount Power.

In 1839 he became an unwilling partner of the British in their ill-conceived, ill-fated first Afghan War—a tragic drama fully recorded in my books *The Hero of Herat* and *The Judgment of the Sword*. Here, in brief, one can only say that the failure of the whole expedition sprang from the curiously frequent British tendency to back the wrong horse, coupled with a prevailing fear of invasion by Russia or Persia, then regarded as ' the bayonet end of the Russian rifle '.

Ranjit Singh, with his shrewd political instinct, disapproved from the first of the whole enterprise, and the risk it involved of stirring up that hornets' nest Afghanistan. Doubting the success of the British, seeing his own disadvantage if they failed, he gave in with a good grace and forwarded the fatal plan to the best of his ability.

In July 1841, before the storm burst and the Afghans repudiated their puppet King, he died from a paralytic seizure, ' as like the old Lion as he had lived '. Deprived of speech, his mind clear to the last, he continued to receive reports and give orders by gesture till he could no more. Though the creed of Guru Nānak forbade *sati*, four royal wives, refusing to survive him, were burnt on his funeral pyre ; and his favourite Minister was only restrained by force from sharing their fate. The ashes, taken to Benares, were strewn upon the waters of holy Ganges.

The whole Sikh kingdom was dismembered by the death of Maharaja Ranjit Singh—the bold adventurer who had begun life ' with a horse and a spear ' ; had risen, through daring robberies and military conquests, to become first Chief, then monarch, of his fellow Chiefs—the first and last Sikh Ruler of the Punjab. He left no true successor. His many marriages—regular and otherwise—had produced eight so-called sons, only one of them actually his own. The mother of his successor, young Dhulip Singh, had never been his wife. The record of the man—as often in the East—scarcely matched the record of the Ruler.

His death released forces of disorder and intrigue that could no longer be held in check. Always he had recognised that the welfare, even the existence, of his kingdom depended on friendly relations with the British ; but he had created two forces that only his iron hand could control : the Lahore Durbar—or Government—and his formidable Army of the Khalsa, that very soon became the real power in the land. His two feeble successors feared their own army more than they feared the British, whose power and prestige had been gravely damaged by the terrible Afghan disasters of 1841. Years of anarchy among conflicting Chiefs, atrocities and a reign of terror, so increased the power of the army that its very omnipotence led to the cause of its destruction.

On December 11th, 1844, sixty thousand Sikhs with a hundred and fifty guns crossed the river Sutlej, their boundary, and declared war, on the now familiar fiction that the British were preparing to invade their country. Consistently they had misunderstood the Company's peaceful aims and actions, that were now proven by their inadequate defence preparations, prompted by the Governor-General's anxiety to avoid even seeming to provoke the Lahore Government.

Roused at last, they made good their decisions in British fashion, at the eleventh hour. The Sikhs fought desperately and with judgment ; the British prevailed only at a fearful price in valuable lives. But the fact remained that within sixty days, at the cost of four pitched battles, a force seventeen thousand strong had overthrown a Sikh army of a hundred thousand fighting men, whose generalship, skill and stubborn courage had been proven on every field. By February the victors had taken Lahore ; a treaty was signed and Sir Henry Lawrence (then only a Colonel), appointed as British Resident, was confronted with a task that few other men of his time could have achieved.

In two years he did the work of ten : but under the strain—after twenty-seven years of India—his health broke down. During his absence the smouldering Sikhs flared up again into a second war.

How the Punjāb was finally conquered and annexed has been told in my book *Honoria Lawrence*. The fighting was the fiercest in British Indian history ; for the Sikhs had fine generals and their army combined the religious fervour of Cromwell's Ironsides with the restless pride of Roman praetorians. To the last, unbeaten at heart, they were furious with their own leaders who had betrayed them into final surrender.

The scene of that surrender—as moving as any in British Indian history—has been immortalised by Sir Edwin Arnold : ' With noble self-restraint, thirty-five Chiefs laid down their swords at Sir Walter Gilbert's feet : and the Sikh soldiers— advancing one by one to the long file of English troops—flung down tulwars, matchlocks and shields on their growing pile of arms, salaamed to them, as to the " Spirit of steel ", and passed through the open line—no longer soldiers.

' Saddest of all was the parting of each horseman from his charger. Again and again resolution failed. Again and again he turned back for a last caress, brushed aside tears unashamed ; expressing, in one pregnant phrase, the key to his manly resistance, his manly submission : " *To-day* Ranjit Singh is dead ".'

THE PUNJAB-PATIĀLA : HIS HIGHNESS YĀDAVINDER SINGH,
MAHARAJA OF PATIĀLA

THE PUNJAB-KAPURTHALA : COLONEL HIS HIGHNESS SIR JAGGATJIT
SINGH BAHADUR, G.C.S.I., G.C.I.E., G.B.E., MAHARAJA OF KAPURTHALA

PATIĀLA:
THE MAGNIFICENT

THE Punjab again—more than fifty years after the death of its first and last Maharaja. Converted, long since, into a great Province of British India, it still remains much the same in essence : the dust, the villages, the mile-wide rivers ; gardens of the great Moguls ; Amritsar and its Golden Temple ; the tomb of Ranjit Singh and the Golden Mosque in Lahore City. Through all the vicissitudes of history they abide—those two unchangeables, the landmarks and the land.

Yet, in a hundred ways of life and aspect, the Punjab of 1941 is markedly a different country from the kingdom that Ranjit Singh conquered and created, and failed to establish. The land itself has been in part transformed by that triumph of irrigation, the great Canal Colony, by motor roads and motor transport in all degrees. The province itself, created by those incomparable brothers Henry and John Lawrence, admittedly boasts an administration the finest of its kind. And within the actual geography of the Province there still remain those independent Chiefs who sought and received British protection from the all-encroaching Ranjit Singh a hundred and thirty years ago. That protection preserved the independence of the Sikh States ; and when the Mutiny storm broke over Northern India, Patiāla—acknowledged head of the Sikhs—proved a bulwark to the British.

In my opening chapter it has been told how the Sikh Chiefs guarded the Grand Trunk Road to Delhi—a life-line for urgently needed troops and supplies. Throughout the siege of Delhi—on which all turned—the Sikh troops proved their mettle many times over ; and thereafter, for signal services rendered, the Patiāla Maharaja inherited the distinctive title ' Favoured Son of the British Empire '.

The three Chiefs east of the Sutlej are Patiāla, Nabha, Jhind, with Kapurthala, farther north in the region of Jalandhar. And the greatest of these is Patiāla, which takes its name from the Sikh Chief Āla Singh who earned distinction under the Afghan Ahmed Shah and held his own against the Lion of Lahore. To him the State practically owes its existence ; but the ruling family, though Sikh in religion and rite, claims descent from the Lunar Rajputs, through a distant Chief Jaisul, founder of the small Rajput State

Jaisulmir.   With Rajput ancestry claimed by Sikh and Maratha
Princes, we find those gallant sons of Kings virtually ruling the
greater part of Royal India.

The present young Maharaja, Yádavinder Singh, is a Sikh
of Sikhs, a splendid figure of a man, handsome and bearded,
standing six feet three inches, his kingly appearance matched by
a goodly equipment of brains and character.   Educated in India,
he has not been subjected to the unfamiliar influences of English
public school and University life.   His Western outlook and
sympathies blend admirably with his Eastern heritage.   His war
contributions, his enthusiasm and rousing speech to his people
have been recorded in an earlier section.

It was only in 1938 that he succeeded his illustrious father,
Lt.-General H.H. Bhupindra Singh, with twenty-one letters after
his name ; and in every way he is proving himself a Ruler of high
promise : a true successor of Patiāla the Magnificent, if on more
modern lines.

Patiāla itself will remain magnificent—unbelievably so, like
many of India's marvels, that, in stock phrase, must be seen to
be believed.   In cold print they read like fantasy or exaggeration.
One can only vouch for the truth as told by those who have seen
the eleven acres of Palace : an immensity of rose-pink sandstone
that would make Versailles look like a cottage, the interminable
façade soaring aloft from redder terrace ; the vast central saloon
furnished with English chairs and sofas, decorated chiefly with
photographs of European royalties in jewelled frames ; three
generations of English Kings set in isolated dignity on the piano ;
bedrooms like reception halls, the bathrooms like ballrooms.

In the fifteen dining-rooms as many dinners would be served
each day on a silver dinner service worth no less than £30,000 ;
the elaborate courses prepared by a hundred and forty-three cooks
and kitchen helpers of whom seventeen chefs were dedicated to
curries only.   Guests were housed in a suite of five rooms and
slept on gold-plated beds.   In the vast garden, with its ivory
pavilions and fountain-filled canals, white peacocks drifted about
like ghosts, and birds of all kinds flitted among the trees.

The Maharaja, though a keen sportsman, was devoted to
animals, above all to horses and dogs.   His kennels, that housed
ninety-five of them—mainly gun dogs—were incredibly elaborate—
tiled walls and electric light ; a dog hospital with an operating
theatre that would shame some military hospitals in India ; and
three Englishmen in charge of the valuable inmates, bought at a
fancy price, in some cases over £300.   Sir William Barton tells
of one that was bought from an Englishman for £200, and the

Maharaja gave him another £50 because he wept when parting
from it. Would £50, one queries, console any true Englishman
for losing a dog he loved ?

The Patiāla court, as held by Sir Bhupindra Singh, was hardly
less resplendent than courts of the Great Moguls : and his personal
magnificence will hardly be matched by those who come after, in
a levelling age. A man of splendid appearance, courtly manners,
with the unyielding eyes and emotional lips of his forebears, he
has been described as a ' direct product of the Middle Ages, of
their magnificence, their courage, their cruelty and autocracy ' ;
a host without equal, given to boundless hospitality and unstinted
personal generosity : a composite character made up of contra-
dictions ; adored by his simple village subjects, whether he
technically oppressed them or no.

For sheer personal splendour, picture him welcoming a Viceroy,
on Patiāla platform, in his superb tiara and emerald breastplate—
the Patiāla emeralds each as large as a dessert spoon. His guard
of honour in maroon with cream facings ; his huge silver coach
for the Viceroy and himself : a blue-and-silver one for the
Vicereine ; and Rolls Royce cars for common mortals : the
coaches escorted by Patiāla Lancers : cars pursuing them at a
respectful distance.

The State banquet in the Palace glittered under vast chandeliers, hundreds of them, lit by electricity, he himself glittering
like any chandelier of them all. His pale-blue turban, surmounted
by a great diamond tiara, was looped with pearls, emeralds and
diamonds. To his diamond necklace, from the Empress Eugénie,
is added a pearl necklace, perfectly matched and shaped, said to be
worth a million sterling.

' No wonder ', he remarked to Sir William Barton, ' that Russia
has always wanted to loot India ! '

Who could pay the assigned cash value for India's incredible
gems is a question that does not seem to arise.

With an income of three millions a year, he was yet credited
with an overdraft bigger than the value of all his treasure ; and
the tale of a characteristic episode gives colour to the fantastic
statement.

Sauntering unattended into a big electrical furnishing firm
in Calcutta, he was piqued at receiving scant notice from the
salesmen. By way of arresting their attention, he glanced
round and asked casually, ' What price the whole contents of
this shop ? '

Startled wide awake, they retired for consultation with a
flustered manager who chanced it at nine lakhs (about £65,000).

' That'll do,' agreed His Highness coolly. ' I am the Maharaja of Patiāla. Send them along.'

They were sent along—the entire contents : and many of the cases still remained unopened when the State passed on to his son.

Yet the man was no eccentric, devoid of money sense. He merely possessed, in an unusual degree, that curious strain in Eastern Princes that impels them to wholesale purchases whether needed or no. If he wanted to impress mere shop-walkers, he would not boggle at the cost.

Sir William Barton writes of him, as a ' striking, forceful personality and a great conversationalist with a keen sense of humour. About a high British official he remarked to my wife : " He was not present when tact was being distributed ! " And his vignettes of fellow Princes were clever and witty.'

Soldier and statesman, a firm friend and relentless foe, he was impatient of officials ; shrewd enough to detect weak points in the first draft of Federation, and to warn his fellows against stepping on to the slippery plank, caring nothing that it made him unpopular in some quarters. For that reason he jokingly called himself ' the bad boy of Federation ' ; but as Chancellor of the Princes' Chamber in 1926 he played an important part in their discussions ; and his influence on Sikh opinion, in the whole Punjab, would have increased had he lived. Patiāla claims a million out of four million Sikhs ; and their fighting tradition, their strong element in the Indian Army give them a political importance out of all proportion to their number.

The present Maharaja may yet take the leading position, religious and political, to which his father was in every way entitled.

The Sikh soldier tradition had remained undimmed—adding to its glory in every Indian expedition and in two world wars.

A minor epic, in the Tirah campaign of 1897, is worth recalling as typical of Sikh courage and resource, resistance and endurance to the end.

Two small forts, on the Samána range beyond Kohāt, were practically encircled by thousands of Pathan tribesmen from the wild Frontier Hills : and a vital signalling post between the two was held by twenty-one Sikhs with an Indian officer. That post the tribesmen were out to destroy, so that the two small forts might be cut off from each other before they were attacked *en masse*.

A simple affair, it seemed, to them. What were twenty-one men without guns against five thousand ? But the twenty-one were Sikhs of a no-surrender breed : and the ingrained hatred of the Pathan dates from far-off days of Afghan invasion. When the two meet in battle, it is a case of no quarter given or asked.

The Khalsa, while it endures, will glory in the memory of that seven hours' resistance against overwhelming odds ; in the knowledge of that, but for a wooden door and weak flank defences, they might even have held out till the relieving troops arrived.

For the first few hours the surging mass of red-hot fanaticism dashed itself, in concentrated rushes, like waves against a rock—with about as much result. But, where thousands failed, two sinister figures crept secretly under the north-west bastion of the post and proceeded to undermine it.

Officers and men in the larger fort could see what those in peril could not. Again and again messages of warning were signalled, but never seen by men who were fighting for their lives.

At last the fated bastion tottered and fell inwards. The wooden door was hacked to bits ; and tribesmen, scrambling over their wounded and dead, swarmed into the little post, to kill—and kill.

Even then a stubborn remnant held out, in true Sikh tradition, till all were dead or dying ; all except one solitary sepoy, who locked himself into the guard-room and blazed away at the baulked, yelling crowd till they fired the place.

So that one unconquerable died a Norseman's death after killing, with his own rifle, a Pathan for each of his dead comrades.

Thus Saragharri fell, to the inexpressible grief and pride of British officers who—unable to help—had seen from afar the column of smoke, the tongues of flame, the swarming thousands and the inevitable end.

In the war annals of that Sikh regiment there are few prouder memories than the heroic defence of Saragharri.

Those were the Sikhs at their finest : and if the peace-time Sikh has his failings—vanity, obstinacy, love of money—so have other peace-time people. For war is human nature at its uttermost ; highest height or deepest depth.

The Maharaja was not destined to see his soldierly people proving their quality once again with Empire troops in yet another world war. He died in March 1938, when clouds were darkening over Europe and hopeful politicians were still making optimistic attempts to avert the inevitable.

While he lay mortally ill, in a vast pillared room overlooking his lake and thronged Zenana Palace, men could hardly believe in the passing of one who had so loved life and good living, sport and spending and the beauty of women. Husband of many wives, father of many sons, no one knew precisely the size of his astonishing family, which was reported to number at least eighty-seven sons and daughters. He himself had probably lost count. Mrs. Rosita Forbes, when staying in the Palace, describes a procession of perambulators containing fifteen or twenty royal infants, ' each pushed, with the utmost solemnity, by a bearded Sikh '. No less than six children, she was told, had been born to His Highness in one week.

And at his death she tells how ' hundreds of women, crazed with grief, rent their clothes, tore off their jewels, beat their heads against floors and walls ' ; seemingly distraught with anguish that may have been more genuine than the usual prescribed lamentation of the East.

The Maharaja, handsome, extravagant, despotic and boundlessly generous, possessed the indefinable quality of effortless personal attraction. Men liked him, women loved him : and his whole State mourned when the lowered flag over his rose-red Palace told them they had lost their Maharaj.

As with the passing of that so-different Prince, Sir Fateh Singh of Udaipur, so with the death of Patiāla the Magnificent, a last remnant of the feudal semi-divine authority of kingship passed away for ever. Most spectacular among the Princes, modern India—of Congress, village ' uplift ' and Delhi Assembly—will not, for good or ill, see his like again.

But the Sikhs of the Punjab, looking to the future, may turn more and more to Patiāla as their national centre : and Patiāla relies confidently on the leadership of Maharaja Yádavinder Singh.

KAPURTHALA:
THE COSMOPOLITAN

THE only other Sikh State of the first importance, though not large—set in the midst of the Punjab, above Lahore—is Kapurthala, a name more familiar than most outside India. For there are few more widely travelled Princes than Colonel H.H. Raj-i-rajgari Maharaja Jaggatjit Singh Bahadur, G.C.S.I., G.C.I.E., G.B.E. He is familiar with most countries in Europe and Asia ; has travelled in North Africa ; and visits Europe or England almost yearly. He must by now be one of the elder statesmen of his Order ; but he carries his age with an ease that is more usual in the West than in the East.

As a boy of eighteen he was extremely stout, weighing as much as eighteen stone. Now, just over seventy, he is noted for ' the immense distinction of his appearance ; slight and clean-shaven but for a small moustache, with the burning dark eyes of a Medici portrait ', resembling those subtle statesmen in build and expression, and possessing ' the most delightful family imaginable '. His well-favoured sons have succeeded in marrying beautiful women, one of them, Princess Karām, being accounted the loveliest lady in India.

But if the Prince is a modern in thought and way of life, he possesses an interesting Sikh temple, dedicated to the Faith of the Ten Gurus, and one of the finest Durbar halls in India.

His Moslem subjects have a mosque in Moorish style said to be unique in Asia : a large claim.

Most of his people are Sikhs, in the soldier tradition, or land-bound peasants like the bulk of the Punjab.

The Maharaja's chief idiosyncrasy is a love of France and all things French, including the language that he speaks like a Parisian ; yet another call for the over-worked word unique. He has, in effect, created a curious fragment of France on the dusty plains of the Punjab between Lahore and the foothills of Kashmir : a tinsel anomaly, perfect in its alien conception and design ; delightful in its stage-like unreality. For it is neither France nor India. It is Kapurthala : a Sikh State, where at certain times processions of enormous elephants still carry the Sacred *Granth Sahib* and a holy one, who intones its noble phrases, high above the heads of the people, while they acclaim their Maharaj. It is

Kapurthala : the delight of travellers for its sport, its attractive ruling family, its cultivated princely host, its incomparable cuisine.

And this Maharaja owns the inevitable jewels of his Order that are intrinsically India : a topaz belt buckle four inches long, of burning amber yellow, said to be the largest in the world ; a crown that surmounts his turban on supreme occasions only ; emeralds beyond price, set in pearls and diamonds—three thousand of them, carefully chosen.

Once, in distant days of his youth, when certain visitors were inspecting his crown jewels, an enthusiastic young woman ex-claimed enviously at sight of those endless pearls of price.

What would she not give to possess even two strings of them !

The young Prince wreathed in them, with a wide jewelled collar, answered—as one stating a simple matter of fact—' Pearls are not for *women*.'

The Englishwoman's comment, if any, is not recorded : and the Prince himself must presently have realised that India's Princesses and Queens are as lavishly looped with pearls as any potentate of them all ; though no doubt the most priceless jewels adorn the sacred person of the Maharaja, for reasons explained when I described the Dussara festival in Mysore.

These wealthy Maharajas, with Parisian surroundings, rose-red Palace and jewels of untold value, seem a far cry from one humble fourteenth-century storekeeper turned saint, with his forest prayers and meditation, his dream of a faith in the God above all gods that should unite Hindu and Moslem and so save India from the horrors of religious persecution and strife.

But if the dream of Guru Nānak did not prevail, other marvels undreamed of came to pass through the inspiration of his devoted life. An acorn fell to the ground : and from it sprang the mighty oak tree of a Sikh Empire : a Sikh nation and Sikh Princes, who have become pillars of the House that *is* standing together ' in the last great fight of all '.

THE PUNJAB-KAPURTHALA : CAPARISONED STATE ELEPHANT

THE PUNJAB : THE GOLDEN TEMPLE, AMRITSAR : POOL OF IMMORTALITY

(From *The Road to Kashmir*, by James Milne)

KASHMIR : DIADEM OF INDIA

Here indeed is the Spirit of India purged from the dross of creeds. These are neither India nor not-India, these sublime impersonal abodes of snow and cloud and a rushing mighty wind : remote from man and his insect activities ; shining witnesses to the Truth that transcends all creeds, they create a world of their own between earth and heaven.—MAUD DIVER, *The Singer Passes.*

As the dews are dried up by the sun, so are the sins of mankind dispersed by the glories of Himalchān.—(A Hindu saying.)

I

' KASHMIR without an equal—Kashmir, equal to Paradise ! ' is a song that countless pilgrims of time have sung to the lazy potent swing of the Jhelum river round Srinagar.

Differently expressed, it is the song of all those whose ' eyes are filled '—in Eastern phrase—with the spring and autumn glory of that enchanted valley, which is yet but an ante-chamber to greater glories, reserved for those who seek them among the higher mountain regions of that incomparable land.

The valley itself reveals fresh aspects and fresh charm with every curve of the sinuous Jhelum river ; now framed in silver-grey poplar stems, now in broken ridges of rock and pine ; crowned always—as with a tiara—by the Shining Ones, pale gold and rose in the last of the sun, or ink-blue under an outstretched wing of storm-cloud sweeping darkly up the stream.

Beyond the valley there remain, for those who venture, the steep track, the mountain torrent, sweeping curves and changing lights of the high snows, more nearly allied to heaven than to earth.

But Kashmir itself, the land, the people, the tapestried background of history—over two thousand years of it—is more than a world-renowned spectacle of mountain, forest and river. It is a vast, composite Indian State, only second in importance to Hyderabad. Owing to its size and frontier position, one-seventh of its revenue is spent in keeping up the largest and best-equipped army in Royal India.

The mountain passes of Northern Kashmir, where the empires of India, China and Russia meet, are highways of the oldest trade routes in the world : the camel caravans of shaggy, tireless Bactrians, laden with rich cargoes, padding at little more than a foot's pace—a seven or eight months' journey—from ports of the Indian Ocean to marts of Turkestan and Central Asia.

Through those same passes, and through Kashmir, every invading host has marched or fought its way, from Persia, Afghanistan, Arabia, down to the plains of the Punjab, leaving in its wake a legacy of death and destruction.

And before the invaders, before the dawn of History, Kashmir reaches back and back to legendary days of Buddhist supremacy ; days of an earlier, mightier race, who can be judged only by the ruins of their temples, that are unlike any others in Hindustan. Their massive simplicity of design, their grace in detail of colonnade and fluted pillar and trefoil arch, suggest a mingling of Egyptian and Greek influence on a people who must have been profoundly religious to have built temples on a scale so noble, simple and enduring.

Of these, the most impressive ruin—Martand, Temple of the Sun—stands on a site more sublime than any other famous building in the world. Bold, simple and immensely strong, set upon a grassy upland, it faces the whole length of the valley in all its changing seasons ; none lovelier than autumn, when the many trees of Kashmir flaunt their sunset glory : walnut and elm, gold-powdered ; poplars clothed in clear amber ; and chenars—the mighty plane trees—aflame from base to summit, outshining and outnumbering them all. A prose-poem could be written on the trees of Kashmir alone. The dignity of the royal chenar, often centuries old : the grace of the spiritual deodar, Tree of God : the shivering poplar, birch and grey-green willow ; and all the host of lesser trees that blossom in spring.

Earlier still, in the mists of world-beginnings, we find the inevitable legend of how this delectable valley came into being.

Originally, it is said to have been one vast lake ; and there is geological proof that much of it must have long been under water. The land was possessed by a huge Snake or Nagar, the god of primitive gloomy earth-worship ; and the lake was haunted by a ' conchiferous Demon ', water-born, who preyed on men and women to the great distress of the country round. Finally, it is told how he uprose in his might and carried away the whole terrestrial globe.

Then were the Devas (gods) in sore distress at losing the Earth Goddess (Prithvi) and all the sacred Védas, their inspired books. So they besought the great god, Vishnu, by some means to rescue both.

Vishnu thereupon assumed the form of a mighty boar, and dived after the conchiferous Demon, bringing up with him the Earth Goddess and the Sacred Books. At one blow he made an exit for the waters of that vast lake ; and the place where he rested from his great achievement was called Varahamulla—the Abode of the Boar : now corrupted into Baramulla where the waters of the Jhelum leave Kashmir. And the land that emerged from the half-emptied lake became the habitable valley of to-day.

So and no otherwise—as Kashmiris believe—did the gods create their world-famous vale, cradled in guardian mountains, watered by a thousand streams, a chain of lovely lakes and a river that demands to be regarded with imagination, because it has temperament.

Born in the highest hills, it descends in foam and spray from the snows. Its winding stream—fed by countless hidden springs —is said to have given Kashmiris the idea for the prevailing pattern on their shawls.

Majestic and serene it flows past Srinagar—a ramshackle, Eastern Venice, clustering on either bank, looking almost as if it had been bombed or shaken by an earth tremor, so many of its balconied houses are just off the straight. And here are old, old temples with worn stairs ; open-ended houses, their roofs converted into flower gardens ; and at intervals the river is spanned by the well-known seven crooked bridges, their quaint arches leaning forward, yet by some marvel holding their own against the volume of water, even when it rises in occasional floods.

In the Golden Age, 327 B.C., India's great Emperor, Asoka, became an enthusiastic convert to Buddhism, ordaining it to be the State religion. To-day no trace of it remains among the people. Only a few temples and great stone fragments attest that the spirit of the Buddha once passed that way.

When the Romans were conquering Britain, a great wave of Scythians came pouring down into the favoured valley that, because of its very loveliness and fertility, could never be left in peace. Like Italy, a ' woman country loved by male lands ', it adds to its own peculiar charm the grace of its women. Their beauty, like those of Malabar, is world-renowned. It may be rarer now, as some assert ; but there still remains the lure of almond eyes, fair skin and an occasional Greek contour of the face —a heritage from far-off days, when world-conquering Alexander passed through Kashmir to possess India, and left behind him enough soldier-settlers to endow Kashmir women with Greek profiles and fair skins for ever.

But here is no traditional counterpart—fair women and brave men. The Kashmiri, in spite of his fine physique, his skill in many arts and crafts, has never been skilled in the art of war. These men of the valley seem to lack even the normal instinct of self-defence. They will patiently endure and suffer, but they will not fight ; and they are chary of the truth. In the words of an American visitor, ' they set such value on truth, that they very seldom use it '. And the neatly turned phrase, no libel, is affirmed by Mr. Tyndale-Biscoe, Head of the famous Mission School that has been a vital influence in Kashmir for close on forty years.

' The Kashmiris themselves ', he says, ' have so degraded the word that it has become almost a term of abuse signifying coward, rogue, slacker and other unbeautiful qualities. I have often told them so to their faces without evoking the least resentment. They know it is true, and it does not greatly trouble them.'

Yet he, of all men, knows that there are scores of admirable exceptions ; and to him belongs the credit of having largely increased their numbers through precept, example and a life devoted to combating every possible and impossible form of prejudice, slackness and thoughtless cruelty common to their kind. For all that, it is not easy to assess them as a race. There are so many variants, from the high and stark regions, where men are hardened by their struggle with Nature in her sterner moods, to the low hills of Jammu, where the people are mainly Dogras— hill Rajputs, proven soldiers.

But these men of the valley have been lapped for centuries in its insidious softness of air and scene : a softness that induces the Kashmiri's pleasure in the passing moment, his placid philosophy of acceptance—' To-day is sufficient. . . . To-morrow may never come.'

But beyond the prevailing atmosphere and texture of his valley, no other form of softness has been his portion. Throughout the centuries he has been a victim : battered into abject submission by invasion on invasion from every warlike race in turn—Tartars Moguls, Afghans, Sikhs.

Buddhism passed ; Scythians passed ; the subtle Brahmins regained their hold on the Hindu mind, and one conqueror after another laid violent hands on lovely Kashmir.

After the Scythians came a far more terrible inflow of Tartars from Central Asia, under a Chief notoriously violent and cruel, known as ' the White Hun '—a word that has become a synonym for all that is most inhuman. The people, it was said, knew of his approach by the flights of vultures, kites and crows eager to feed on those who would be slain. His passing merely heralded a dreary sequence of tyranny, cruelty and religious persecution. Only here and there a brief respite ; only one Golden Age, one great king of their own, some twelve hundred years ago, Lalata- ditya, who conquered Tibet, invaded Central Asia and sent embassies to Pekin. In thirty years he raised his kingdom to a height of glory never attained before, nor ever equalled since.

After him, there followed inevitably the too familiar iteration of weak rulers, murder, treachery, internal strife, for the matter of five hundred years—a trifling period in the large stride of history. That unhappy race threw up no fine leaders to mould a strong national character. Its people remained at the mercy of any conqueror who coveted their covetable country. Truly Kashmir itself—the whole magnificent region—is greater than any of its rulers ; its loveliness undisfigured by stroke on stroke of the oppressor.

Almost it seemed to promise relief when a Moslem Ruler, in the fifteenth century, ousted the decaying Kashmir dynasty : but too soon the unhappy Hindus came under the flail of Moslem fanaticism, persecution and wholesale slaughter. They were either converted by force or slain if they refused to change their faith. Hundreds, in despair, burned down their own homes or committed suicide. Hundreds tried to flee the country ; and, failing, flung themselves over precipices to escape a worse fate.

Notorious, as tyrant, was Sikander Khan, the idol-breaker, who destroyed all their sacred places and cynically used the material to build mosques and *ziarats*.[1] Religion as the prime cause of war and man's inhumanity to man ranks among the major anomalies of creation.

One merciful breathing-space was vouchsafed them in King Zain-ul-ab-ul-Din ; no persecuting fanatic. He would indeed fain have become a Hindu ; but the Brahmins could not accept him, Hindus being born, not made.

He therefore remained a Moslem, but he was tolerant towards Brahmins. He repaired many Hindu temples and revived Hindu learning.

He made great conquests, including the wild country of Tibet ; he built many palaces and public buildings. Better still, he encouraged learning and all the fine arts. His court was thronged with poets and musicians, artists and singers. Best of all, he gave unhappy Kashmir an oasis of peace and prosperity that lasted for fifty years : a period spoken of, even now, as the happiest in their history.

It was a genuine blessing when the sixteenth century brought most of India under the enlightened dominion of the Great Moguls, who came to love Kashmir and set their seal upon it in gardens of deathless beauty. Akbar himself conquered the country without much serious opposition : and for close on two hundred years it

---

[1] Moslem shrines.

R

remained under Mogul rule, which—as we have seen—was just and wise and free from tolerance.

Three times Akbar visited Kashmir. He settled the land revenue and built the fort of Hari Parbat ; its midday gun still the timekeeper of the valley. He also laid out the lovely *Nasim Bagh*, Garden of the Morning Winds. Wisely it was designed without set flower-borders ; only grass and aisles of splendid chenars ; and in springtime clumps of white or purple iris open their curved petals, faintly scenting the air.

Of the valley people in general Akbar formed a poor opinion ; and he was a shrewd judge of men. In scathing terms he told them the unflattering truth :

' You Kashmiris,' he said, ' have stomachs to eat, but not to fight. Men ? Faint-hearts not lion-hearts. Therefore skirts for you.'

So he bade them eat their victuals cold, and exchange their Oriental finery for a loose shapeless garment hanging to their ankles : a garment they still wear centuries after. Who shall compute the insidious effect on the character of even stalwart men ? Dress can have a queer, unmistakable effect on the mind ; and the Kashmiris might well owe a grudge to Akbar, for all his enlightened rule. But so completely had they been battered into submission that they probably never gave it a thought.

Among Mogul Emperors the sincerest devotee of Kashmir was Akbar's son, Jehāngir, Lord of the World : a lover of woman, a lover of Nature and a lover of good wine, to his own detriment, though alcohol is forbidden by the Prophet. Jehāngir was supremely an artist in life and temperament : an original character, as revealed in his own curiously frank, translated journals. He records his own weakness and the debt he owed to his favourite wife, Nur Jahān, Light of the World, who gradually persuaded him to take fewer cups of wine in the day and eventually helped to save his country from a serious revolution.

As an infant she had been left on the roadside by her parents, on pilgrimage ; had been picked up, and saved to become the favourite wife of an Emperor and, in her own right, a very great lady indeed : not to be confused with her daughter-in-law, Mumtāz Mahāl (Glory of the Palace), wife of the next Emperor, Shah Jahān, who immortalised her memory in the world's most exquisite and impressive shrine of love and sorrow, the Taj Mahāl, at Agra.

Enchanted alike by the beauty and sterner splendours of Kashmir, Jehāngir returned there again and again ; making the journey in springtime along the Road of the Emperors that enters

the valley over the Pir Panjāl Pass : a vast cortège of elephants,
baggage ponies, gaily-covered litters for his imperial harem—
all the gorgeous magnificence peculiar to the Kings of Hindustan
in transit from splendour to splendour. The *serais* of to-day have
forgotten those wondrous royal visitations : five hundred elephants and thirty thousand coolies, mere items in the train of an
Emperor who was supposed to be ' marching light ' for his summer
change of scene.

Two exquisite gardens were added to the Valley by Jehāngir,
with his artist's eye for trees and flowers, birds and fountains, for
the towering heights beyond, and the reflections, mirror-clear, in
the silver waters of the Dhal Lake.

Nishāt Bagh, Garden of Delight—approached from the lake,
as are they all—is at its loveliest in April, the incomparable month,
here as elsewhere. Beyond a gateway flanked by masses of
Persian lilac, that lovely garden climbs the hillside in seven
terraces. From the highest of these a cascade of waterfalls comes
splashing down to the lake, escorted by statuesque chenars in
youngest leafage. Everywhere sheets of pale mauve and purple
iris, blossoms of peach and cherry and pear, strike the authentic
note of spring in Kashmir. Here and there the flash of a sky-blue
kingfisher, the gleam of a golden oriole. From the highest grassy
terrace the view of waterfalls, lake and mountains beyond, is but
one among many, each one so enthralling that it seems to surpass
the rest.

There is here no beautiful pavilion comparable to that in the
Shalimar Bagh, or Royal Garden, as its name signifies. Set on a
tank, it is colonnaded with pillars of black marble exquisitely
carved. Between the pillars a sparkling cascade falls into the
quiet water disturbed only by the soft splash of many fountains
rising and falling. The grass round the tank is shadowed by
guardian chenars, many of them two or three centuries old. For
even now none may fell these royal trees without permission from
the Maharaja.

While that imperial monarch reigned over most of India, the
battered Kashmiris enjoyed comparative peace. There followed
him only two more Mogul Emperors : Shah Jahān, King of the
World, who sleeps for ever with his Queen in the Taj Mahāl ; and
Aurungzeb the Terrible, in whose reign power declined and
violence increased. Governors in outlying provinces became
more independent and high-handed. Officials took to fighting
among themselves, and maltreating Hindus. Once more Kashmir fell into violent disorder ; till, in 1750, that beautiful and
unhappy country came under the worst and cruellest rule of all.

The Afghans, descending on it from Kabul, found the far-famed valley an earthly paradise, and proceeded to make of it an earthly inferno.   Notoriously the most ruthless tyrants in creation, they filled the land with governors who laid upon the people, especially on the Hindus, burdens impossible to be borne.   They thought no more of cutting off heads than of cutting flowers ; and when they wearied of slaughtering Kashmiris wholesale, they would save themselves trouble by tying numbers of them up in sacks and flinging them into the lake.   Such cruelties were practised that many died under brutal ill-treatment, or killed themselves in order to escape from it.

No wonder they turned almost hopefully to the next invader, Maharaja Ranjit Singh, Lion of Lahore, who came with his Sikhs to oust the Afghans in 1819, when England was settling down after the battle of Waterloo.

With the Sikhs came Raja Gulāb Singh of Jammu—the hill State south of Kashmir—their own Man of Destiny, with whom they were to become increasingly familiar before many years were out.   With his help, Ranjit Singh finally conquered and annexed the country.   So once more Kashmir came under Hindu rule ; but by now, paradoxically, the bulk of its people had become or been converted into Moslems.   Irony has pursued that hapless race down all the corridors of time.   As Hindus they were set upon and ruthlessly exterminated by Moslems.   When the bulk of them had turned Mussulman, they found themselves ruled and persecuted by Sikhs.   If these were less barbarously cruel than Afghans, they were harsh and rough masters, who subjected the conquered to every conceivable form of extortion and oppression ; so that again hundreds fled from the country to avoid their ruthless rapacity.   Could these be the disciples of Guru Nanāk, preacher of tolerance and seeker after unity between the rival creeds ?

Sikh mastery endured for twenty years ; a brief interlude in the tragic record of their long martyrdom.

In 1839, as I have told, the death of Ranjit Singh threw the whole Punjab into disarray.   In Kashmir the Sikh army of occupation mutinied and murdered the Governor.   A strong hand was needed to quell the upheaval : and once more Gulāb Singh of Jammu appeared on the scene.   With five thousand men he quelled the rising ; appointed a Governor of his own choice ; and in effect made himself master of the covetable valley, though it still belonged, nominally, to the enfeebled Sikh government at Lahore.

The chance of his life came to him when the Sikh army forced the British into a major war and suffered a major defeat.   It then

KASHMIR : JHELUM RIVER AND TAKT-I-SULEIMAN

(From *The Road to Kashmir*, by James Milne)

KASHMIR : NANGA PARBAT (DEOMIR), HOME OF GODS

(From *The Road to Kashmir*, by James Milne)

came out that the Lahore treasury could not meet the full indemnity demanded by victors, who, like Robert Clive, might well have stood astonished at their own moderation. History has few parallels to the forbearance of the English at Lahore. The Sikhs themselves marvelled at it : no slaughter, no loot permitted in a rich, conquered city. But the treasury was not rich ; whence came the chance of Gulāb Singh. Astute and miserly, having no quarrel with the British, he offered to produce the necessary sum—three-quarters of a million sterling—on the condition that he should be nominated Ruler of Kashmir ; that country having passed into British hands with the whole Sikh dominion.

After due consideration, the offer was accepted as the simplest way to get the money and solve a difficult problem. The treaty of 1846 transferred the province of Kashmir ' for ever, an independent possession, to Maharaja Gulāb Singh and the heirs male of his body '.

Undoubtedly a great day for Gulāb Singh. Thirty-eight years earlier he had begun life as a common soldier in an obscure fortress, drawing three rupees (six shillings) a month, and his rations. Now, still under sixty, he found himself absolute monarch of a magnificent kingdom amounting to eighty thousand square miles.

As for Kashmir itself, many have marvelled that this lovely land—actually ceded to the British as the fruit of a strenuous war—should have been virtually sold to a mere hill Raja for a paltry sum, considering the country's untold potential value. At the time, it was argued that the East India Company had no right to ' sell ' a country that it was in no position to conquer and could not effectively hold.

The answer is that the British had then no thought of annexing the Punjab, nor any prevision of a second successful Sikh war. It was necessary to keep some kind of hold on Kashmir as the only trade route between British India and Central Asia : immemorial route of the invader. Only a single strong· Ruler on the spot could securely hold the Border passes : and Gulāb Singh was the one Chief equal to that demand, also the only one who could produce the necessary cash. Undoubtedly, if the question had arisen three years later, after the second Sikh war, the Company might have reached a different decision.

But, as things turned out, the only feasible arrangement, at a difficult moment, was afterwards seen to be a master stroke of policy—killing two birds with one stone : the Sikh power weakened, in the event of any further rising, and a friendly, subordinate power established on the most important frontier of the Empire. In many respects external independence was the best policy. The fine race of Dogras, like the Gurkhas of Nepāl, have not been enervated by skin-deep civilisation, which often takes away with one hand what it gives with the other. And all four Maharajas of Kashmir have been men of striking character.

True, Gulāb Singh, with all his ability, had a notorious reputation in the Punjab for cruelty, duplicity and savage abuse of power. But in that line there was probably little to choose between him and the Sikh Governor whom he would replace. And the British could keep an eye on their nominee. Only a strong Ruler could hold together that ' curiously compounded mixture of people and countries '. For the peasants were Moslem ; the intellectuals were Brahmins—christened Pundits by Akbar ; the landowners were mainly colonising Sikhs or Afghans ; and their new Maharaja was a Dogra Rajput, unpopular owing to his reputation for oppression and avarice.

He was, in fact, opposed by the Sikh Governor and a handful of feudatories, when he set out to take over his new kingdom. British troops, or rather Sikh troops, must come up from Lahore, led by Colonel Lawrence himself : ' the extraordinary spectacle ' —as he afterwards wrote—' of a few British officers leading a lately subdued, mutinous army through as difficult a country as there is in the world '. But being British officers, with a Lawrence for their leader, the thing was done : Maharaja Gulāb Singh was duly settled on his purchased throne : and the long-suffering Kashmiris, numbed into indifference, waited to see what would happen next.

The condition of the country, when Gulāb Singh took it over, was deplorable, apart from conflicting elements of race and religion ; but he was an able man, untroubled by tiresome inhibitions as to ways and means. By good management of Kashmir's fertility and magnificent forests, he soon recouped his purchase money ; organised, on British lines, an army of Dogras, Moslems and Sikhs ; and proceeded, in his masterful fashion, to impose peace on his unwieldy kingdom.

He put down crime with a strong hand, by punishments relentless and often cruel : but he achieved his end. Crime became so rare that practically no police were needed, except in the capital and a few other towns. Of how many civilised lands could that be said ? In other respects he left the country much as he found it ; the Brahmin Pundits, or landlords, continuing to ride roughshod over the peasants. It was now Hindu over Moslem ; and, as always, the innocent paid the price for later Mogul persecutions. Slave labour, enforced by soldiers, ruined the land. State monopolies were legion and mulcted by the Brahmins, which did not greatly trouble Gulāb Singh.

He died early in 1857, and was succeeded by Maharaja Ranbir Singh, a man of noble presence, as his portrait [1] bears witness. Sir Walter Lawrence wrote of him as ' one of the handsomest men I have ever met ' ; and in every way he was a complete contrast to his father. He was extremely popular with his people, and with all the British who came to Kashmir for work or pleasure ; delighting in all manly sports ; devoted to his family, simple and moral in his personal life. A Ruler of the old-fashioned type, dear to the East, he would sit daily in Durbar, receiving and answering petitions, keeping in personal touch with his people : a practice impossible to combine with modernised methods of rule, yet eminently in accord with Eastern ideas of kingship.

Unhappily this admirable monarch was served by officials of a less enlightened school, neither desirous nor capable of the immense effort required to remove the terrible effects of centuries-old misgovernment, aggravated by the harsh cruelties of Afghan and Sikh. The Maharaja did what he could. Improvement was steady, but it was slow work. The whole State had got into the grip of grinding officials : an ill fate for any country. It was a wise Burmese philosopher who reckoned among ' the three greater evils, fire, flood—and officials '. Those of Kashmir were products from a bygone age, ' when men of honesty and public spirit had no more chance of survival than a baby in a battle '.

The handsome and admirable Ranbir Singh died in 1885, leaving to his successor a fair crop of difficulties, increased by a terrible flood and famine that had saddened the last years of his life.

2

The advent of Sir Ranbir Singh's successor, in 1885, brings us to comparatively modern times.

The new Maharaja, Major-General H.H. Sir Partāb Singh, lacked the splendid appearance of his two forerunners. Short and thick-set, he was addicted to wearing a large turban that drooped persistently over one enquiring eye. In his own different fashion, he was, like his father, a Maharaja of the old school, though ruling on more modern lines with the help of three Ministers, Home, Revenue and Chief Minister—his able brother, Sir Amar Singh. Most courteous, yet most inscrutable of men —like fine old Sir Fateh Singh of Udaipur—he was kindly but shrewd. By some means he contrived always to know what happened everywhere in his State ; but he kept his own counsel.

[1] See Frontispiece.

He would talk most politely for hours, and tell the interested listener precisely nothing. Deeply devoted to the Royal House of Windsor, he gloried in the fact that King Edward, King George, Queen Mary and the Prince of Wales had all visited Jammu. Belonging to a generation less chary of expressing sincere emotion, he never lost a chance of publicly stating his loyalty to the British Throne and all connected with it. Yet neither he nor his brothers ever crossed ' the black water ' : so rigidly they adhered to orthodox caste rules. Even moving about India was, as we have seen, a cumbersome, elaborate business. But he owned a cherished map of London : and thoroughly knew his way about it—on paper.

In his daily life he was simple and frugal, like most of his kind. Leaving his inner palace at 7 A.M., he would listen, till 10 A.M. to reports and extracts of papers. Then an hour would be devoted to bath and *puja*—a word that means more than prayer. It includes any form of worship, meditation or talk with holy men ; and even officials may take part in it.

At 11.30 he would eat the first meal of his day : a veritable feast of some fifty or sixty dishes. No alcohol, no meat ; but many kinds of vegetables, bread, rice, cakes, sweetmeats and sour milk-curd, his favourite food. Unstinted butter enriched every dish, and the wonderful meal would often last an hour.

Then came Durbar—the real business of the day—till two o'clock, when he would return to his inner palace till five. Then he would enjoy his exercise, rowing or riding, till eight. His last meal—dinner—at 10.30 was no silent affair, as the Hindu meal is ordained to be ; but enlivened with much talk, jesting and laughter.

After all that, he retired to his inner palace and his many ladies. But in spite of their number, they gave him no son : a very real grief to him, as Maharaja and devout Hindu, for whom a son, to perform his funeral rites, is the one sure passport to paradise.

So it was the son of his brother, Chief Minister Amar Singh, who must come after him. His Brahmins, having potent influence, persuaded him to adopt a boy ; desiring, for their own reasons, to oust the true heir in the male line, his brother's son, Sir Hari Singh. But the British Government refused to recognise the adoption owing to the phrase in their treaty with Gulāb Singh, ' the heirs male of his body '. Sir Hari Singh, being a son's son, fulfilled that condition ; so the plot failed—and he was nominated heir to the throne.

The Maharaja himself, though influenced overmuch by superstition, by his priests and his women, was a very individual and attractive personality with a real gift for friendship. All who knew him well spoke of him with affection. A very complex character, he had known much and suffered much. He was greatly respected in India and loved by his people. It pleased him that his Imperial Service troops—no Kashmiri among them —had the honour of guarding the Northern passes into India. As a young man he was not strong in health. His doctors, at one time, gave him only a few months to live; but he out-witted them by reigning more than forty years and living till he was seventy-four, his activities increasing with age. Though he avoided alcohol, he was, like many Rajputs, addicted to opium: his wits and his outlook brightened by the daily ' opium peg '.

Again, like Sir Fateh Singh, he was resolved to maintain the seclusion of his beautiful country : and would allow no railway to be built up the Jhelum Valley. But, before he passed, the motor car was, in a measure, defeating him. Kashmir, fated to invasion, a magnet to all the world, could not be saved from its final invaders—English families from India and inescapable tourists from America and from every other country. Financially, in many ways, it is a profitable invasion ; though it tends also to deteriorate the Kashmiri in its own more insidious fashion.

Considering the Maharaja's personality—his devotion to the Crown and all things British—it was unfortunate, if no more, that a tangle of circumstances, early in his reign, required direct British intervention in the interests of good government and the safety of a Border State at a moment when the Russian threat to India was causing acute political anxiety. There had been trouble with the tribesmen north of Gilgit: and undoubtedly certain Pundit officials were in league to oust His Highness in favour of his brother, Sir Amar Singh.

Taking advantage of the Russian ' scare ', they flagrantly forged letters to incriminate Sir Partāb Singh as being in secret corre-spondence with Russia. The Indian Government was not much impressed by their seeming show of zeal ; but the more cogent facts of inefficient administration, baneful Pundit influence and the urgent need for frontier defence, moved them to drastic, if reluctant, action.

For the time being, the Maharaja was practically superseded, in favour of a Council. His brothers, Amar Singh and Rām Singh, with British advisers, were to overhaul the State under supervision of the Resident: His Highness being nominally President of the Council. British officers remodelled the Kashmir army ; and others were employed mainly in connection with woods

and forests—a profitable State activity—and schemes for converting Kashmir's immense water-power into electric power, reclaim-
ing the land and preventing floods.   The last was mainly in charge
of a Royal Engineer with a large staff of Englishmen, Americans
and Canadians.

It is noticeable that very few high appointments were given to
Kashmiris, probably not without reason, though we have it from
Sir Walter Lawrence that, for brains, the Kashmiri Pundit has
hardly his equal in India.   Another British officer, called in for
land revenue settlement, was that very Sir Walter Lawrence, as a
young civilian—no relation to the Lawrences of the Punjab.   His
settlement work was an admirable achievement carried out in the
teeth of much local official antagonism ; a task demanding years
of untiring work, resource, firmness, tact and courage—qualities
in which the Englishman is seldom lacking.   More : his settlement, when achieved, became a charter of liberty for the down-
trodden Kashmiri peasant : a charter that was his due after
centuries of cruelty and oppression.

For that active intervention in State affairs the Indian Government—Sir William Barton admits—has been heavily criticised ;
but he adds that undoubtedly ' the situation had got out of hand ;
and intervention, especially in view of frontier complications, was
justified '.   In every State department improvement was rapid and
lasting.   The benefit to Kashmir was unquestioned : and in 1905
the loved Maharaja reassumed full control, with Sir Amar Singh
again as Chief Minister, an army to take pride in, a peasantry
content and fairly treated for the first time in its history.

No portrait of Sir Partāb Singh would be true to life without
mention of His Highness' curious passion for the purely English
game of cricket.   He took it up quite suddenly, practised assiduously and even engaged a professional eleven, that he himself
might learn the great game, and play it in his own arbitrary
fashion.   Always it was planned ahead how many runs he must
make.   On his birthday they must amount to the exact number
of his years : and howsoever the rules might be strained to prevent
a premature loss of his wicket, he never seemed to notice the
deception.   He would sit for hours contentedly watching ' the
wonderful game of cricket '.   Intensely patriotic, and proud of it,
that was his notion of showing sympathy with England.

The yearly summer cricket match, Kashmir v. Visitors—three
days of it—was for the Maharaja the event of the season.   Even
when nearing fifty, he must personally captain his own team and
take his turn at the wicket ; his short figure buttoned to the neck
in a blue brocade coat above crinkled muslin trousers, his large

turban lop-sided, bare feet encased in silver slippers, an incongruous-looking bat tucked under his arm.

From pavilion to wicket he was conducted in procession, between his Prime Minister and A.D.C., escorted by armour-bearers. Then there began elaborate divestings. Two men rolled up his sleeves. Two buckled on his pads that went oddly with the brocaded coat. Two more adjusted the gloves, while another took the bat and made the correct chalk mark. That done, the procession filed back to the pavilion, leaving their Maharaja fearfully and wonderfully arrayed.

As to the game, it was definitely ' not cricket ': bowling underhand ; runs made by proxy ; and not less than twenty-three of these must be scored before His Highness could be declared ' out '. This was no such simple matter, though loyal subjects served him slow long hops and the field missed the softest catches. Still harder was the lot of the batsman when His Highness bowled ; aware of serious British cricketers watching him do all he knew to lose his wickets, short of tumbling over them—in vain. It was hard to say whether the Prince or his audience derived most amusement from his privileged version of cricket as it is not played.

Many and lovely are the roads of Kashmir valley, but the road of all others for traffic and charm is the River Road—the Jhelum itself, that flows through Srinagar under its seven bridges. Up and down the placid stream goes the traffic of that beguiling ramshackle Eastern Venice : flat-bottomed, slow-moving boats of the country, heaped with pale gold from the mustard fields, or piled high with grain and vegetables from floating gardens of the lake ; lumber-laden barges creaking and crashing down towards India ; walnut *doongas*—houseboats of the country—flat-bottomed, enclosed by a wooden framework walled with matting, thatched with emerald-green rushes, and a pile of scarlet chillis in the prow ; the skimming *shikara*, gondola of Kashmir, curved at stern and prow, with sofa-like seats, the boatmen as clever with punt and paddle as any Venetian gondolier ; little fishing-boats, often drawn up near the bank, wide nets outspread, meshes glimmering in sunshine like dragonfly wings.

Entering Srinagar by the River Road has a fascination peculiarly its own. Thus the Maharaja enters in spring after wintering in his lower hill kingdom of Jammu. Thus the Viceroy enters on State occasions : an event well-described by Miss Fitzroy, who had the good fortune to experience it on a viceregal tour.

The royal barge, built with the gracious sweep of a gondola, is propelled by twenty-four men fore and aft, in scarlet livery, wielding the heart-shaped paddle of Kashmir. In the midst a stateroom, walled with yellow, green and orange papier-mâché work, is roofed with a scarlet carpet for the Viceroy's party.

Down the wide, main stream sails the slow-moving barge between flat-roofed brown houses, first isolated, then crowding to the water's edge, as one enters actual Srinagar, the most haphazard city on earth. ' It sways and climbs and crowds and tilts and hangs ' against a background of wooded slopes and high, unconcerned mountains. Built mainly of timber and narrow bricks, its prevailing tones are brown and cream colour ; its quaint appearance far more beguiling to the eye than any pomposity of marble and stone ; its delicately carved balconies and arches leaning at perilous angles over the stream.

Near the first bridge looms the great pile of the Maharaja's Palace, standing out importantly into the river ; spacious carved verandahs overhanging it ; the gold-roofed Sikh temple gleaming close by ; the banks crowded with lesser barges, to welcome the Lord Sahib.

Lower down, wide steps of the *ghāts*, or washing-places, are thronged with onlookers, gaily clad ; or laid out with a wonder of carpets, rugs and shawls, from China, Bokhara, Yarkand, in the richly blended tones of the East, blue and purple and rose. Everywhere shops and shop-fronts display a bewildering variety of wares : furriers, jewellers, woodcarvers—among the best in Asia ; one merchant, with a sense of human appeal, describing himself as ' Suffering Moses of Old Persia '. But the traveller is warned to beware of the hospitable merchant's Persian ' breakfast ' ; twenty-four courses, all fearful and wonderful, often nauseating to the Western palate ; yet—without damage to courtesy—not one can be refused.

And, to greet the Viceroy, all the seven crooked bridges are adorned with flags and bunting. Across one of them—gold on scarlet cloth—is blazoned the loyal welcome, ' God save the King ' ; and beneath it, in all innocence, ' God help the Viceroy ' : no distinction suspected between the identical-seeming words.

By then, Sir Partāb Singh's reign was nearing an end. In 1925 he died : and the lovely, if difficult, kingdom of Kashmir passed under the rule of his nephew, H.H. Maharaja Sir Hari Singh Bahadur, more modern-minded than his forerunners, and prepared for his princely rôle by having served several years on the State Executive Council.

Lacking the splendid appearance of his handsome grandfather, he is none the less a man of commanding aspect ; tall and athletic,

KASHMIR : HILL ROAD BEYOND KASHMIR
(From *The Road to Kashmir*, by James Milne)

a keen polo-player, his very definite personality linked with a friendly ease of manner and a nimble sense of humour. The face is dominated by an aquiline nose, the jaw noticeably broad, the fine dark eyes close-set under strongly marked brows. Highly educated and well-informed, he is one of the most wide-minded of Indian Princes ; animated and observant, competent to hold his own in any conversation, with a complete command of the English language.

He has built himself a new Palace, Gutāb Bhwan ; and he is the first Prince to restrict the rigid purdah of the Ruling Family. He prefers London to Paris, having no knowledge of French. Rightly he argues that, in order to feel at home in any country, one must be familiar with the language. There might have been a better understanding, in these difficult days, between English and Indians, if the white men and women destined to spend most of their lives in the country, had taken the trouble to learn more than the essential imperatives of household Hindustani.

In the season, Sir Hari Singh lavishly entertains the English visitors, who increasingly invade his Garden of Eden, and he appears to enjoy their society. It may be courtesy ; it may be his own enlightened interest in men and things. Though susceptible to modern ideas, he is inclined, like his uncle, to restrict European or Indian enterprise from too freely opening up his lovely valley. He is credited with ideals of good government ; but there are those who have criticised his tendency to leave over-much power still in the hands of a Brahmin Pundit oligarchy, to let his Ministers handle matters that his subjects would prefer him to keep in his own hands. But he chooses his Ministers well ; and acts on the principle that men do their best work when they are not irked by overmuch supervision.

Many of his early troubles arose from the simple fact that the Kashmiri Moslem, under better treatment, has developed a hitherto unknown sense of self-respect, while the Pundits were still disposed to treat them as serfs : and the ferment was increased by outside stimulus from the Nationalist Moslems of the Punjab militant—very much so, in the troubled time of the early nineteen-thirties.

A wave of disaffection spread through the State ; and in 1931 a warlike body of Moslems from the Punjab entered Kashmir. British troops were needed to quell a rising that put a Hindu Maharaja in a difficult position. Backed by British and Indian troops, he maintained his authority over his extremely mixed population, appointed a British officer as his Chief Minister and instituted widespread reforms : relieving the peasants from the age-old tyranny of forced labour, establishing more schools, and credit societies to curb the baleful activities of the *bunnia*.[1]

Already he had been trying to placate the Moslems by increasing their official appointments. Now he went further and agreed to give them a reasonable share in governing posts. Disturbances quelled, a peaceful future still depends mainly on the crux of making Hindu rule acceptable to a Moslem majority. It is the position of Hyderabad reversed : and, given the moral support of the British Government, there is every possibility of a peaceful solution that may be reasonably expected to endure.

In the last Great War, Kashmir's Imperial Service troops were maintained at a strength of 60,000 : and on the outbreak of the present war, the Maharaja was notably among those Princes who gave the lead to India's magnificent response in money and troops, as told earlier in ' The Princes of India and the War '. The looming threat is to India, as to the whole world : and few, perhaps, have a country better worth fighting for than the Maharaja of Kashmir.

With this inadequate portrayal of his kingdom, we complete my portrait gallery of Indian Princes and their States ; a gallery such as no other land could produce. And it should not be forgotten that there are close on six hundred more in Royal India, many fine personalities among them, who must of necessity remain unrecorded. Even these fifteen major principalities cover a vast area of the country.

From farthest South to utmost North we have followed their records, personal and historical, culminating in Kashmir and the majestic Himalayas, the stupendous Hindu Khush, Abode of the Gods.

In its blend of grandeur and delicate loveliness, of the stark wild and the pleasantly civilised, there is no land comparable to it anywhere, unless it be Canada, which is on a ten times mightier scale, except as to the actual mountains. But Canada lacks the languorous dream quality of the Valley ; lacks the tapestried background of legend and history, the array of manifold great personalities. And in India the personal element—as I have shown many times—colours and dominates everything. ' It reckons in ancestry, names, titles, princes, kings, emperors ; for that has been the teaching of its whole chain of history.'

Kashmir has had many lovers, has given delight to many lovers ; but in neither aspect can any be said to have excelled her Mogul Emperor lover, Jehāngir, who died on his autumn

---

[1] Money-lender.

journey down from the land he treasured more than all the jewels of his kingdom : died fittingly—as men seldom die—in the last camp from which the traveller can look back to the vanishing snows of Himalchān.

The river running far below—a tumble of foam in its pebbly bed—is here walled in by forest-mantled slopes, splashed with the first gold of autumn ; and away at the far end, a glimmer of peaks and domes in the last faint flush of sunset—the Shining Ones.

Here they brought the dying Emperor and laid him down, to take his leave of mountain, river and sky. And it is said that when his attendants asked him if there was anything he wanted, he closed his eyes and turned away from the too familiar crowd of ignoble, self-seeking, insincere time-servers ; away from life itself and his loved Queen-Empress. One longing consumed him : and he said with his last breath, ' Only Kashmir ! '

ROYAL INDIA : WHAT IT MAY BE

In the future of the States lies the answer to the future of India. In their history lies the true story of India's social and political life ; and in it, so I think, lives her destiny.—MAJOR-GENERAL J. C. F. FULLER, C.B., C.B.E., D.S.O.

WE come at last, inevitably, to the large and complex question— What of the future ?

An ultimate federation of States and Provinces has been accepted in theory by a British Parliament, little versed in Indian history, customs or policies, and by a group of advanced Indian politicians. Yet it still remains unworkable in practice ; and must so remain, while it implies one idea to political leaders of the Provinces (British India), and a fundamentally different idea to the vast and varied world of Royal India.

The greater Princes, firm adherents of the Crown, may well pause and ask themselves what is likely to be their own future in a changing India, ever more impressed by the political upheavals of Europe, and increasingly responsible for the trend of her own destiny *within the Empire* : a stipulation essential to any working federal plan in which the Princes will agree to pull their weight.

But Congress, the dominant political party of India, has quite rankly other aims in view.

What then ?

Clear answers are far to seek ; and prophecy is vain. Yet men will for ever be trying to read the stars—men of the East above all. For India lives largely by the stars. No marriage without exchange of horoscopes ; no journey without advice from astrologers as to an auspicious day. The more enlightened Maharajas may have passed beyond such influences ; but for Hindu India, as a whole, the stars rule the major events of life.

Whether or no they rule the future, unseen forces are shaping the destiny of India ; and much depends on the degree of unity that her Princes can arrive at among themselves, if their interests are to be safeguarded in the proposed new régime.

Federation is hard enough to achieve under the best auspices. How then shall it be attained among so many—Hindu, Moslem, Jain, Sikh : hampered by their countless taboos, prejudices and conflicting beliefs ?

The Rajput States have never pulled well together, or their gallant history might not have been so frequently darkened by tragedy. The age-long gulf between them and the Maratha Chiefs has never been bridged ; nor has Rajput rule ever quite recovered from the terrible blows inflicted by the Marathas in the eighteenth century. Neither side looks favourably on the idea of any close alliance, even for desirable ends ; and the lasting feud between two great neighbouring races remains one of the tragedies of Indian history.

Not much brighter is the prospect of harmony between the major States and their lesser fellows, who are often virtually in a different era : nor can the greater Princes all feel sure of having their own subject people behind them. In some instances their authority has weakened ; and though they have power to deal drastically with disruptive elements, neither police nor frontier bar can prevent the infiltration of revolutionary ideas. Yet their princely status must at all costs be maintained, not for personal reasons alone. With centuries of autocratic rule behind them, they are custodians of the culture and welfare of the peasant masses. Any revolutionary political change might spread discord and famine which no power on earth could control.

The portraits—past and present—that I have essayed, must make it clear that, both as men and Rulers, the Indian Princes have a decisive part to play in the moulding of India's destiny. They speak nominally for eighty million people. They maintain among them an army of forty thousand troops who have proved their fighting quality in two world wars, and in several Frontier expeditions. Even their most prejudiced opponents must concede that the heroism of their warriors, unequalled in a thousand years, may well influence the future. They take, on the whole, a broader, more realistic view of defence problems than do most Congress-minded Indians, whose weapons are words. For the Indian tongue works like lightning, but the Indian mind, burdened with age-old grievances, moves slowly in rutted grooves.

The Princes, men of authority themselves, accept and respect the prevailing power of the King-Emperor, from which the Congress Party proposes to cut adrift. The States are also aware that British sentiment and the most experienced among Indian Civil Servants are in full sympathy with them ; both sides clearly recognising that failure to cope with revolutionary groups—violent, and noisy, if not formidable—might plunge them into a common ruin.

Hence the purposeful insistence by Sir Ganga Singh of Bikanir, on the need for a Princes' Conference, that was eventually summoned in 1916, with a view to giving the States a formal voice in the government of ' All-India ', as conceived by the India Office in London.

Even then the Maharaja foresaw a Federal Chamber, representing the States and the Provinces of British India. Ever alive to the interests of those Rulers who were ' Not Highnesses ', he urged that they should by no means be excluded from any federation, lest they become ' weak links in an otherwise perfectly strong chain and find themselves in a position of stagnation '.

Rightly the Princes prize the certainty that, so long as they keep their own obligations, they can rely implicitly on the assurance given them by King George V, when he reaffirmed the definite promise of Lord Canning, in 1862, that ' the integrity of the States should be preserved by perpetuating the rule of their Princes '. On these uncompromising words the King-Emperor set the seal of his Royal resolve ' ever to maintain the privileges, rights and dignity of the Indian Princes, who may rest assured that this pledge is inviolate and inviolable '.

Finally, Lord Irwin, as Viceroy, announced that ' whatever proposals be made, it is essential, on every ground of policy and equity, to carry the free assent of the Ruling Princes of India. Any suggestion that the treaty rights they regard as sacrosanct can be lightly set aside, is only calculated to postpone the solution that we seek.'

The importance of these pronouncements, Royal and Vice-regal, can hardly be over-stressed ; and it remained for the Chamber of Princes, that same year, to speak its own mind on the resolution passed by India's National Congress, proclaiming ' complete independence as its goal '.

To that resolution the Chamber opposed its own : ' So far as the ideal of independence is a matter affecting British India only, it is no concern of ours . . . but in so far as it is an ideal that is likely to affect the whole of India, we regard it as inconsistent with the treaties that bind us to the Crown and also contrary to the true interests of the country '.

That astute and realistic declaration, in effect, cut away the ground from under any plan for Dominion status on the lines laid down in an Imperial Conference three years earlier ; and supplied a much-needed support to rational political elements all over India. It virtually stated that the Princes would not tolerate a '*Vakil*[1] *Raj* '. It proved the value of the Chamber as a means of giving authority and publicity to their point of view.

It had, by then, been eight years in working order ; yet neither in form nor in procedure had it fulfilled their real hopes and wishes. In sittings largely controlled by the Political Secretary to Government, they were often hindered from discussing matters of real

[1] Lawyer rule.

importance to their States. But the Chamber had at least given them a common meeting-ground, and so put an end to isolation.

None the less, as constituted, it possessed no active powers with which to protect the rights and privileges of its members. Many in British India looked askance at it ; and it had suffered some loss of prestige from the aloof attitude of several important States— Udaipur, Mysore, Baroda, Kashmir, Hyderabad and others. These, while in sympathy with its main object, were withheld from adherence by a feeling that their sovereign status would be diminished by allowing even their own Chamber to mediate between them and the Viceroy, as representative of the King-Emperor.

That direct link with the Crown is the Princes' most cherished privilege and sheet anchor. Fully alive to the uncertainty of their future position in any new system of government for British India, they are implacably resolved not to put themselves in the hands of Congress Ministers. Yet the Princes' Chamber, without universal support, must inevitably lack full authority and practical value.

The problem is no light one for men who have deserved well both of India and the Empire. To the Hindu Princes India owes the preservation of Indian sovereignty—two thousand years of inherited tradition, culture and religion ; while British Indian politicians—ignoring their services to the country—would utilise them merely as subordinate allies to help dominate the British ; a false position into which the States will neither be persuaded nor coerced. They know—as do all men of Eastern experience —that a scramble for power must inevitably follow such a gradual transfer of power as the India Parliamentary Act involves. They also realise that most Congress-minded politicians accept the creed of democracy mainly as a convenient means to secure power for themselves. The Princes have seen that the country as a whole has derived little benefit from the first instalment of the Montagu reforms. They know that there can be no grafting of Parliament and party government on to a land lacking England's tradition of good-humoured contest ; a land where antagonisms cut too deep for the West to understand ; where, as yet, the great mass of inhabitants are illiterate.

India is a land of peasantry ; and the power they wield is expressed through one of her oldest institutions, the *Panchayat* or council of five, that builds itself as a pyramid, from the smallest village up to the Maharaja, whose autocratic rule is thus seen to rest on a democratic basis. For proof of that seeming paradox, witness the amazing reforms made in many of the larger States —Mysore, Baroda, Bikanir—while even some smaller ones have become, as it were, laboratories of political experiments. For example, in the minute, but notably advanced, State of Aundh we are told that an attempt is being made to recreate, on Indian soil, some of the institutions of ancient Greece.

In depicting the Princes, I have clearly shown how State service gives larger scope to ambitious and capable men than service in British India ; and how many of their chosen Ministers have exhibited statesmanship of the first order, and have gained European reputations. That these things are not the outcome of democracy on Western lines, they must recognise clearly enough ; while, in British India, they have seen for years three parts of the land divided against itself, agitating for this or that, multiplying endless debates and committees ; displaying an ineptitude in tackling realities, often with farcical results of a Gilbert and Sullivan order. They have also no doubt observed that most of India's recent political advance has been achieved within the States, while they themselves were being denounced as anachronisms, hinderers of progress towards a self-governing India that frankly aims at their liquidation.

Yet, in spite of it, Royal India remains—with its antiquity and achievements, military and political—the strongest and most stable element in the land. If the Princes themselves are not enthusiastic for vote and ballot-box, the best of them are well versed in the theory and practice of good government. It is an Indian Civil Service officer who writes that ' many of the Rajput States are better governed than the Provinces. Customs and duties have enriched them. The Chiefs are well educated ; their sons have been to Eton and other first-rate public schools. The best of them are benevolent autocrats and remarkably efficient ; while British India is suffering from a corrupt democracy—the worst form of government.'

Indeed, any intelligent traveller through the States cannot fail to be impressed by an increasing sense of kingly duties balancing the sense of kingly rights. More and more the best of them recognise that the strength and safety of a Ruler and his State can only be maintained by the loyal affection, the contentment and co-operation of his own people.

During many troubled years before the present war, when British India was in a ferment of political discord, affecting several of the States, it became clear to the majority that, in order to remain strong and stable, they must become a recognised and unified body, or press for a reformed Princes' Chamber to which all could adhere. Only so, it was thought, could the Princes retain the full powers that would keep them in the forefront of Imperial affairs ; a position as important for India as for themselves. Hence, no doubt, the unexpected pronouncement at the First Round Table Conference in 1930.

That first Conference ' spread on the top of Mount Pisgah '— staging a view of the promised land—met in an atmosphere of tension heightened by the frank hostility of Congress politicians. Their decision to boycott a Conference that held no prospect of immediate Dominion status, had landed them in jail ; and their absence handicapped the Moderates, who were unable to foresee the probable attitude of the Princes, now holding the key to the situation.

A formal assemblage in the House of Lords preceded the actual Conference in the great drawing-room of St. James's Palace : a gathering unique of its kind.

Among the Princes present were the Rulers of Kashmir, Bikanir, Dholpur and Bhopāl, under the leadership of Sir Sayaji Gaekwar, Maharaja of Baroda. With them were distinguished Ministers representing Mysore, Hyderabad and Udaipur. For their spokesman, the States had chosen Sir Ganga Singh, a Chief of great political experience and sagacity. Moslem delegates had their own leader, the Aga Khan ; and with them sat two distinguished Indian women. British representatives included Lord Sankey, Sir Samuel Hoare and Lord Reading.

The case for India was opened by Sir Tej Bahadur Sapru, a Moderate politician of balanced mind and character. His masterly arguments and brilliant oratory, in favour of an All-India Federation, with responsibility at the centre, were followed by a direct appeal to the Princes that they should join hands in the only form of government he considered capable of uniting their diverse Motherland.

The effect of his speech could be gauged by the impressive silence that preceded the normal outburst of applause.

As it subsided, the Maharaja of Bikanir stood up, handsome and soldierly, charged with a fateful decision.

He emphasised the infinite variety of India ; the need to seek unity ; ' not through the dead hand of an impossible uniformity, but through an associated diversity '. To that end, he declared, the Princes would be willing to take their place in a federal system of government composed of the States and British India, though their final answer must obviously depend on the structure of that government and on certain necessary safeguards for preserving the rights and interests of the States and their subjects. There could be no coercion in any form. The Princes could only come in of their own free will and on terms that would secure their just Treaty rights, preserving their safety for the future, and their direct link with the Crown. The Central Imperial Government, he insisted, must retain its hold on all matters concerning Defence, Foreign Policy, Finance and power to intervene, should federation or government show signs of premature collapse. Given these assurances, the Princes would ' freely and honestly ' lend themselves to any workable scheme for effective association between the States and British India.

' I am inspired by one thought,' concluded the Maharaja, ' service to my beloved King-Emperor and devotion to my Motherland. Bábar, first of the Moguls, when he set out on the crowning adventure of his life, placed his feet in the stirrups of opportunity, his hands on the reins of confidence in God. I would commend to you, on the threshold of our great enterprise, the words of Abraham Lincoln, in circumstances not remote from these : " With malice towards none, with charity for all, with firmness in the right—as God gives us to see the right—let us strive on to finish the work we are in ".'

Here was a genuine lead, a frank declaration of goodwill, that came as a surprise to all concerned, and closed the first Conference on a note of optimism as unexpected as it was welcome to worried politicians, weary of endless intellectual talk that seemed to lead nowhither.

That was in November 1930 : and twelve years later the fateful decision still remains undecided, the goal of All-India Federation still remains ' a blessed word ', a pious hope, not yet translated into a working concern. The Princes, though in sympathy, still remain aloof, and disunited ; unsatisfied as to those essential safeguards that alone would justify them in so gravely jeopardising the future prospects of their whole Order.

The lofty idea had not been broad-based on realities. Its advocates had ignored the fact that Federation can only be achieved with success—as in the U.S.A. and Canada—where all States concerned have the same political form and economic objectives.

Canada, for instance, had involved no change in principles of government ; no risk of weakening at the Centre ; no cleavage of opinion comparable to that which has been since revealed among the States, great and small, Hindu and Moslem : a cleavage so deep that it weakened their position at later Round Table Conferences and their power to uphold their own rights, in view of Congress antagonism. Committed to Federation, in principle, they had found the working plan ' not at all the same pair of shoes ', as expressed by the late Jām Sahib of Náwanagar.

In his last public speech as Chancellor of the Princes' Chamber, he spoke his mind on the subject with characteristic honesty and point :

' If I find myself—as I and some of my friends do—unable to accept the present federal scheme, it is not from any hostility to British India, but from the simple instinct of self-preservation. I wish British India all good luck in its endeavours ; but its problems are not our problems ; and no good can come of trying to confuse the two. The real truth is—and no one who has studied the proceedings of these Conferences can deny it—that the kind of Federation of which (in 1930) our representative Princes signified their provisional approbation, was very different indeed from the kind that now holds the field.'

For that reason—and that reason alone—their early enthusiasm had subsided. Not a single Prince has made a forward move. Many are now obviously disillusioned. They see the safeguards on which they had insisted—Defence, Finance and Foreign Relations—being whittled away : the thin end of a dangerous wedge. They are not at all sure of a welcome from British Indian politicians. An inimical Congress frankly regards Federation, backed by the Princes, as a death-blow to their main hope—complete independence.

Meantime the greater Princes have been urged, even pressed, by Government to walk into the Federal parlour. But the more they look at it the less they seem to like it ; possibly suspecting a suggestion of the spider and the fly. Result—a deadlock ; and the problem still unsolved. Is it ultimately soluble ?

Lately Indian statesmen have been reminded that ' constitutional forms do not express the whole of a nation's life, that a conflict between rival political schools may have a chance of being resolved if brought out into a larger air and viewed in a more ample light '.

Needless to say there was, and remains, much moderate opinion between the extreme elements on both sides ; but moderate opinion seldom carries the same weight as the fervent views of Right and Left in the day of decision.

There remain, also, ninety million Moslems, with their Mogul heritage of power, concentrated in Hyderabad, Bhopāl and the North-West Frontier, watching the trend of events : preparing, in their practical fashion, for the obvious possibility of revolutionary activity in British India, or a weakening of the strong Imperial hand at the centre. Against either contingency they are fortified by a Moslem Federation of their own : Hyderabad, Bhopāl, the Punjab and the North-West, with feelers towards Afghanistan and beyond, among the Moslem peoples of Irān, Irāq, Saudi Arabia, Syria, Palestine and Turkey. Always in India—though tolerance grows with wider knowledge—one has to reckon with that cleavage of creeds. In the words of Major-General J. F. C. Fuller, a profound student of Indian life and thought, ' democracy and theocracy are two world orders that refuse to amalgamate, unmixable as oil and water. . . . Until India is de-theocratised, democracy is no more than a will-o'-the-wisp that must land it in a slough of despond.

' That is not to imply that her people must become agnostics or callous towards religion ; but that the idea of God must cease to impose itself on everyday life with such force that the idea of men is crushed out of existence. . . . A readjustment of her religious views would cleanse Hinduism—which is founded on this most exalted conception of Deity—from crude superstitions and unholy practices that have collected round it in three thousand years.' [1]

Such, more or less, is the opinion of most thoughtful Hindus to-day, notably of that profound philosopher, Professor S. Radhakrishnān. One may almost say that the readjustment is already in progress. Nor is this brief religious digression unrelated to the political problem of a hopeful attempt at federation between so-called democratic Provinces and autocratic States, with a Central Government strong enough to ensure that neither shall encroach upon the other. But Congress India is opposed root and branch to central Imperial authority ; and without it the Princes will never play their part in Federation ; for, without the Crown, the Treaties—their sheet anchor—must cease to exist.

The present Federal scheme must automatically end in extinguishing all that they stand for ; and they know it. Equally they know that, as factors in a future Imperial India, their importance can hardly be overrated. They will always remain one of the strongest among many links between Britain and India. They take a personal pride in their devotion to the King and to the British connection ; and for that very reason—most creditable to themselves—they are at daggers drawn with Congress politicians. Hence the deadlock, the tacit opposition, armoured against argument or persuasion.

Meantime the British Government—with more persistence than imagination—has pursued the impossible policy to which it

[1] Major-General J. F. C. Fuller, C.B., C.B.E., D.S.O., *India in Revolt*.

was pledged : the bestowal of full parliamentary government on a ' terrifying combination of democratic forms with caste, kismet and mediaeval autocracy '.

The true solution, however drastic, would seem to be a swing towards the other extreme, aristocratic rule, which is what the mass of Eastern peoples best appreciate and understand.

In plain terms, let the unwieldy Provinces be divided up and converted into States under carefully chosen leaders, so that all India may once again be ruled by Princes. No retrogression need be involved, since the greater ones—as I have shown—are moving with the times.

This bold suggestion, put forward by Colonel Graham Seton Hutchison in his provocative book *Arya*, must now be considered as an eventual possibility, since it contains the ingredients essential to any working Federation—the same form of Government procedure and social system in all the States concerned. It would aim at preserving India's historical and racial genius for personal rule. A ' Monarchical Federation ' would impose on all the Chiefs of Indian States far higher obligations and a larger measure of responsibility towards All-India. It should also spur them to eradicate the corruption, the nepotism and cruelties, in less advanced States, that have given Indian rule a bad name. The suggestion would at once remove the main stumbling-block to Federation : ' the impossibility of welding the constitutional forms of British and Indian India into one national unit '. It would recognise the sovereignty of the Indian people ; and it would, of necessity, be founded on the basic principles of Indian culture and philosophy.

The borders of certain lesser States might be enlarged, on geographical or racial lines while the more unwieldy Provinces could be divided up on the same principle and entrusted to leading men, who had proved their capacity for statesmanship, and their goodwill to co-operate in a Princely Federation.

' There is no lack ', writes Colonel Hutchison, ' among the lesser Rulers, or among Indian political leaders, of men fit to be entrusted with the government of such States.'

The present Princes would be secured in their own domains : a fundamental condition. ' No attempt should be made to produce a Europeanised India ', except in so far as the Princes themselves have adapted the ideas of constitutional monarchy to suit their own country and people. It seems superfluous to add that no form of government ' by counting heads ' could ever hope to prosper in India.

If a solution so fundamentally sane should ever come within

the sphere of practical politics, the details of administration, as suggested by Colonel Hutchison, give this challenging proposal a workmanlike air. Central Authority would be vested in a King-Emperor's Council (London), replacing the present India Office : a Council composed of nominated Indian Princes, leading experts and others representing the various racial interests : the British Cabinet to be represented and the Viceroy to be *ex officio* member. This Council should have power to nominate Rulers of the newly created States, and to it Ministers would report developments, so as to keep, as far as possible, an even rate of progress throughout the whole Federation. The Chamber of Princes, already existing, could recommend appointments, work out details, and be of inestimable service in many ways.

In so brief a space it is impossible to quote the full proposed structure of this genuinely All-India conception ; those who are interested can examine the details in *Arya : the Call of the Future*, by Colonel Graham Seton Hutchison, D.S.O., M.C., published by Hutchinson & Co., London.

But points of detail are secondary to the first vital question— Can a Princely Federation of All-India be regarded as an ultimate goal ? At present even the most optimistic mind can hardly envisage the possibility of persuading Congress to look favourably on a federated India of independent States, within the framework of the British Empire. Its votaries block the path of true progress by their refusal to put social reform first, political reform growing out of it, if Indian political economy is not to be a house founded on sand. Political reforms, when the time is ripe, need not—in fact should not—be borrowed either from Moscow or from the West. Sir Walter Lawrence, after twenty-one years of India and much association with the Princes, wrote : ' The Indian States— with certain modifications and improvements—rather than the Provinces, would be the true model for administration of the new India '. In those twenty-one years he lost his heart to Rajput Chiefs and to Kashmir—the best of the land, human and scenic.

Sir William Barton, equally experienced, cites the Rajput system ' with its foundations deep in human nature ' as a model that, with some re-shaping of its internal structure, ' might still be adapted to the needs of a progressive community, combining it with the patriarchal element '.

Major-General J. F. C. Fuller, author of that admirable book *India in Revolt*, holds the opinion that, whatever the future form of government may be, it can only prove successful if it be based on Indian philosophy and culture. Lord Lloyd is also known to have approved of the Princely Federation idea, though the road from approval to attainment may ' wind uphill all the way ' ; and the views of Colonel Seton Hutchison have already been made clear. The significance of these quoted opinions lies in the fact that so many Englishmen—Lord Zetland is perhaps another—all reared on democracy, should so unanimously see the wisdom, in fact the necessity, of an Indian India, a kingly India, as the only possible basis for a Federation that can be counted on to endure.

We must never forget that Mr. Winston Churchill—although a member of the Conservative Party—led the Opposition in the House of Commons while the Government of the day was pressing through the India Act, implementing the decisions of the Round Table Conference, and the earlier Montagu reforms. Mr. Churchill is not only a Prime Minister who towers above his predecessors as a man of intellect and imagination, possessed of amazing gifts in the widest field of action ; he is also an eminent historian. His political wisdom and the judgments ensuing therefrom have been based on profound study and unique experience of public office. His masterly speeches on the India Act, preserved in book form, prove his uncompromising hostility to the Federal ideas, as embodied in the Government of India Act.

Among Indians, the wise Maharaja of Bikanir saw clearly, long ago, that the real need of the States was ' not for immediate popular institutions, but for certain fundamentals of responsible good government '. These he classed under seven headings ; postulating, as essential, a frank recognition by each Prince of his supreme duty to his subjects—beneficent rule in keeping with their general interests.

It is common knowledge that many States are already ahead of British India in the matter of social and educational reforms. Dealing with their own people, they are free to initiate new measures not yet attempted in the Provinces ; to make valuable political experiments that may possibly establish new principles to guide the world. They reap also many advantages of beneficent one-man rule. A Prince who is impressed by some new invention or theory is free to finance it and ' get on with it ', unchecked by any formal budget, by endless debates and the intrusion of varied interests. He is unhindered by *non possumus* discussions and the ' counting of noses '. Freedom from the toils of red tape gives a flavour of adventure unknown to the victims of files and pigeonholes. But these Chiefs of progressive States are no mere dreamers. They are practical men, alive to the danger of putting the cart before the horse or of building the roof before the walls.

They have besides, in some ways, conserved more of the old traditions than has British India.

We have already heard the voice of that sane and stalwart reformer-Prince of Kolhapur : ' Educate, educate. Uproot prejudice and superstition. Only by means of social progress, can political progress become a natural growth from within.' Such has been the experience of England and America. But natural growth must proceed in Nature's unhurried way.

Much of all this has been said many times over, without visible result. Congress still aims at immediate political advance, and Congress, though a minority, is a power in the land, not to be placated by any reasonable compromise. It takes two to make a bargain, as to make a quarrel. Hence the cautious attitude of many far-seeing Princes, who wish the best for their country, but not at the expense of breaking their link with that brotherhood of nations, the British Empire.

Well might Sir William Barton write in his *Princes of India*, ' The magnitude and complexity of the problems involved are startling. Nothing but goodwill and harmony of purpose can solve them.' That was written eight years ago ; but neither goodwill nor harmony seem yet to be conspicuously in evidence, except here and there among the more broad-minded.

So the tug of war went on with no definite result ; till once again, in 1939, as in 1914, the outbreak of a European war changed, in a lightning-flash, the whole atmosphere of India. It proved the futility of trying to drive a wedge between the Crown and its ' perpetual allies ', the Princes. It stirred the martial races of India—the Punjab leading—to offer themselves and their resources with the promptness and ardour of former years. Again, as before, the common enemy, seeking to dislocate and disrupt the Empire, only welded it more closely into one great family, ' drawing the threefold knot firm on the ninefold band ', as Kipling has it. From all sides came a spontaneity of giving and serving that has no parallel in history. ' That our House stand together ' is the unshakable resolve of all. In fact, a spirit emerging from the welter of war, is bringing men to recognise that a sick world can only be made whole when nations and individuals learn the art of working *with* and not *against* each other ; that ' co-operation in the art of living can alone make the modern world safe to live in '.

Safety may not and should not be man's highest aim. It is danger that strengthens all the fibres of character : and the bed-rock virtues are, after all, the military virtues. But the fine art of living and working in unison breeds more than safety ; and it need not involve merging into a lifeless uniformity. Each man ' or nation can remain individual, while respecting the outlook or creed of his neighbour : an approach, if no more, to the ' unity in diversity ', which is India.

There—reverting to our main theme—is her opportunity, and Britain's no less. India's challenge to the West cuts deep ; dynamic thought, over against dynamic action. Rooted in her past, yet transcending it, only a god can say what lies ahead of her. Working with England, she may yet lead and lift the thought of the world.

' Ask us to work *with* you, British and Indian together,' said a Hindu Professor of Economy at Mysore. ' Both have much to forget . . . but it has got to be done. We must go on together. It is too late to separate now.'

An appeal so patently sincere ought not to fall on deaf ears ; and already in many of the States British officers are working with Indian Princes in complete accord, identifying themselves with State interests as Englishmen seem peculiarly able to do ; proving their racial gift for adaptation that ensures survival and, in this case, points the way to a permanent link essential to the welfare of both races.

In British India, as yet, genuine association still seems to be regrettably hampered by ' inferiority complex ' on one side, and, on the other, by a certain racial lack of sympathetic understanding. For there is a measure of truth in a recent criticism on that head : ' The basis of half the political trouble in India is that although Indians, on the whole, understand the English fairly well, too many of the English—while all out for justice and fair play—do not even want to understand Indians '. They fail to see that the emotional East needs love and understanding even more than fair play ; the stimulant of personal leadership, personal example, such as they recognised, revered and loved in Sir Henry Lawrence. Too often the appeal of the West is to pocket and profit ; while the true East more readily respects and responds to a higher appeal. The spirit that animates Government or Ruler is nowhere more sensitively perceived than in India ; nowhere more certain of evoking response.

The word spirit is used advisedly. India sets more value on things of the spirit than on the efficient brain, the well-run machine. Indians, as a whole, neither desire nor admire mere efficiency. They prefer the ups and downs of their own taboos and decrees. The Hindu finds too much monotony in first-class administration. It has been said by one of themselves that ' he doesn't want the best of anything. He prefers the second best. He likes something left to chance ' ; which is true of many Englishmen. In fact the people everywhere have no desire for a first-class world. They gird against bureaucratic restrictions and impositions. They want a human world—variety in uniformity. They want joy and mystery, freedom and authority, not a rigid fate. Much the same might be said of artists everywhere. For the artist relishes life, with its chances and changes, its accidents and uncertainties, its unexpected joys, even its desperate demands ; and most Hindus are artists in their souls.

Leadership, as always, is the supreme necessity. Could but the hour and the man coincide, a Princely Federation might carry India to heights beyond any yet attained. Great Britain, in this war, has found her leader. Aristocrat, soldier, artist—the trinity of leadership—Mr. Churchill epitomises in himself the finest qualities of the race. Can India hope for the same good fortune ? Diversified by many races and religions, the true type becomes, even among her greater Princes, harder to find. Rajputs have the leader spirit in their blood. I need only mention the Maharajas of Bikanir, Náwanagar and the immortal Sir Pratāp Singh. But it is almost inconceivable that any princely leader would be accepted by Congress ; a prejudice in part responsible for India's unsolved problem.

There are those, no doubt, who would lay the blame for that, as for every ill, on the broad shoulders of England and over a hundred years of alien rule. The British have, no doubt, made many mistakes—too little social intercourse, too much purely materialistic education—but so have all the fallible nations of earth. It is a truism that the man who never makes a mistake rarely makes anything else : and Great Britain, down the centuries, has accomplished many marvels ; her achievements in two world wars, not being the least.

The benefits that have accrued to India, from more than a century of peace within her borders, are writ clearly enough for all the world to read. It does not behove an English writer to enlarge on them. But one may be permitted to quote an American verdict as not being biassed either way.

Mr. Paul Cravath, the lawyer millionaire, had been touring India with a business friend to see what they might do, between them, in the matter of railway contracts. A chance meeting with Mr. C. B. Fry, the famous cricketer, gave them an opportunity to see, not only the Provinces, but the inner working of several Indian States, whose Rulers were known to him.

When they parted, Mr. Cravath said heartily : ' Well, sir,

very many thanks for all you have shown us. I can only say that, after having seen so much of India, I will never again run down the British.' That last is the prerogative of Congress politicians, who continue to throw on British statesmen the onus of solving India's complex problem in the teeth of their own persistent opposition.

And so, after much not wholly irrelevant digression, we find ourselves, like Alice in Wonderland, back again at the front door of the house. In other words reverting to ' Royal India : What it may be '.

Hindus and Moslems alike have come to recognise that the future of India lies with the Princes. Colonel Hutchison's practical suggestion appears to be confirmed by that stalwart young Moslem Ruler, the Nawab of Bhopāl.

Comparing democracy, in its workings, with India's normal aristocratic manner of rule, he admits that ' both are open to temptation, both can be a menace to the people. Why then quarrel about forms ? ' And pertinently he adds, ' Why initiate methods of administration so far unknown to the country ? Why not reform ourselves, where reform is needed, yet retain our indigenous system, which has stood the test of centuries ? . . . A fully democratic Government can only be successful where a very large number of the people know what is best for them. . . . I am afraid that, at the present stage of our moral, mental and physical development, this is not the case with us. . . . You cannot alter these conditions by a wave of the magic wand. You need centuries of persistent honest work ; and I think it would not be practical politics aspiring to rule, with any success, a mediaeval people by twentieth-century methods. . . . I am convinced that the success of an Oriental people lies in their remaining Oriental. We have already had too many Western ideas forced upon our Eastern minds.'

There speaks Princely India—the practical Moslem brain, with its Afghan heritage of strength, unhindered by the complexities and inequalities of Hindu caste distinctions ; upholding personal rule rather than the ballot-box and the ' Talking Shop ', as the key to successful government of India at her present uneven stage of social and cultural development. And it may safely be inferred that the most thoughtful and advanced among his fellow Rulers would echo his sane conclusion.

Certainly no Western mind is qualified to counter it. British opinions already quoted are affirmed by Sir William Barton, to whose ' long service and shrewd judgment ' Lord Halifax has paid eloquent tribute. Of the Princes he writes, ' whatever scheme of government may be ultimately evolved, it is beyond doubt that their future is assured '.

Strong in that belief, it is England's first duty to give them a clear lead towards an ultimate Princely Federation, were it only by the half measure of creating new States, where feasible, and forming other areas into Congress republics : their Presidents to rank with Princes in the Central Government. In such a case, through the· prevailing atmosphere, the chances are that they would ultimately become Princes in fact.

It need hardly be said that so drastic a solution would not everywhere be popular. It would be opposed by extreme elements on both sides. But, in the words of Colonel Hutchison, it would be ' a project worthy of the British people, worthy of the Monarchy of which the Empire is the greatest and most enduring exponent ; worthy, not least, of All-India '.

In the changed atmosphere produced by united effort, a Princely Federation might fittingly be an outcome of the present war.

Finally, if All-India is to become a reality, it behoves the Princes themselves to recognise the importance of their own first duty—to lead their people, which implies fitting themselves, one and all, for that high function. There lies the prospect of a lasting solution. The road may be long ; an uphill path beset with many obstacles. But obstacles exist to be overcome. It is my own hope that the issue of present discords may be a true Federation of Princes : in name and in fact—ROYAL INDIA.

Parkstone, Nov. 27, 1941